THIS IS MY DAMN ADVENTURE

Patti Jo Ruskin

Nightengale Press
A Nightengale Media LLC Company

THIS IS MY DAMN ADVENTURE

Copyright ©2005 by Patti Jo Ruskin
Cover Design ©2005 by Rodney Connor and Steve Connor

For information about Nightengale Press please
visit our website at www.nightengalepress.com.
Email: publisher@nightengalepress.biz

Library of Congress Cataloging-in-Publication Data

Ruskin, Patti Jo, 1966
    This Is My Damn Adventure / Patti Jo Ruskin
    ISBN: 1-933449-00-4
    Memoir
        Copyright Registered: 2005
First Published by Nightengale Press in the USA

October 2005

10 9 8 7 6 5 4 3 2 1

Printed at
Lightning Source Inc.
1246 Heil Quaker Boulevard
La Vergne, Tennessee 37086

This Is My Damn Adventure

Acknowledgments

The completion of this project ends a journey that has taken over 8 years. This process was not an individual event and its ending must be the beginning of my gratitude to all of those who made my damn adventure what it was!

First and foremost, to my husband, John, for being my first reader and my most gentle advisor. Thank you for putting up with all of my obsessive behavior over the past 17 years. I would do it all over again in a minute with you by my side! You are my Everlasting!

To my mother, Rita Slattery who had to re-live a lot of the hard times in order to help me put them away for good. You have taught me how to be the wife and mother that I am today. The sacrifices you made to keep our family together are nothing short of remarkable. I love you with all my heart.

To my sister, Kelli Trainor, who had to stifle sobs at work as I read her parts of my first draft. You are my best friend and I hope I have done justice to your story as well. You will always complete me and I thank God for you everyday.

To my brother, Ed Slattery, who will carry on our great name. You have always wanted the best for me and I would not be the person I am without you. You made me a great athlete and your advice has been invaluable over the years. You have had your own adventure which was very different than mine, but I hope you know how very, very proud I am to call you my brother.

To my children, Erin and Joe, who now have a collection of stories to share with their children some day. You are the reason

I am so happy with my life. You have had to deal with so many changes in your short lives that I hope have made you stronger and more resilient. You are the light in my life and the laughter in my heart. I love you both so much.

And lastly, to my first real friend, B.Babes, Brenda Murray. You helped me begin this story by including me in your wedding. Who knew that my gift of a poem would lead to so many stories. Thank you for your unwavering friendship and for sharing your family and their comedy. 35 years and we are still together! Love you Bren!

Table of Contents

Part 3
Getting Under Way

August 15, 1996

    I have no idea where one starts once they give the crazy idea of writing about one's life a chance, but I am finally at a point in mine to begin. My family has joked for years as different things have happened that we have yet another chapter in our family book. Life is too short to hope that someone else remembers the good, the bad, and the ugly times that make us who we are.

    I can look back and know with confidence that my family, especially my parents had everything to do with the person I have become. Since it seems my life could be a comedy, a tragedy and a drama all wrapped into one, I am not sure how my story will be categorized. Mark Twain once wrote, "Write what you know about," so that is what I will do.

Patti Jo Ruskin

Chapter 1

My Arrival
Early September 1966

The air was as crisp and clear as if you had ordered it special. The familiar smells of burnt leaves and grass being mowed for the last time filled their small house on Union Street. Fall was creeping into the Midwest with brilliant colors of red, orange, and yellow. The ground below crunched with each step under the added weight of Rita's ninth month. She could hardly believe how fast this one went. Her first two seemed to take longer, but for some odd reason this pregnancy flew by.

It was early September in Illinois and that meant Rita was just days from delivering her third baby. She could hardly believe her and Tom's good fortune. They had wanted kids more than anything but for so long it seemed that this was not to be.

Rubbing the girth that lay beneath her shirt, she tried to recall the frustration of those first five years of trying and failing to conceive. To think of how close they had actually come to adoption. Tom was so excited the day they heard that they had been accepted as adoptive parents. That joy was no match for the day shortly after that Rita had found out she was pregnant.

Walking up the stairs and into the house, she stopped to glance at the photos that graced the entry way of their first house in town. There was Ed, a fat, happy baby that welcomed with open arms the arrival of his baby sister, Kelli just 18 months later. Now, two and a half years later, here she was ready to deliver again. She could not help remembering the pain along with the joy of Eddie and Kelli. Dr. Breisch had let her go natural but because she was as slim as she was, she had torn with both births.

As she remembered the pain she looked again at the miracles on the wall and without a doubt knew she would go through it all over again for this one. It was her hope that it would be better this time. She had felt good about Dr. Madiota from the first time she had met him.

She labored her way around the living room picking up the scattered toys left behind by her sleeping angels. She caught a glimpse of herself in the mirror as she passed through the hallway. Her tall thin frame was hardly affected by the birth of the first two babies. Her long slender legs had lost nothing of their shape and other than the round ball in her tummy, she did not look thirty-three, though she certainly felt it at times. Eddie and Kelli were typical toddlers and kept her on her toes. She sat down heavily at the kitchen table and glanced out toward their new yard. They had left their rented farm house and bought the perfect little house in Dwight, Illinois, now that Tom was selling insurance.

She sighed heavily and could not deny the pit she felt in her stomach when she thought of the past year and all its changes. There was the sale of Tom's land to his brothers. Had they done the right thing? She knew Tom well and she knew although he loved farming, they had to have more income. He had always been such a people person and she knew if there was one thing he could do it was sales.

There on the table were the insurance books that he studied religiously. She knew there were things she should be doing but she was enjoying the silence of the house while the kids slept.

The silence was interrupted by a rustling sound that was all too familiar. Oh how she hated these old houses especially in the fall. It seemed every field mouse from Illinois to Iowa had found a home in their house in the country. By the sounds of things one had found its way into town too. She laughed to herself remembering the scene in the kitchen just yesterday. A mouse had squeezed its way behind the oven and wielding a broom and very little courage she had tried to shoo it out from behind its hiding place.

Being all of four and using some new words of Daddy's, Eddie shouted for her to sweep the little bastard his way. She could hardly tell Tom she was laughing so hard. Eddie had become quite the little protector of his women. He absolutely idolized his baby sister and that made her heart swell. She knew there would be plenty of times that this undying love may not always be as easy to show.

The afternoon sun was warm through the window and she closed her eyes and stretched her tired back. She had not realized that she had dozed off until she heard the padding of little feet down the stairs. She opened her eyes just in time to see a chubby little face with a new burr haircut coming into the kitchen. Before he could open his mouth to tell his mom that Kelli was up, a very impatient scream came from upstairs. Her moment of quiet would not return again until all were in bed many hours later.

Two Weeks later

As Tom came in the front door he tried his best to be quiet. He knew when he started selling insurance it would mean working around other people's schedules, but he had felt especially guilty leaving Rita with the kids tonight. Setting his keys in his dish, he took off his ring and watch as he looked around at the immaculate house.

She had done it again. Every inch of the house was sparkling. Hoping that tonight would finally be the night, she had knocked herself out cleaning. She was two full weeks overdue and this was the third cleaning spree since her due date. Bless her heart. He knew how frustrated she was getting and he wished he could do something to make it easier. Everything was ready except the baby.

He entered their bedroom and was struck by how pretty she looked lying there. He was not used to seeing her with the added pounds but he could honestly say he had never loved her more. He crawled in beside her and it was not two hours later that he felt her stir next to him.

"I think I'm starting, so I am going to run in and shave my legs," she whispered.

This made absolutely no sense to Tom who was more than a little groggy, but he was exhausted and she had said it was just starting so he dozed off again.

The screams from the bathroom woke him this time, and with his heart in his throat he raced down the hall to find Rita doubled over in the tub. He knew the plan, but as he looked at her in the tub, his mind went blank. Helping her from the tub, he tried to focus as he ran through the mental list of things to do.

Once Rita was dressed he ran to call Delores, Rita's sister, to stay with the kids. He had Rita in the car when Delores drove up and he damn near ran her over leaving the driveway. They had to get to Streator, and it was a 30 minute drive.

Rita's pains were very regular and coming quickly. They did not speak until they hit some railroad tracks that he should have remembered were there. In the rush to get there, they came up too fast for Tom to even brake. He was sure from the scream Rita let out that she'd had the baby right there in the car.

"We need to get there alive, Tom!" she growled through clenched teeth.   Dr. Madiota met them at the door and within seconds they had taken Rita down the hall. The relief Tom felt was overwhelming. He sat down in the waiting room of St. Mary's and took the first deep breath he allowed himself in over an hour.

He let his head rest back on the cold, vinyl chair and thought back to the last two times he was in this same position. Tonight or is it actually today he would have his third child. He and Rita had quite a time after Kelli was born. Knowing that they did not have room for another baby and with just 18 months between Eddie and Kelli they had to do some kind of birth control.

He could laugh now, but at the time he did not find too much humor in the rhythm method. It had actually put the most strain that they had ever had on their marriage. He truly believed that God knew what he was doing. Those six months were a time of change for all of them but he knew that he had made the right decision by leaving the farm.

The buzz of the lights in the deserted hallway brought him back to the task at hand. Just as he was standing to stretch, he caught sight of the doctor walking toward him. It was just after midnight and he had come out to tell Tom that he had a baby girl.

A huge grin spread across his Irish face and his blue eyes sparkled.

"We have our Patti Jo," he said as he hurried to go meet his new little girl.

6 weeks later

Rita looked around her hospital room and tried to stop the tears from coming. The ache she felt in her heart was a perfect match for what she felt lower from her surgery. Who would have thought that she would be back in this damn hospital just six weeks after giving birth? She closed her eyes and remembered the day she left with Patti in her arms.

Dr. Madiota was signing her out and as she signed the final papers she laughed and told him,

"I'll be back in about a year for number four."

She was so grateful to him for making it so easy on her. Knowing her frame was so small he did not wait for her to tear and instead gave her the necessary episiotomy. Her uterus just had not bounced back and never would. She could not believe how exhausted she felt. She knew she was supposed to go home tomorrow but she honestly did not feel like she could get out of bed on her own. She had read a lot about hysterectomies, but she never dreamed she would be recovering from one.

Rita heard a faint cry from a newborn and felt the tears start again. The doctor was adamant about her not taking care of the kids for at least six weeks. But how could she not have her babies for that long? Just this past week had felt like forever. Eddie was staying with Tom's brother Francis, and his wife Norma out on the farm. Norma had brought Eddie to see her just yesterday and fresh tears ran down her cheeks thinking of how fine he seemed.

After just a few minutes of visiting, he had looked at Norma and said,

"Well Norma we better get going." Rita felt like she had already been replaced. From all reports he was having a wonderful time with Doug who was just a few years older than Eddie. She wondered if they truly understood what was going on. Kelli was with Aunt Delores and Patti, who was exactly six weeks old today, was with Rita's sister, Betty. She knew how hard all of this was on Tom, but if she wanted the kids back soon, she knew her focus, for once, had to be on herself.

She drifted off to sleep with a new determination to get her strength back, and a deep feeling of thankfulness for the three babies who waited for their mommy and daddy to come and bring them home.

February 1967

The snow had been falling all night with absolutely no end in sight. Tom thought it was a lot later when he first woke because of the brightness of their bedroom but he realized when he pulled up the shade that it was just before dawn. Mother Nature had created the most beautiful winter wonderland he had ever seen. The trees looked as if they had been sprayed white over night. The branches sagged wearily under the weight of the new fallen snow and it was hard to tell where the yard stopped and the road started.

He let Rita sleep since she had been up with Patti most of the night. She had run a fever and had the worst cold he could remember any of the kids ever having. He hoped she was better today because by the look of things outside no one would be going anywhere.

He went downstairs and turned on the radio. The Streator station was listing all the closed roads and schools that surrounded Dwight. It certainly would be a slow day in the insurance business so Tom enjoyed his morning coffee and the peacefulness that the snow had brought. It had been a long time since they had been hit with a blizzard of this magnitude. Looking out the window, he was sure there was at least a couple of feet already on the ground.

The phone interrupted his thoughts. Some of the guys were helping clear the roads and wondered if Tom could lend a hand. They were meeting up at Metzkes, which was the blacksmith shop off of Main street. It was best known for the daily Euchre tournaments that occurred as regularly as the welding. He dressed in as many layers as he could find and left Rita a note. He would surely be back by lunch time as he would need to check on things at the office by then too. He was out the door before 7:00 a.m. and started to trudge through the snow on the long walk uptown.

Rita woke to the congested, nasally cries of Patti. She was so tired. She heard the heater kick on and could not help but notice how chilly it was in the house. She was greeted by a coughing, runny-nosed Patti who did not look very rested.

As she picked her up she could feel the heat from her clammy little body. Poor thing! She had been really sick the last day or so. Eddie and Kelli were just waking up. Realizing what the night had magically done to their yard, they were shrieking for Mom.

"Come and look Mom!" As Rita pulled up the shade, she could hardly believe her eyes. She had never seen so much snow in all her life!

"Can we go outside? Can we go outside?" Ed was shouting.

"Just as soon as we get some breakfast," she said as she read the thermometer. One hundred and two first thing in the morning! Boy was it going to be a long day she thought as she read Tom's note. She had a feeling that snow clearing was not the most important task that the men had on their minds, but she could do little about this. She could not dwell on this thought for too long though as she noticed the first dark spots leaking through on the butt of Patti's new little sleeper.

Several hours later she had finally sat down. The snow had stopped, but not before dumping four feet in a 48 hour period. Patti had given in to sleep at last, after a very cranky protest. Eddie was outside in his new red snow suit and was having the time of his life. The snow literally dwarfed his little round body as he made one angel after another.

Kelli had just come in and her cheeks matched the color of Ed's snowsuit perfectly. She was now snuggling under her blanket on the couch and was dozing off for her afternoon nap.

Rita was waiting for Dr. Steineche to call her back. She just hated to bother him on a day like today but she was really worried about Patti. Her fever had stayed at 102 all day and she had diarrhea now to add to her misery. She knew Dr. Steineche was an older man but she would do whatever he said. She had not heard from Tom all day but she was sure he was not in any danger. It made her angry just thinking about him so she opted to put him from her mind.

The phone only had to ring once before she picked it up.

"Hello" she said anxiously hoping it was the doctor.

"Hi Rita, this is Dr. Steineche. I can get to the house if you can clear the walks for me," he said in his direct manner that she had grown accustomed to.

"I'll start shoveling right now Doctor and thank you so much." Rita hung up the phone and was dressed for the snow in no time. Eddie was 'helping' her as well as any four-year old could. She had her work cut out for her and if she thought she was mad at Tom earlier, she was fuming now. With every thrust of the shovel, her anger increased.

The fresh snow was heavy and she was forced to take it off in layers. It was actually quite pleasant outside and she began to perspire under the weight of the heavy clothes. The road out front was deserted even though the plows had cleared one lane. Route 47 had never looked this abandoned, but no one in their right mind would go out on a day like this. She put the shovel aside to rest for a minute and noticed a man walking towards her.

"You look like you could use some help," he said as he approached the walk carrying a shovel of his own.

"Be my guest!" Rita yelled, as together they cleared a path. They were just finishing up when a small figure appeared down the block. Dr. Steineche was walking at a good pace for a man his age. He wore a black hat and overcoat which hung well below his knees. His rubbers were packed with snow and appeared white from where Rita stood.

"How's the littlest Slattery doing?" he asked as he made his way up the path that had been cleared in his honor.

"Let's go in and check," Rita said as she turned to thank the stranger who helped her. He had already made his way towards the road when she waved her thanks. With a tip of his hat he was gone. To this day she has no idea who he was but she would never forget his help on that snowy day in 1967. Patti was given a shot much to her disapproval and returned to her old self long before the snow melted. Tom did make it home thanks to John Metzke and his tractor. Much to Rita's chagrin, he showed up right in the middle of the examination rambling on and on. With one look, Rita made it clear that he should go in the bedroom and shut the door. One thing was for sure; the blizzard of '67 would forever be etched in Rita's memory.

1967 was also the year that Rita's youngest brother, Bill, joined the Army. His new wife, Carol, was working in Dwight at William W. Fox Developmental Center as a secretary. They were anxiously waiting to find out where she and Bill would be stationed. She was devastated when Bill was assigned to Germany and the tour had to begin "unaccompanied" as the Army so coldly put it.

In terms that only Carol understood, this meant she could not go with her new husband. Her and Bill had been renting a cute little place out in the country. Carol hated to be alone while Bill was off in another country. Carol spent quite a bit of time with Tom and Rita especially in the winter months. Rita welcomed the visits since her adult conversation was extremely limited.

Carol's visits gave her and Rita a chance to get to know each other. Carol loved the kids, but it was Patti whom she always held during her visits. Patti would nuzzle up with those chubby little cheeks and Carol would succumb to her charm and always pick her up. Carol would no sooner have Patti in her arms than WHAM! Sour milk was all over Carol's perfectly ironed work outfit.

It wasn't just Carol whom Patti chose to throw up on. Almost everyone had been a target of her projectile talent at one time or another. But Carol was always a good sport about it. It was just two months after Bill went over to Germany that he sent for Carol. She was sad to leave home, but Rita was sure she was more than ready to leave the sights and smells of Union Street behind.

Chapter 2

There's No Place Like Home
1968
123 West Chippewa

To his little eyes it looked like a mansion. Standing on the front walk, Eddie looked up at his new house. Mom and Dad had told him that this would be the house he would grow up in. Shielding his eyes from the sun, he glanced at his new front yard. The afternoon sun was hard at work casting shadows on both sides of the sidewalk that split the yard in half.

Just up the street he heard the loud clanging of bells and stepped back to the Walnut tree just in time to see the four o'clock train rumbling through downtown. Boy was it loud. 'I wonder if I'll be able to sleep through that,' he thought, as his attention was diverted to a car pulling in next door. It was a big blue station wagon and the woman driving waved as she drove into the driveway rather fast.

"You must be Eddie!" she yelled, as she grabbed some groceries out of the backseat. As she approached him, he looked over his new neighbor. She was not as tall or thin as his mom but she had a really friendly way about her. She wore her hair short and she seemed quite out of breath.

"Is your mom home?" she asked as she made her way up the front steps. She did not have to go far because Rita was standing just inside the front door.

"Hi Edie!" she called opening the screen door.

"Did you meet Ed yet?"

"I sure did and I'll have to round up all the kids so they can get to know each other." Eddie listened a while as she talked of her kids.

He lost track of what she was saying rather quickly. He had never heard anyone talk that fast in his whole life. At least he might have someone to play with. It sounded to him like she had quite a few kids. He walked down the skinny driveway which led to their small garage. He glanced up at his bedroom window with a proud smile. He finally had his own room. Mom and Dad told him that Kelli and Patti would share the bigger room once Patti was out of her crib. But he did not mind the smaller room a bit. He came around the back of the house just in time to see his Dad go into the garage.

"Hey Bum, what ya doing?"

"Nothing. Just kind of checking out the neighborhood."

"Did you meet the Clausens yet?"

"Just the mom." Tom smiled as he said, "I thought I heard Edie."

He had been trying to organize the garage for over an hour and he was not making much headway as he shoved another box aside. Standing up to stretch, he stepped out of the garage and looked out into the backyard.

"Quite a bit bigger than the old yard, don't ya think Bum?" Eddie just nodded as his eyes glazed over a bit. He was already picturing the football games, the baseball games, and all the golf balls he would be hitting in this awesome yard. It stretched clear out to the alley and was bordered by beautiful Lilac bushes. The yard on Union Street could not hold a candle to this one. He would miss that house, but there were a lot of things he could do without. Like the scary man who mowed yards that lived next door, and the fact that he always had to stay back from the road.

Looking around, he could hardly believe that they actually lived here. This was his yard, and his new bike was in his garage! Realizing that he had not answered his dad, he looked up and smiled as big a smile as his toothless mouth could muster.

"It's gonna be great, Dad!" Running up the back steps, he

stopped and turned around. Taking one more look around, he took it all in. He felt so lucky because he knew at that moment that no matter where he went, he would call this house his home for as long as he would live.

It did not take the rest of the Slattery family long to realize that they too, were home.   It seemed like the neighborhood had been waiting for them all along. Tom and Rita made fast friends with John and Edie Clausen, their next door neighbors.

The Clausen house was a constant flurry of activity with their seven kids coming and going. Cathy was the oldest at 17, and then came Gina, who was 16 and the newest driver of the bunch. Tom's drain pipes didn't stand a chance under the weight of the Clausen station wagon. Paul was the oldest boy and had just turned 13. Cheryl had just turned 11, and was completely taken with Patti. Cindy and Mark were just 15 months apart at nine and seven. Mark was the closest to Eddie's age, but Mark did not seem to be into sports as much as Eddie would have liked. Their youngest was Mary who was 4; exactly the same age as Kelli, and they became instant best friends.

As if Edie did not have enough to do, John's father also lived with them. Actually, it was John's childhood home and after John's mother died, he and Edie moved in with John's father. He was known as Grandpa to everyone who knew him.

Patti was just about two and quickly made her little presence known in the neighborhood. They had only been moved in about a week when John and Edie had found her perched on their kitchen table thoroughly enjoying the peanut butter that she, without so much as a second thought, had helped herself to in the cupboard that was just her size. It had taken Edie quite a while to get all the peanut butter removed from her kitchen, but she was more than used to cleaning up after her clan so she took it right in stride.

Next door to John and Edie lived Donnie and Jeanette Tock and their three kids, John, Rich, and Barb. Their kids were all older than the Slattery's kids but they still became very good friends. Barb was one of the many girls on the babysitting list along with all of the Clausen girls that Tom and Rita used on a regular basis. Ellen Seibold lived on the east side of us. She had two children, Zeke and Mary, who were much older than us.

Patti became a permanent fixture on Cheryl Clausen's hip and Rita was getting used to apologizing for Patti's little antics. Cheryl had just gotten a new pair of glasses that she absolutely hated. Edie had thought they were very "in" with their beige colored frames and square shape, but Patti had taken care of them in one quick swipe. Although Rita was mortified, Cheryl was ecstatic!

It was the fall of 1968 and with the departure of summer came the all too familiar sounds and signs that cooler days would soon be upon us. The trees on Chippewa took on bright yellows and reds while the locust sang their song of changing seasons. The sky was that perfect blue of fall with white puffy clouds completing the scene.

Rita looked out her kitchen window that faced the Clausen's driveway and the west side of their house. She heard giggling from below and stretched over the sink to see from whom these cute sounds were coming. Once again Patti was providing entertainment for Mary and Kelli. She had taken her diaper off and decided to use the driveway for her newest bathroom. Rita tried to be firm, but found herself trying not to bust out laughing as she yelled out to them.

"Patti! You know better than that! Kelli, help her get her diaper back on and bring her in here!"

As she watched them, she could not help but laugh. She watched Mary stifle her giggles with a chubby little hand clasped firmly over her mouth. Mary had gratefully accepted Patti as part of the deal of having Kelli as her new best friend. She was not quite as tall as Kelli and where Kelli's hair was dark. Mary's hair shone like spun gold in the summer sun. They both shared the same short cut, but where Kelli's curled, Mary's hung as straight as the stripes on her shorts Edie had made for her. Mary had sturdy, stocky little legs which were usually covered with band-aids. Her face was round and sprinkled with freckles that these last warm days had distributed on her nose and cheeks.

For all their opposites, they got along like sisters from the start. They were together constantly and usually had an average of two or three major arguments daily. They were really good at including Patti.

Hearing the screech of the back door, Rita relinquished her dishes duty and met her girls as they entered the kitchen. Patti toddled in on the heels of her big sister and Mary. She was rubbing her eyes with hands that had not seen soap since last nights' bath. 'Nap time is just around the corner,' Rita thought with a relieved sigh.

"Eddie?" Patti asked as Rita's thoughts returned to her oldest. Eddie had just started First grade a week ago. Thinking of him, she felt a tug at her heart. He had adjusted to the new house so fast and with so many kids in the neighborhood, she knew he had not had any problem making friends. But she still worried. She had taken him to school on that first day and watched in horror at the number of kids on the playground. Rita had just 10 kids in her class in Kinsman, Illinois. Kinsman had a population of 100 people. She could not imagine leaving her first born to fend for himself in this frenzy of children.

She remembered saying aloud, "They will kill you, Eddie!" He had wiggled up on his knees on the front seat to see what she was looking at with such amazement.

"I'll be fine Mom!" he had said with such confidence that Rita knew he would be. And now after just the first couple of weeks he wanted to walk to school. The Dwight Elementary School was just three blocks from Chippewa Street and Eddie saw this as a perfect chance to show his independence. He was growing up so fast, and it would be only another year before her Kelli would start Kindergarten.

Answering Patti, she explained that he was a big boy and would be going to school all day now. This seemed to suit Patti just fine and she was off to play until Rita called the girls for lunch. Rita had set Patti in her high chair and Kelli at the table.

She decided to finish her dishes while the girls ate. She did not hear the usual chatter behind her and growing suspicious she turned to find her little sweeties asleep at the table. Patti had her head on her chubby little arm and had made her peanut butter sandwich into a pillow much to Rita's dismay.

Kelli had fallen asleep sitting up and her head kept nodding forward inching closer and closer to her Spaghettio's. She deposited them both upstairs on the double bed and decided she could sneak in a nap of her own before Eddie came home at 3:00.

Lying down, Rita reflected on how full her days were with Kelli and Patti at home. This house was quite a bit more work than they had originally thought it would be. She did love the house but she could not believe how much work was involved maintaining both the inside and the outside. There were so many things they wanted to do to it, but they had their hands full now just making the mortgage payments.

Tom was keeping very busy selling insurance. Sometimes too busy! Most of his appointments were in the evenings and Rita missed him. He was doing great though. Ron Wilder had called just this morning to invite them out to dinner this Saturday night. Ron and Rosemary had been so good to Tom and Rita. Ron owned his own insurance business in Dwight and had taken a chance on Tom. She thanked God it was paying off. They had become very good friends and they just adored the kids. Their oldest daughter, Pam, had been so excited when Tom and Rita had asked her to be Patti's Godmother.

Realizing that she had too many things to do to be napping, she got up and made what seemed like the 100th trip down the stairs. She set to work on the dishes that had been started at least three times that day, but she was determined to finish them this time.

It had been a great night but Rita cringed at the mess left in the kitchen. Tom had already made his way upstairs, but Rita did not want to face this mess in the morning so she set to work getting the kitchen back in order. They had had John and Edie over for dinner and they ended up playing cards until well after midnight.

Rita could not stop giggling as she stacked the dishes to be washed. They had all had plenty of martini's and Tom and John had bonded quite a bit. Rita looked out her kitchen window and saw her neighbors through their dining room window. They were turning their lights out and Edie was still giggling too. They headed through the dining room and waved their goodnight to Rita as they headed upstairs.

Thinking again of what had cracked them all up so much, Rita put the dishes away. They had been standing on the front porch thanking John and Edie for coming over. The lamp post with its name plate that declared the occupants of this fine house was burning brightly just below the porch. It was providing the nightly entertainment for the mosquitoes. As John began his descent, he started to stumble down the steps. Like a runaway truck, he gathered speed as he hit each step. Somehow he managed to stay on his feet. He hit the last step and grabbed the lamp post just in time to right himself.

As he swung around to face his neighbors, his usually slicked back hair fell on his forehead as he yelled, "I CAN HARDLY WAIT FOR THE HOLIDAYS!" This was the first of a lifetime of many, many wonderful times with John and Edie.

With Rita's busy days, she found herself needing a car very badly. She was getting tired of being stranded and found that she was more than a little stir crazy without a means of transportation. They found Rita a 1939 dark blue Chevy with a really bad paint job. It was $100.00 and Rita was thrilled to death. She buzzed all over in "Old Susie" and the car more than paid for itself in a very short period of time.

She was able to pick Eddie up from school, do the grocery shopping, and get out of the house whenever she felt like venturing out. The car was beginning to show its age though, and Rita found out more than she cared to about repair bills. She was determined to drive "Susie" until her wheels came off.

Rita almost made that wish come true soon after. One day Rita loaded up the girls and after picking up Eddie at school, decided to run up to the dime store. She proceeded around Hager's Lumber yard passing Moyemont's Plumbing. She started to brake for the familiar turn before the Village Hall which led behind the stores on Main Street. As Rita applied the brakes, all that she felt was the brake pedal hitting the floor. She began to pump the pedal harder using both feet now, but absolutely nothing happened. The panic Rita felt was beyond anything she could remember. Eddie was in the front seat and the girls were in the back with no seatbelts.

The only words she could get out of her now very constricted throat were, "GET DOWN NOW, KIDS! MOTHER HAS NO BRAKES!"

Eddie managed to jump in the backseat and was trying unsuccessfully to get Patti to stay down. She was a nosey little thing and insisted on popping her head up to see what had mom so crazed. Rita knew they were approaching a stop sign and started praying that there were no cars coming. The only thing that she saw to stop them was Boyers' Buick Car Dealership straight ahead. A fleeting picture of the front end of "Old Susie" smashed into the front door of Boyer's flashed through Rita's mind. 'Wouldn't that make a wonderful headline for next week's Star and Herald,' Rita thought as her mind raced for what to do.

"Please God get me through this!" she silently prayed. As they approached the intersection, she turned left hoping with all her heart that the road was clear. The tires were squealing as she made another quick left avoiding any traffic feeding into downtown from Mazon Avenue. They were now on East Main Street.

She was beginning to slow down and she said another quick prayer that no one tried to back out in front of her. She could not pull into a parking spot yet because she was afraid she would jump the curb and ram right into the front of one of the stores on Main Street.

As they passed Art's bird Store, the local tavern that boasted selling swallows, Rita gathered her courage and told the kids to hold on. She had turned the car off and they were now quietly coasting as if everything was fine. She pulled "Old Susie" into a spot in front of the dime store and with a lurch, bounced her off the curb. The old Chevy came to its last stop that day on Main Street. Rita and the kids watched as Kenny Jensen towed the first of many "Old Susie's" to that big junkyard in the sky!

The days moved by faster than anyone wanted and before we knew it, the 60's gave way to the 70's. Tom and Rita watched as Richard Nixon was re-elected for another term as President. Vietnam had succeeded at dividing the nation and Tom and Rita thanked God every day that their kids were too young to be caught up in all that was so wrong in the country. Everyone had an opinion and it was a perfect way to find yourself at odds with your best friend or neighbor.

Tom was against war of any kind but his was a personal opinion. All he had to do was close his eyes and he was back in Korea again. He had spent the early part of his 20's in Korea between 1952 and 1954.

The 18 months Tom spent over there were some of the longest months of his life. After all of their training and preparation for war, they had learned that peace had been declared while they were on the long ship ride over. He would never be able to forget how lonely he was during not one, but two Christmas's.

At the time, Tom was dating Joanne, Rita's younger sister. He wrote to her faithfully but was never really sure of her true feelings until he returned to Kinsman in 1954.

It was then that Joanne broke the news to Tom that she had fallen for a guy while Tom was away. His name was Ken Turner and he was from Dwight. Tom thought his heart would never mend, and much to Tom's disappointment, Ken and Joanne were married within the next year.

It was not until 1955 that Tom started dating Rita and realized that this daughter of Emmett and Eileen was truly his soul mate. They were married in the fall of 1957 on a bitterly cold day in November. Joanne was a bridesmaid in their wedding and by that time Tom and Ken had become friends. This was a true testament that God works in mysterious ways. God certainly had a plan for Tom and Rita and obviously the Korean war played a part in it.

Every night as pictures flashed on the Nightly News, Tom wondered how many thousands of lives were being altered and often destroyed by the lunacy of this war that was not even the USA's to fight. They really did not know anyone personally that the war had affected, but it was emotional enough just letting the images of strangers into their living room night after night.

Tom and Rita replaced "Old Susie" not long after that fateful trip downtown. They stayed with the Chevy name but opted for a beige 4-door this time. It was a good car and had served its purpose as a second car well. It was nice to have when the kids had a babysitter too.

Most of the babysitter's Tom and Rita used were old enough to drive so they were allowed to take Rita's car to the Dairy Queen or to take the kids out for Pizza. One night in particular, Jamie Stevenson was babysitting. Jamie was the daughter of good friends of Tom and Rita.

There was a dance at the Legion that Tom and Rita and John and Edie had gone to. The old Chevy was parked across the street in front of the house facing west.

After a fun night of drinking and dancing Tom and Rita made their way home with John and Edie who had driven their car. Getting out of the car, Tom looked around and realized that Rita's car was not across the street where they had left it . He had had quite a few drinks, but he was sure that the car was on the street when they left for the dance.

Once they got inside they asked Jamie about the car but even she had not noticed it being gone. She had not taken the kids anywhere since they had had T.V. dinners that night.

"We better call the police," Rita said as she paid Jamie. About that time John came to the door.

"Tom, I think we found Rita's car," he said in that deep voice that was like no other. As Tom and Rita walked out on the porch, they followed John's gaze across the street to Mary Smith's house. There, tucked into her shrubs that lined her front porch, was Rita's car. From where they stood they could see its back end was badly damaged.

"What in the hell happened here?" Tom said as his glow from their night out started to disappear. He stormed inside and was dialing the number to the police when the doorbell rang again. He was already talking to the dispatcher and she was sending someone over right away. Rita answered the door and recognized the two good looking young men instantly. One was a Phelan boy, and one was Joe White's son. Both were from Kinsman and their parents were longtime friends of Tom and Rita's.

Kevin looked so mad and he allowed Mike to start rambling before Rita could even get them inside. The smell of liquor was enough to make Rita step back as they both started to explain how Mike had hit Rita's car and then got scared and left it in the bushes across the street. Through the melee, Tom and Rita deciphered that the boys had been at a party in Dwight. Tom stood trying to hide his smirk as he listened to the tale unfold. Mike had taken Kevin's car to go see his girlfriend. When Mike took Kevin by the house where he had hit the car, Kevin's anger mixed with embarrassment when he realized that Mike had hit his insurance man's car!

As if there was not enough confusion already, the doorbell rang again and this time it was the Dwight Police. Kevin Phelan was sitting on the couch in the entry way apologizing to Rita! Jamie was used to being out late on her babysitting nights, but she had never seen anything quite like the scene she was witnessing at the Slattery's tonight.

Rita kept apologizing to her, but she would not have missed this for anything. Oscar Beier was the policeman on duty and he was more than a little amused by the scene as well. He was a favorite of almost everyone in town and he was very well liked by the young people. Mike was on the phone with his Dad who from the sound of things was not taking the news too well.

"Tom, my dad wants to talk to you," Mike said as he handed the phone to him. Oscar was talking quietly with Rita, asking her what she wanted to do with the car.

"Should we wait until morning to push it out, Rita?"

"We might as well do it now since I'm sure the entire neighborhood is up anyway!"

Tom was off the phone as the boys both anxiously waited to hear what the father's had decided.

"Your dad is willing to pay for the damages through his insurance, Mike. Oscar, if you can forget you heard anything about a hit and run, we can fill out an accident report right now and be done with it," Tom said as he smiled at his old friend.

"Whatever you want to do, Tommy."

Rita finally got Jamie home while the men wrote up the accident report. As she dropped her off, Rita yelled, "I'll understand if you don't want to sit for us again, Jamie." Flipping her long hair out of her eyes, Jamie replied, "Are you kidding Rita? That was more excitement than I have had in a long time!"

She waved goodnight and went inside as Rita laughed the whole way home. Her luck was sure not going so good with cars, but she was very thankful that no one had been hurt. She made a mental note to call Jamie's mom, Irma, first thing in the morning. She was sure Mary Smith would need an explanation as well.

As she pulled into the drive, she waved goodnight to Oscar who was just leaving. Tom met Rita at the door with the two young men close behind.

"Be careful, you two." Tom yelled as they both watched the dented car pull away.

"Just another memorable night at the Slattery house," Rita muttered closing the door and heading upstairs to bed.

Chapter 3

The Golfer

Summer 1970

Ed watched in the side mirror as the dust billowed out from behind the Rambler. The blue vinyl dashboard of the station wagon was as thick with dust as the air outside. They had not had the Rambler for too long and it was still a new car to Eddie. Tom and Rita knew that with 100,000 miles on it, it was far from being new. They had found it up at Boyer's and it seemed to be the perfect car for a family of five.

Ed breathed in the familiar smell of dust mixed with the smells of the country. It all meant that Ed was going to spend this Saturday doing the only thing he could think of these days. The thought made Ed's stomach do a little jump. They had just turned on to the gravel road leading out to the golf course and Dad had told him that they could play eighteen holes today.

It was a perfect day. The sky held a few white clouds but nothing that would bring rain. Mom and the girls had asked him to go to the pool in Odell with them, but swimming just was not how he wanted to spend his day. It had just been a year since Ed started golfing but already, he knew he was starting to get the hang of it.

As they drove past the fields, the plush green canvas of the seventh hole came into view. They had had lots of rain and the course was as green as the stripes on Ed's tube socks. They both noticed a threesome just getting ready to tee off and Ed waved when they turned towards the road. He recognized all of them. Glenn Funk, Chuck Watters, and Ikey Watters were Dad's golfing buddies.

"Looks like they got an early start," Dad said.

Dad played on Sunday mornings when most of the other male members did. Mom was not too happy since this standing Sunday morning golf date meant that we did not get to go to church as a family, but Ed understood all too well. In fact he was a little jealous, and if they allowed kids on the course on Sunday mornings, he would be out here too.

They were pulling into the parking lot now which sat directly in front of the small clubhouse. The building looked like an ordinary house with its white paint and brown roof with the trim around each window to match. Eddie could see the putting green to the right of the clubhouse and he felt the itch to get out on the course. He knew they had to sign in and he hoped that this time he would not have to wait for Dad to have a drink first. They entered through the Pro-shop and saw Terry Cole walking down the two steps that lead into the bar.

"Hey Terry!" Dad said as Terry made his way behind the glass display case. Ed said hi and watched Terry take a pull on his cigar. He was a good looking man with dark hair and even darker eyes. His face showed the lines of his days in the sun but the color blended perfectly with his other features. He did not smile very often and as Ed looked at him he thought about how mean he could look at times.

"So the Slattery boys are going to play a little golf today?"

"Yep! Pick out a couple sleeves of balls Eddie, I'll be right back."

Eddie let out a disappointed sigh as he watched his dad head for the bar. He knew what this meant. If he was lucky, they would get out on the course in about an hour. He climbed the two steps and saw Dad sit down on a stool. Eddie ordered a coke and was heading out the door to the patio when he heard his Dad.

"Hey Bum! If you want to play, why don't you head out on your own."

Ed was sure there had to be some mistake. Did he hear him right? He turned and looked at him.

"You mean I can go play by myself?"

"Sure! You've been out with me enough times."

Eddie was beaming. He was going out on the course by himself for the first time! He almost ran to get his clubs. It did not matter to him that his clubs were actually his mom's old set. As he set up to the ball, he tried to concentrate on everything that he had learned during the lessons Terry had given him on Friday mornings. Terry had started a junior golf clinic free of charge and Ed had not missed a lesson.

He teed off from the men's tee and clobbered it. He was sure they had watched from the clubhouse. As if confirming his thoughts, Dad stuck his head out of the patio door and yelled "Nice shot, Bum!" Eddie gave him the thumbs up sign and he hurried to where his ball was. He finished the first hole and continued on to what he thought was number two. What he did not realize was that he was missing most of the holes on the front nine. The layout of the course was a bit confusing and he had played only the holes he could see.

He finished up on number nine and was back in the clubhouse within the hour. Dad had not seen him come up on number nine, and he was quite surprised when he walked in to the clubhouse.

"That was quick," Dad said as he focused his attention on the bottom of his now empty glass. Dad's drink of choice was a very dry martini, which consisted of two shots of Vodka on ice. Motioning for another, Dad turned his now fuzzy gaze toward Ed who was explaining his route around the course. They all had a good laugh about Ed's abbreviated round, but he had had the time of his life, even if he did not play the course the right way.

That day was the beginning of Ed's life long passion for the game of golf. It would only take him two years before he started winning tournaments. Although Dad was not the best golfer, he taught Ed everything he needed to know to be a champion. Ed could out drive Dad before long but he would never outgrow the lessons Dad gave him at D.C.C.

Who needs tonsils anyway?

July 1971

As she lifted her heavy eyelids, she had to blink several times before her eyes focused. She felt like she had bricks on her eyes and she fought hard to keep them open. She tasted the saliva forming in her mouth and without thinking started to swallow. She winced in pain as she remembered why she was lying in this strange bed. Large tears began to spill from her eyes and she tried hard not to swallow the lump in her throat.

"It's OK sweetie." Kelli turned to see her mom near her bedside.

"It hurts," she managed to mouth to her mom.

"I know sweetie. We just have to give it a chance to heal in there." Kelli noticed her mom looked really tired as she watched her reach up and scratch her forehead. Rita looked at the clock on the wall of the recovery room for what seemed like the tenth time in the last ten minutes.

She was just beginning to feel the effects of the past couple days. She could finally let go of the knot that was pulling at her stomach. She hated the fact that Kelli had to be under general anesthesia and she was more than a little relieved to see those big blue eyes open, even though they were blinking back tears.

She would be able to take Kelli home today if everything checked out with the doctor. Rita watched as Kelli drifted back to sleep. She rested her head on her arm and to her surprise, was awakened by the doctor. The procedure to remove Kelli's tonsils had gone fine. The doctor told Rita that they should have been removed a year ago.

Rita related that after Kelli's first six cases of strep throat she had asked Dr. Thomas about this and he did not believe it was necessary to remove her tonsils at that time. Kelli was able to go home thank God. As a special treat Mom had stopped at the Dairy Queen on the way home. The doctor told Kelli that she would know by how her throat felt as to when to start eating real foods.

Mom had ordered a cheeseburger which to Kelli looked

like a steak dinner after the last four days of hospital food. Kelli had ordered strawberry ice cream, but she wanted to sink her teeth into that cheeseburger more than anything. She took a small bite, but had to spit it out. It would be another week before her seven year old throat was ready for anything other than Jello, ice cream, or pudding.

Chapter 4

Eddie's Little Brother
Summer '71

"Where are you guys going tonight, Mom?" I asked looking up at Mom who was putting on her makeup.

"Out to the V.F.W. for a ROTO dance," she answered as she dotted her face with makeup.

"Glenn and Anna May are coming here for drinks before we head out." I was in my usual spot while she got ready, sitting on the toilet in the upstairs bathroom. Through the open window, I could lean over and see down to Clausen's driveway.

The hum of a lawn mower drifted in the window from somewhere down the block and the breeze coming in the window held the sweet smell of freshly cut grass. I could not help the lonely feeling that enveloped me almost every time I knew Mom and Dad planned to go out for the night. I wished that I could go with them, but just like most of their other nights out, it was not a family thing.

Mom took a drag off her cigarette that sat perched in the Caesar's Palace ashtray on the marbleized counter. I traced a long forgotten drip of light blue paint on the cupboards that sat underneath the marble counter. I opened the top drawer to the right of the cupboards and sifted through Mom's jewelry. The bathroom was decorated in different shades of blues. I counted six shades from where I sat. My tanned bare feet rested on the waste basket made from recycled magazines.

I closed my eyes and took a deep breath. The smells were always the same when Mom was getting ready; the clean smell of her soaped skin just after getting out of the tub, mixed with Right Guard and the lingering smell of smoke from her Kent cigarettes. The bathroom kept this smell long after they had left for the evening. Even though she wasn't, the smells would still be here when I would come up later to get ready for bed.

I could hear Eddie through the closed bathroom door.

"I am old enough to stay with the girls!" Eddie protested to Dad who was dressing in their bedroom. He would be turning nine at the end of the summer and just hated the fact that he had to be with a babysitter!

"I know Eddie, but we would just feel better if someone was here to help you with the girls," Dad was saying in that voice that was a clear sign that this was not up for a whole lot of discussion.

"Fine then, I'm going to the Dairy Queen," he yelled as he thudded down the stairs.

"Eddie, you wait for Cindy and the girls!" Mom yelled from the bathroom.

"SHE is baby-sitting us? Jeeeez!" Eddie whined from the base of the stairs.

"Go get your shoes on sweetie, and tell Kelli that it's time for you to walk to the Dairy Queen."

"OK Mom, have a good time." At the bottom of the stairs, I turned and yelled back up, "Love you!"

"Love you too Bum! Be good for Cindy," Dad yelled. Cindy Clausen was one of our usuals. Eddie actually preferred Cindy to Cheryl Clausen who Eddie thought was a ditz. I was sure Eddie probably had more of a crush on Cheryl than anything else. Cindy was at the door and we all headed down the street towards the Dairy Queen.

I was quickly becoming Eddie's little brother wannabe and I had plenty of scrapes and bruises to show for it. I would be starting Kindergarten in the fall and I was already a tomboy. We turned up Washington Street and just as we were crossing Delaware, Eddie turned to me, "I will race ya?"

"Give me a head start!" I said as I took off at a dead run.

I turned back just before reaching the other side of Delaware Street to see if he was coming. This was when I felt myself starting to fall. I turned back around just in time for my head to hit the curb. Eddie was beside me before I got up and the look on Cindy's face was enough to start me screaming.

"We have to get her home NOW!" Cindy yelled as she picked me up and started running back towards Chippewa. I could hear her whispering, "Please be home Tom and Rita, Please be there!"

Eddie was already in the house and to Cindy's relief, Mom and Dad met us at the end of our sidewalk. My right eye was swollen shut and it hurt worse than any punches Eddie had ever landed. Glenn and Anna May Funk were in the kitchen. Dad set me up on the file cabinet in the dining room and Mom got on the phone to the doctor. I had to keep an ice pack on it and I was crying so hard that I could hardly get my breath. Dad made me stop crying.

"Be tough now, it's not that bad. You just look like Eddie landed a good punch to your face."

Glenn and Anna May left and we all took off for the emergency room at St. Mary's in Streator. Dad carried me inside and just as he was about to open the door I saw a sign with a dog on it. For the first time since my fall, I forgot my eye. I was terrified of dogs and asked Dad if there were any dogs in here.

"No sweetie, there are no dogs in hospitals," he said as he chuckled all the way to the desk. I remember the secure feeling I had when I was in Dad's arms. I loved it when Dad carried me. It was as if no one would ever hurt me. I was too big to be carried, but that night even though my eye hurt, I felt so lucky to have my mom and dad home.

I had to wear a patch until the blood that had pooled around my eye went away. It was black and blue until I started Kindergarten and it would leave a small scar. This was only the first in what would be a long line of injuries usually caused by trying to be the brother that Eddie always wanted.

Chapter 5

The Kindergarten Kid

August 1971

As I walked through the big doors at the end of the hallway, I could hardly believe that this day had finally come. I was starting school! Mom and I did not have to go far since my classroom was the first one inside the door. The room was crowded with anxious parents and apprehensive Kindergartners. Looking around the room, I could not stop the huge smile from forming. I could not believe how big it was. I had not been to any nursery school, so this was my first look at the big time.

A nice looking woman with a nametag that I could not read was introducing herself to my mom. So this was my teacher. I heard her say her name was Miss Andersen and she bent down so we were looking right at each other.

"Hi Patti! Why don't you let me help you find your cubby and your table and you can color at your seat until everyone else gets settled." I liked her already. She had a big smile and her voice was sort of soft, not loud like the teacher's on the TV.

She took my hand and we walked by a long workbench with real tools on it. Straight ahead, I noticed that my room had its own bathroom.

'Wow this really was some room!' I thought as she turned towards the back wall. I saw lots of hooks for jackets and she showed me what this "cubby" thing involved. It was a long red shelf with small square boxes cut out of it. Each cubby had a different name on it and Miss Anderson showed me to mine. I noticed some of the letters on the cubby next to mine, but I had never seen that name that started with a 'B' before.

As I followed my new teacher, I noticed she had one of those neat shag haircuts like my mom. She showed me to my table and I took out my brand new crayons and pretended to start coloring. There was so much going on in the room that I gave up trying to color. I noticed two boys with their moms and wondered what had happened to mine. As if she knew I was thinking about her, Mom whispered in my ear.

"Are you going to be O.K. Sweetie?" Mom asked in a different voice than her normal one.

Part of me wanted her to stay, but I felt fine about this huge play place. She kissed me and I noticed one big tear slide down her face. I watched her as she walked out the door and realized this was a lot harder for her than it was for me. I was, after all, her baby and her last one to leave home.

I let go of my sad thoughts about mom and sat back taking in my new Kindergarten room. At the far end of the classroom, tall thin windows lined the wall. Looking out, I saw Mom drive by. She was looking back towards the window of my classroom on her way home. She would be back at 3:00 and that was only a few hours away. Kelli was going to meet me outside my room, since she was just up the hall in Mrs. Meyers' class.

I felt so grown up just knowing that I was in the same school as Eddie and Kelli. Eddie was farther up the hall in Ms. Voyles' fourth grade class. I turned around to check out what was on the other side of the room and I found a real live kitchen that was just my size. There were cupboards and a sink and even a stove. They all sat on carpet, and across from the kitchen were lots of dolls. They sat in strollers and one was propped up in a cradle.

Hearing loud screams, I turned around and saw the two boys that I had noticed earlier. Both were crying and one, who seemed really upset, was clinging to his mom.

"Now John, you will be fine. Just stop this right now!" his mom was saying in a quiet voice.

She looked older than most of the other moms. Her son was

just a little guy. He was shorter than I was and I wondered if maybe he was four instead of five. The other boy would not sit in his chair and I could hear him telling his mom, "I just want to go home!" His name was Dean and he was supposed to be sitting at my table.

Turning completely around in my chair, I stared as another reluctant Kindergartner came through the door. She was a little chubby and she had the longest red hair that I had ever seen. Her eyes were red and swollen and they had little white dots all around them as if she had been crying all morning. She was walking behind her mom who looked as nervous as the little girl. Her mom was a small thing and she had some of those cat eye glasses that she kept adjusting nervously.

I watched as Miss Anderson talked with the mom and slowly worked her way to the red haired little girl. She must not have liked what her new teacher was saying because her red hair starting going back and forth as fresh tears flowed from her swollen eyes. I really did not understand why these kids were so upset. I mean this was GREAT! We were in THE school now, so what was with all the tears?

My attention was diverted from the newest arrival by some disgusting sounds from Dean's area at our table. He had gotten himself so upset that he had thrown up all over himself, his mother, and a boy named Joe Call. Miss Anderson came over to him and got a really weird look on her face. She went over to the wall and pushed a button.

"Can you send Fred down to Room #1, Mrs. Condon? We have had a little problem with one of our new students!"

Dean's mom, who was really tall for a lady, was very nervous now and kept apologizing to Miss Anderson. In all the commotion, I had not realized that the little red haired girl had sat down at my table. She was making those hiccupping sounds that you make after you have cried too much. Her striped top matched her blue shorts that served as a resting place for her long hair when she sat down in her chair. I noticed her mom was gone and I figured it was a good idea not to talk about it.

Realizing that I was going to have to make the move, I asked her what her name was. I watched her bottom lip quiver as she whispered.

"I am Brenda." I tried to sound grown up when I announced in a strong voice, "Hi, I am Patti Jo Slattery."

We both watched as Miss Andersen helped clean up Dean, Joe and his mother. Dean seemed to be losing his battle with keeping up his protest. He sat down next to another little girl whose eyes looked a little funny. She had a really round face and did not say anything. Her name was Annette, but Brenda and I were already talking to each other so we sort of ignored everyone else for a while.

A little man entered the room pushing a garbage can, and carrying a container of pink stuff. He recognized Brenda right away and she called him Fred. When he turned around, I almost screamed. He had a perfectly normal left hand but where his right hand should have been, he had this hook thing.

My mouth dropped wide open as I watched him shake this pink stuff on the area that Dean had polluted. He was amazing! He used this hook thing as if it were a hand. The room smelled really bad but Miss Andersen was talking to all of us and telling us to come and sit on the carpet in front of her desk.

I am not sure how we got that way, but I found myself hand in hand with Brenda. I had found my first friend.

We had decided on Monday, Friday night would be the first night for Brenda to sleep over at my house. I was so excited I could hardly sleep all week. We had been making plans all week and we had decided that Brenda should bring two suitcases. One would be filled with her Barbies. She had so many more than I did and she had all the newest outfits for them too. The other would hold her coloring books and crayons. I had lots of these but there was just something about coloring in other peoples' coloring books that made it more fun.

Ever since that first day of school, we had been inseparable. It had been two months since the beginning of our friendship and things were going great. After that first day she had finally dried up and it was not long before she was enjoying herself.

As for myself, I was having the time of my life. I did not care too much for those dittos we had to do sometimes but the free play was worth the wait.

After what seemed like the longest week ever, Friday finally arrived and I watched as Brenda's mom pulled into the driveway. I ran out and grabbed Brenda as if she was a long lost friend. She smiled shyly as she looked at her mom.

She was a little quiet but then so was her mom. It always took her a little while to become used to things, but I was sure once we got playing she would lighten up and enjoy herself. Besides, this was her first sleep over, if you do not count her times with Grandma Humbert or her Aunt Phyllis.

Mom had come out onto the porch and was reassuring Delores that we would have a great time. Mom and Dad were not going out and Dad was supposed to be working late so we had nothing but time to play.

"We'll be home tonight too, Rita, so just give us a call if you need anything," Delores said as she got behind the wheel.

I watched Brenda as she turned around to look at her mom. She raised her arm to wave and I thought I saw that same look of panic that she had that first day of school. Before she could get herself worked up, I grabbed her by the hand and we ran up the steps.

"Which one of these has the coloring books?" I asked as her face broke into a smile again.

Before long the living room floor was a carpet of Little Lulu, Flintstone, and Raggedy Ann coloring books. Kelli walked in and stopped to see what we were doing.

"Hi guys! Whatcha doing?" she asked as Brenda looked up from her coloring.

"Brenda, this is my sister Kelli." I watched as Brenda quietly said hi. Brenda studied Kelli as she picked up a crayon and began helping me with my picture. I watched too, as Kelli expertly used her left hand to color perfectly in the lines.

I knew that Brenda had an older brother. Wayne was Eddie's age and they played together quite a bit. As far as I knew, it was just the two of them. I watched Brenda as her gaze went from Kelli's face to mine and back again.

"Do you have any sisters?" Kelli asked without looking up from her picture of Raggedy Ann.

"I would have had one, but she died," Brenda said matter of factly.

"That's too bad." Kelli said in a quiet voice. Kelli looked at me as if to say 'oops' and I just shrugged my shoulders at her. I wanted to know more about this, but I knew we should get talking about something else.

"Let's get out the Barbie's!" I said a little too loud. Brenda seemed to snap out of her momentary sadness and she returned to playing without another word about the tragic news we had just heard. W e had been playing for about an hour when I heard my dad's car pull in the driveway.

"Girls, start picking up in there, we are going to eat soon," we heard Mom holler from the kitchen.

We were gathering up the crayons just as the front door opened. We both looked up to see my dad standing in the entrance to the living room. He had on brown slacks, a striped shirt and his dark brown tie. I loved to see him all dressed up in his suit. He looked tired and his tie hung loose around his neck as if it had been set free in the car on his way home.

"Hey girls! This must be Brenda! How are you?" I hurried to my feet to get the usual kiss and hug that was as welcome as his smell of Old Spice.

"Hi Bum! How was your day?" he asked as he began to take his wallet out of his pocket. Dad had his glasses on, which meant he had been in the office this afternoon.

"Oh it was great and Brenda gets to stay over----" I stopped in mid sentence as I turned to see why Brenda had not said anything. She had that panicked look and her face was as red as her hair.

Looking at me, she let go of the tears that had been building just under the surface.

"What is wrong sweetie?" Dad said as he bent down to her level. She was crying really hard now and those little white bumps were showing around her eyes again.

"What did you do, Tom?" my mom asked as she came into the living room through the dining room entrance. My dad just shook his head as he looked at Mom apologetically.

"I want to go home," Brenda managed to choke out through her hiccups of air.

"Oh, Man!" I said, as my wish for a super fun night began to disappear.

"What is it?" I asked as gently as I could through my frustration.

"I just don't want to be here," she said as a huge tear trickled down her round cheek. With that, Mom was on the phone to Delores. Before we were even able to pick up, Delores was pulling in the driveway.

"I'm so sorry about this Tom and Rita," Delores said as she bent to pick up the suitcases.

"I just wish I knew what I did," Dad said as he settled in his chair. He was stirring his martini that Mom had made him while he had helped us pick up.

"Bye Brenda. Maybe we can try another time," I said as bravely as I could muster. I had received one of those looks from Dad when I started complaining about how bored I was going to be all night, so I thought I better just hush. I waved from the front door and watched as they pulled out of the drive.

It was not until years later that we would find out that Dad had indeed brought on Brenda's crying fit. She had not met him before and I guess with his glasses on he scared her to death. Dad never let Brenda forget about that day. Every time we told the story Dad had to rub it in. "I knew I was scary looking Brenda, but you really knew how to hurt a guy."

Before long, all three of us kids were going to school for the full day. The big house on Chippewa was in need of a face lift so in order to pay for the remodeling, Mom decided to go to work. Dwight did not offer a lot for a stay at home mom wanting to return to the work force, but Mom put applications in all over town.

After several weeks, she got a call from the Coil Factory in town. Although this was something Mom had no experience in, she was more than willing to try. She had no idea what to expect and she was so nervous that first day.

Once the kids were off to school, Rita took some extra time getting ready. She chose her new purple pantsuit for her first day on the job and she held her head high as she entered. She knew many of the employees, but she knew the minute she walked in that she had over-dressed. The place was very dark and the noise was overwhelming.

She was given her assignment to begin winding wire coils that are spun onto spools as big as a bushel basket. She tried to disguise her shaking hands and began to wind the coil.

From where she was working, she could see out into a large walk-way. She could not help but notice the whispers and stares as the workers watched their new co-worker. It wasn't long before the first spool was filled. Instead of automatically stopping, the machine needed to be slowed down to remove the spool.

As Rita watched in horror, the spool spun off of its spot it front of her as the machine began to make the loudest noise she had ever heard. She watched as the spool bounced out into the walkway. They all stood and stared. Her embarrassment was almost debilitating as she asked herself, 'Why hadn't they told me what to do?'

Her supervisor managed to shut down the machine as the workers around her continued to watch her every move. No one was injured, but the sneers and laughter from her co-workers cut into her with more hurt than if the wire had. She learned by fire on the job without any help or support.

She spent that first day after work uptown at the dime store.

She bought two pair of jeans, tennis shoes and several blouses to wear so she did not ruin her good clothes. She did her job and took her lunch, which she usually ate alone for several weeks.

After about a month she had fallen into a routine although she hated the job more than anything she had ever done. One Friday afternoon she was at the vending machine when three of her co-workers approached her.

"When are you going to get it?" they asked, almost sneering at her.

"Get what?" she replied.

"You don't belong here. You never have and you never will." Rita collected her soda and sat alone.

The next day, she received the best news she had ever had. Donnie Andreasen wanted her to start working for him at their new clothing store uptown. She approached her supervisor and told him she was giving her two-week notice since she was offered a job at LeDon's selling shoes.

"We have never had anyone give a two week notice here," he said with a shocked look on his face.

"None of us thought you needed the money, Rita. We couldn't understand why you were working."

As she headed for the door, she turned around with her finger extended and said, "If I did not need the money, I would have walked out of here that first day. I would rather smell dirty feet all day than work under these filthy conditions with these nasty people!" She walked out of the Coil factory and never looked back.

Chapter 6

The Longest 6 Months of Her Life
February 1973

I woke to the familiar sounds of the radio coming from the bathroom. Dad was obviously going through his morning routine. Something did not feel right though. As my feet met the cold hard wood floor of our bedroom, Dad came into the hallway.

"Morning sweetie," he said a little tentatively.

"Where's Mom?" I said sensing that something was wrong.

"Let's get Kelli and Ed up and I'll tell you what is going on," he said avoiding my question. 'She died' was all I could think. For those few minutes, I began to picture my life without my mom and I felt the sobs beginning.

"Sweetie, it is OK," Dad said as he pulled me onto his lap.

We were all sitting on Ed's bed and we looked into Dad's bloodshot eyes and waited for the worst.

"Mommy fell at the VFW last night and she broke her hip. They had to do surgery and she will be in the hospital for about two weeks while it heals."

"Is she going to die?" I asked quietly.

"NO stupid," Eddie said disgusted, "you don't die of a broken hip." He hesitated and looked up sheepishly at Dad, "Right, Dad?"

"No No No. She is just going to have to let it heal. She will be on crutches a while so we will have to help a lot." And so we all began a crazy couple of weeks with Aunt Dode and Uncle Bob. Eddie stayed with Glenn and Anna May Funk out on their farm. For the first time ever, I was forced to wear dresses to school. We wrote to Mom daily and could not wait to see her. I had never been away from her and I was not being a real good girl for Aunt Dode. It was fun playing with Jeff who was just 3 years younger than I was and we did see Dad every day.

I have never seen a more welcome sight than Mom sitting in the car that day they came to pick us up. I had been sitting, looking out the window facing Waupansie Street for at least an hour when they pulled up. We had to be very careful around Mom and we absolutely could not sit on her lap.

She brought home two sets of crutches so that she could keep one at each landing of the stairs. Dad had put in railings going down to the basement to help her. No matter how hard I tried, I was always bumping her. Church seemed to be the hardest since I could not sit still to save my life.

I can still feel the sting from the back of Dad's hand as I put the kneeler down on Mom's leg again. I was a hazard but it was Mom who felt the sting of Dad's words. Tom had been given strict instructions from the doctor before Mom left the hospital.

"Tom you must not let Rita feel sorry for herself. If she starts, she will become very depressed and it can affect her recovery," the doctor said matter of factly.

Sure enough, one afternoon, not long after Mom had been home, Dad walked in to find her weeping at the kitchen table.

"I can't do this, Tom," she said with a heavy sigh.

Mustering more anger than he felt and denying himself the desire to fold her in his arms, he made the doctor proud when he said, "Knock it off, Rita. If I ever come in this house to find you feeling sorry for yourself again, I'll walk right back out."

The anger she felt at him for those words could not be measured. How dare he say that. The anger was enough to straighten her back bone and suck up her self-pity for the next few months on those damn crutches.

Ed played golf every chance he could get. It was the summer

of 1973 when he won the Junior Club Championship at Dwight Country Club. His first trophy was going to be engraved with his name, so it was a few weeks later that he ran in the house to show off his first trophy. Mom was the only one home. She was cleaning the bathroom upstairs and stopped at the sink to see what Ed was bounding up the stairs with.

She watched him enter the bathroom in his short-sleeved shirt and jean shorts. His face was freckled from his days on the golf course and his blue eyes were sparkling above his proud smile.   He was holding a small trophy with a male golfer. The golf club was extending out from the trophy, and as they would soon find out, was not glued into the hands of the small statue.

"Let me see that!" Mom said as excited as Ed was. She reached for the trophy and watched in horror as the golf club came loose. It disappeared down the drain of the sink before either one could make a move to catch it. She could not speak, but Ed found his voice immediately. The tears came instantly for both Mom and Ed, but no matter what she tried to say, Ed could not be consoled.

He slammed into his room and would not talk to her. She called Terry at the Country Club and explained what had happened. It was not even an hour later that Terry dropped off an identical club to the one that was now making its way through the pipes of the house. Mom set the trophy, which was now restored to its original state, just outside Eddie's room. In the years ahead, Ed would win more trophies than his room and the house could hold, but not one meant as much as the little one that sat outside his room that afternoon.

Chapter 7

Just call me L.B. (Law Breaker)
1974

I was now a third grader and had finally made the move to the big hall. My teacher was Mrs. Fanelli and she was beautiful and young. Her long black hair was always worn down and curled and her flawless dark complexion offset huge brown eyes that were perfectly circled by long lush eyelashes. She wore short skirts and sometimes her tops were low cut and you could see that little line between her boobs.

Our principal that year spent quite a bit of time checking on our room. He was tall and thin and twitched constantly. He was a blinker with a pointy nose and chin. His walk was easily and frequently ridiculed, with his feet pointing out so his heals almost touched. He used to stand really close to Mrs. Fanelli whenever he came in and most of the time she could be seen backing up.

Even though I had never been in trouble he instilled the kind of fear that only an elementary school principal can. Ed and the rest of the Jr. High kids would always make fun of him.

Ed was in seventh grade, but he was all the way down at the other end of the school. He played on the basketball team and I felt so cool because I knew all the older kids.

My favorite was Kathy Bednarik. Her mom was a fourth grade teacher and I used to visit them a lot. Kathy always included me since I hung around Eddie all the time. Third grade was hard work and I was trying so hard to get this multiplication thing down. Brenda was not in my class, but she was right across the hall so we played together at every recess.

One afternoon after all our work was finished, Carol Leskanich and I were playing a game in the back of the room on the carpet. Carol had brought back a ruler and a small pink eraser that had seen lots of mistakes.

I watched as she balanced the wooden ruler half on the table and half off. The thin gold strip was beginning to peel away from the edge of the chipped ruler. I felt that mischievous grin of misbehaving as I watched Carol place the worn pink eraser on the end of the ruler that was steady on the table. I had seen the boys do this, but not when Mrs. Fanelli was in the room. Carol turned her petite frame around, and saw that Mrs. Fanelli was turned around with her back to us. Carol gently hit the part of the ruler that was off the table and I watched as the eraser flipped up and came down on the carpet.

Mrs. Fanelli was busy taking down the bulletin board over by the sink. She had on a bright orange suit that showed that line between her boobs. Quite a few of the kids were finished with their work so there were different things going on around the classroom.

It was now my turn to try the ruler trick and I set it up but this time I was going to see how far I could let it fly. I had watched Greg Schou flip it all the way across the room so I did not hold anything back when I hit the dangling end of the ruler.

What happened next could only happen to me and if I tried a million times probably could never hit that target again. I knew the eraser had gone far but I hit the ruler so hard that I could not follow the eraser's destined flight. Carol was laughing so hard she was snorting out loud. I quickly looked over to where Mrs. Fanelli was standing to ensure my escapades went unnoticed.

I watched in horror as she dug into her orange suit and retrieved the pink eraser from somewhere lower than where that line ended between her boobs. Carol continued her laughing fit and Mrs. Fanelli's cold dark stare met mine. I felt the flames of guilt creep their way up my neck and face. The first beads of sweat were breaking out on my forehead and I knew she knew it was me. The ruler that had catapulted the eraser, was now on the floor at my fidgeting feet like a smoking gun.

She walked right over to us and I could see her nostrils flaring. Her chest rose with each furious breath.

"Whose eraser is this?" she said through clenched teeth. Carol raised her little hand, but her eyes never left mine.

"And how, may I ask, did it get down the front of my blouse?" Her eyes followed me as I reached down to pick up the ruler.

I did not have to say anymore than, "I did it." I felt the lump lodge in my throat as tears began welling up in my panicked eyes. My legs were shaking so much that I steadied myself on the table.

"You march yourself right down to that office and put your nose against the wall. When the principal comes out, you tell him why you are there!"

When I turned around, every kid in my class had stopped what they were doing. You could have heard a pin drop, or perhaps an eraser fall, it was so quiet. Each stare held the grateful look that it was me and not them in this predicament.

I had never been in this much trouble in my life. The thought of having to tell my principal what I had done was enough to make the tears come in heaving succession before I even reached the fifth grade rooms.

As if life was not bad enough, it was just the time for the junior high to change classes. As I stood there with my nose against the hard blue textured wall outside the office, Wayne Zimmerman, Brenda's brother, came out of the boy's bathroom.

"What did you do, Patti?" I didn't answer him since all I could do was cry. 'Great,' I thought, 'Now Ed will know and then everyone else will too.'

I stood there for what seemed like a week and then I heard Mrs. Fanelli's familiar heels coming down the hallway. Clip clop clip clop. I did not look at her and she did not speak to me. I smelled her perfume as she whipped her long black curls around and pushed through the glass door of the office. Instead, she went right into the principal's office and shut the door.

At eight years of age, I was afraid I was going to die of a

heart attack right there in front of the office. I had stopped crying by then, but I had the after effects which brought on uncontrollable hitched breathing and disgusting hiccupping sounds. On the other side of this wall my fate was being decided. Would it be a spanking at school, more public humiliation, would I ever see the blacktop four squares again? All I could do was wait. I could not even think of how I was going to explain this one to Mom and Dad.

I had closed my eyes and when I opened them, there was my principal standing with the door open.

"Go into my office." Mrs. Fanelli sat in the chair across from his desk. I could not even look her in the eye.

"I'm very sorry, Mrs. Fanelli." My voice cracked on her name and the tears started again. She handed me a kleenex as my sentence was delivered.

"You will lose all recesses for the next week," he continued, "Instead of going outside, you will come and stand outside of the office, just like you did today, with your nose against the wall."

I shook my head up and down since I could not manage to form words over the lump in my throat.

Mrs. Fanelli and I left the office together and everyone stared when we walked back into the room. As I got to my desk, Carol looked at me with her eyes full of an apology which made me feel better.

After school I got out of the room as fast as I could. I stopped by Mrs. Bednarik's room just up the hall. I loved her and she always let me help her after school. She could tell something was wrong as soon as I walked in.

"Rough day, Patti?" I nodded and walked into a much-needed hug. She was rounder than my mom and not as tall. She felt just right at that moment.

"I got in big trouble!" I mumbled into her sweater. I proceeded to share the entire story. I watched her as I highlighted every detail from the orange suit, to the feel of the blue textured wall on my nose. She had grabbed a Kleenex half way through my story and she now had the Kleenex over her mouth.

I was sure I had changed her opinion of me forever and I thought I heard her start crying. On closer inspection, I watched her shoulders start shaking. At first I did not think that she was listening to me. I kept thinking how much I had upset her when she let lose with the loudest laugh I had ever heard!

By the time I finished the story, she was doubled over her desk with her head resting on her arm, just laughing. The tears were streaming down below her glasses and I watched as she removed her glasses and used the Kleenex to dry up the tears from her laughing fit. She even wanted me to re-enact the ruler trick! I did not see the humor here at all, especially since I still had to tell my mom and dad. She kept going on and on that I had made her day by telling her my story.

"Only you Patti Jo, only you!"

It turned out to not be as bad to tell Mom and Dad as I thought. They felt like my punishment at school was enough and that hopefully I had learned my lesson. Little did I know that I had given Mrs. Bednarik the makings for a story that was told to every one of her fourth grade classes until her retirement.

My grade school days continued and I slowly worked my way down the hall. I got my first male teacher for fourth grade. His name was Mr. Nelson and he was not the friendliest man I had ever been around. We started to change classes for different subjects and this was pretty neat. Brenda and I were still best friends and we took turns spending the weekends at each others' houses. Her Mom and Dad rarely went out and I loved the fact that they were home when we were there.

My mom and dad went out regularly both Friday and Saturday night. Dad's drinking was not social anymore. We could all pretend that it was, but I knew that everyone's dad did not come home from work smelling like vodka. Everyone else's dad drank water or milk at dinner, not his third vodka martini.

The real estate market was in a terrible slump and Dad's drinking was not helping his sales. He was no longer selling enough insurance or selling real estate like he was in the beginning and he was not bringing home enough to make ends meet. He would clerk estate sales on the weekends, but this did not bring home too much. The best part about the sales was helping Dad. He would let Kelli and I write the numbers on the tickets and I went with him as often as I could. He clerked for Harry Wollgast. Harry always wore a cowboy hat and I loved to listen to him get going with his fast auctioneer voice.

My mom had started at Fox Center as the Volunteer Coordinator. William W. Fox Developmental Center was a state facility for Developmentally Disabled children. She was trying hard to use her meager salary to cover what Dad was not bringing home.

So many times I overheard Mom's strained voice talking to the credit card representatives when they would call about a late payment. I would hear her and Dad talking about Dad getting another job. It did not make sense that if they did not have enough money that they would still go out so much. But it was never talked about. So I just tried to pretend that it was all OK.

We were all on our way to becoming professionals at pretending. The one thing I could not fake was my nagging worry. I just wished that my Dad was more like everyone else's. I did not want him to smoke. I did not want his eyes to look cloudy and blurry. His beautiful blue eyes began to look red and strained and his hands shook worse everyday, but we all just kept on pretending.

Mom and Dad's friends, without even knowing it, both alleviated the problem and added to it. We went on fun camping trips to Marseilles and Lake of the Woods, where it was acceptable for the adults to drink during the day and even heavier at night. The difference was that the Frobishs, the Perschnicks, the Byers, the Telfords and the Funks made Dad seem like one of the gang. I loved those camping trips because we could all just blend into a great group of people who knew how to have a great time.

Chapter 8

Stan Musial and the Broken Water Hoses

Summer 1975

I had been sitting in the big blue Ninety–Eight for the past hour. I could not wait to get on the road. We were heading to St. Louis for vacation. I could feel the splash of the hotel pool already. I had my activities all organized. Two word-find books, my Nancy Drew mystery and a bag of munchies waited in the seatback of the blue Ninety Eight. Dad had been tinkering with the car all morning to make sure it was ready for the trip.

The poor car had been through a lot in the past year. Usually cars are totaled after hitting large bucks, but not ours. I watched the sun glint off the new hood and remembered the accordion shape it had taken after the impact with the deer. It looked as good as new now and I could hardly wait to see it cruising down Route 66.

They were predicting record temperatures this week so our trip to Six Flags would be a hot one. We were going to the Arch and on a boat called the U.S.S. Admiral.

We had not been on the road two hours when the first signs of trouble appeared on the dash. The red glare of the temperature light shone like a beacon of impending doom. We instantly stopped the elbow war in the backseat and gauged Dad's mood as he watched the red needle inch closer to the left indicating that the engine was hot. Mom saw the smoke from under the hood first and told Dad who let loose with a slew of words under his breath.

We were just past Springfield when we pulled over to confirm that we had a broken water hose. We all knew to stay quiet and not complain. The best way to handle this situation was to lay low and wait for Dad's pursed lips to relax.

We were no strangers to car trouble. We had driven to Canada, and Colorado and found ourselves in this same situation on those trips as well.

We were fixed and back on the road in no time and we were splashing in the hotel pool before dark. I loved when Dad and Mom would swim with us. I think I looked as forward to swimming as I did anything else on our vacation.

Our first day took us to Six Flags. The forecast came true as the temperature reached 100 degrees. I remember the plastic juice containers in the shape of an orange and grapes. Their melted forms on the bench told the true story of the heat as Mom and Dad waited in the smoldering shade for us to hit all the rides.

That night we got all dressed up and ate at the Stoffers Restaurant. This place was fancy! The restaurant was on the 82nd floor and was surrounded by glass windows from floor to ceiling. We waited quite a while, but finally we got a table by the window. The coolest part was that the floor rotated so that those tables closest to the window got a birds-eye view of St. Louis. I remember looking right down into Busch stadium. Kelli had crab legs, Ed had a steak and I had the most expensive cheeseburger of my life.

The fun continued the next day as we boarded the U.S.S. Admiral for a day cruise on the Mississippi River. This boat had it all. There was a band on every floor and a full game room for the kids. Mom and Dad were so good about letting us use a seemingly endless supply of quarters.

Dad could talk to anyone and he had met some people who had been to Stan Musial and Biggies restaurant. He had mentioned wanting to check this out so we made our plans as we left the boat that afternoon. The traffic was so bad as we left the Riverwalk and we all held our breath, praying the car would start. The car did start, but now we had to head uphill from the riverfront.

Dad held the steaming steering wheel with his handkerchief as we picked up speed to climb the steep hill. He had the AC blaring when the familiar red glow of the temperature light lit up the dash.

Dad's voice was stern as he yelled, "Hold on kids!" Eddie shoved my head down as he peeked over the velvet seat. We were flying through red lights, blaring the horn to alert other drivers. Mom was saying a Hail Mary in the front seat as the smoke began to billow out from underneath the hood. Drivers were blaring their horns right back at us as we somehow managed to reach level ground.

For the next hour we found ourselves in the familiar plastic chairs of a service station.

With the second water hose in three days and the hope of meeting Stan the Man, we entered the huge dining room at Stan Musial and Biggies. Stan Musial had played for the St. Louis Cardinals from 1941 to 1963. He was one of the games greatest hitting stars and had been elected to the Hall of Fame in 1969. Eddie was rattling off these stats as we sipped cokes from huge glasses that we would get to take home. We had been seated quite a ways into the dining room which was packed with families hoping to meet the Hall of Famer.

All of a sudden, there seemed to be a commotion at the entrance to the dining room. A hush had fallen over the dining room. I had no idea who I was looking for, but I followed Eddie's stare until it reached the tall man across the room. None of us were really sure what got into Dad, but before we knew it Dad was on his feet. He was waving his hands and yelling. There was nothing we could do but watch.

"Stan, Stan, I'd like you to meet my family."

Mom was pulling on the jacket of his leisure suit to no avail. Dad was on a mission. Stan was not sure who this man was that was making this scene, but he must have known that this loud man would not stop until he got over there.

Stan Musial walked right past at least 10 tables to meet the Slattery family. Dad was so proud of us that he could not stand to wait for Stan the Man to talk to all those other people. I know they were all wondering who we were and what connections we had. All they really needed to know was that Tom Slattery was in the house with his family.

Dad started a new job as a Security Guard at Dresden Nuclear Plant. This worked fine for a while. He wore a uniform and for a while it seemed like this was going to work. I don't think there was one thing Dad liked about that job. Just like before, we all pretended that it worked. His drinking slowed some, but his stomach was giving him major problems. He had developed a bleeding ulcer and so the call-ins began. Sometimes they were legitimate sick days, but mostly they were hangovers.

We sat and watched as the different colored freight cars whizzed past. The vibration of the speeding train could be felt in the front seat of the Rambler. I tried to read the words on each car as they passed between the railroad signs, but I would never be able to get anything but a headache. It never failed that every time we were heading to Kinsman to see Grandma and Grandpa Coughlin, we would have to wait on a train.

It had been a while since we had been out to see them. I loved their old house in the country, but Mom had been waiting years for them to move to town and it was finally happening. They had bought a small brick house on Philmar Street in Dwight, just across from the Dwight High School, so we were going out to help Grandma go through things before the sale.

Grandma had been having quite a bit of health problems lately, so Mom was anxious to have them both closer. It would be neat to ride my bike over to see them.

As we pulled into their drive, the sun reflected off the silver gas tank that sat behind the house and blinded me for a split second. As my eyes focused again, I could see Grandpa through the front picture window and he turned to see who was coming. With a wave he lifted his tall frame from his favorite chair and headed out toward the kitchen to greet us.

As mom swung the car around to park, I smiled looking at the green swing that sat outside of the back door. It was one of my favorite things at Grandma's house and every time we were all there it would be tipped over at least once each visit.

Grandma was opening up the back door just as I approached and she brought me into a warm hug. I could have spent the whole day with my face against her soft, smooth cheek. Cool satin and soft, worn leather all wrapped into one. I breathed in her familiar smell of face powder and soap and as I walked in the kitchen, I found myself in another, stronger hug from Grandpa. His face was a little rough where he had not shaved and he smelled of his snuff and Ben Gay. Mom had already reminded me not to kick over Grandpa snuff can which he kept by his chair to spit in. I don't remember a time when I did not spill it, but Grandpa never got upset.

Mom got busy with Grandma, while Grandpa and I went outside to the old tractor shed. The smells were always the same. Corn cobs, oil, fresh air and gasoline all mixed together. The old tractor sat looking lonely under the overhang from the old barn. Grandpa helped me up and I spent the next half hour 'driving' the tractor and putzing around with Grandpa.

I walked back in the kitchen to find my mom and Grandma sitting at the table having coffee. I saw the wad of tissues next to Mom and she let go of Grandma's hand to wipe away a fresh tear. I hated to see her cry and I was never sure what was wrong. I was afraid it was the same thing that we never talked about. Dad. I was glad she could talk to Grandma. I just wish she could have talked to me about what was going on.

Chapter 9

The Saddest of Summers

1976

Grandma and Grandpa moved to town in March of 1976. Grandma had been having trouble with her stomach for months, but they were not sure what was wrong. Grandma and Grandpa went to church with us on Easter Sunday. At the time none of us knew that this would be the last time that Grandma would go to church at St. Patrick's in Dwight. She went to the doctor the next day and they found a tumor on her colon.

She spent several weeks in Carle Clinic and they felt like they had got all the cancer. Within a month it returned with a vengeance, and Grandma Coughlin came home to her new house for her final months.

As if things were not hard enough for my Mom already, now she had to prepare herself to lose her mom. I remember Mom, and her sisters Delores, and Betty, setting up a schedule of nights to spend with Grandma, since Grandpa could not handle everything alone.

With school out and the weather getting warmer, I spent more time than ever down at Grandma's. The town was gearing up for the Bi-Centennial, 4th of July Celebration. They were planning a whole weekend of events including a carnival, parade, and entertainment all right across the street from Grandma and Grandpa's at the Oughton Althletic Field. I could hardly wait. Mom had spent the last few nights down at their house since Grandma was failing quickly.

I planned to decorate my Stars and Stripes bike for the parade and I already had the baseball cards in my spokes. Mom had bought red, white, and blue streamers and pinwheels for Kelli and I so I was counting the days until the parade. Mom had not worked much the past week and I realized why that Thursday morning. She had come back to our house to help get us all up and ready.

Grandma was not expected to live through the day and she wanted us to go by and see her one last time. I could tell from her eyes that she had been crying a lot. Mom went on ahead and I rode my bike down behind her.

The cars were parked one behind the other in Grandma's driveway and even more were parked in front, half in the grass and half on Philmar Street. It looked like a party, but I knew it was far from that. My Uncle Bill was standing out front staring up at the tree and I startled him out of his thoughts with the loud consistent clicking of baseball card in the spokes of my tires.

"Hi Patti Jo!" He looked a lot like Grandpa Emmett since they were the same height. They had the same square jaw line and full lips which were now trembling, trying to hold back tears. I walked in and made my way down the hall with Mom.

"Grandma can hear you, but she won't answer. Just tell her you love her," Mom said in a strangled voice.

Grandma was lying in her bed and as I bent over to those soft smooth cheeks, Grandma's smell was still there. I took a deep breath in and held it so I wouldn't lose her smell as I kissed her for the last time. The priest was there with Grandpa, and all of Mom's sisters and brother, Bill. I did not stay, since Mom thought it would be better if I went for a quick bike ride. When I returned, the black hearse was in the driveway. I kept on riding. I hated that thing with a passion. How could Grandma be alive one minute and dead the next?

It was hard to get the same excitement about the weekend when I knew that Grandma was gone. I wondered if we would get to do anything fun at all.

What a long day it had been. All day I just rode my bike around the same few blocks that bordered Grandma and Grandpa's. I didn't know what to do with myself. We had come back from

Grandma's to find food everywhere. Our green bar was covered with baked goods, buns, breads and casseroles. I was ready for bed, but as I walked out of the kitchen and turned to head up the stairs, something caught my eye in the dark living room. I looked and saw my Mom on the couch. She had a drink in her hand and her long legs were outstretched and crossed in front of her.

"Ready for bed, Hon?" She asked in a thick, sad voice. She sniffled and I asked if she was OK

"I'm just sad, sweetie." The fear I felt was almost paralyzing. Not her too. Please not her too. I remember being so scared that Mom was now going to start drinking like Dad. I was not used to seeing her with a drink in her hand and I climbed the stairs with another worry on my young mind. It just became a natural thing. That consistent stomach lurch just when I felt like everything was going to be OK.

I heard Dad's loud snore coming from their bedroom. I was beginning to notice the difference between his drunk snores and his sober snores. I knew tonight his snore was a drunken snore. He and Mom's nephews had imbibed quite a bit out on the patio at Grandma and Grandpa's house. It wasn't as bad when anyone else who seemed normal got drunk along with Dad.

Everyone was dealing with Grandma's death in their own way, but it seemed Dad used drinking to deal with just about every situation. How much did my mom need him tonight? How much could she take? I prayed she would stay strong for all of us.

I would remember that Bi-Centennial weekend for the rest of my life not for the history surrounding it, but for the sadness it brought to my house.

Two weeks later

The familiar smell of flowers was almost sickening as we entered Von Qualen's Funeral Home. I wore the same dress I had worn two weeks earlier. It was my light blue jumper and I was wearing light nylons with my new thick soled sandals.

I sat down in one of the familiar folding chairs and watched as Keith Von Qualen opened the door for most of the Slattery family. His voice never rose above a whisper and I thought of what a sad job he had. I was really sick of having to be sad and always having to be dressed up.

We were back here because Grandma Slattery had passed away. I should have been sad, but the truth was that I never knew her except for the childlike person we visited in the nursing home. We had pictures of her when she was full of life, but she never looked like that when we saw her in the Livingston County Manor. Usually she smelled like pee and her hair was all messy. She never once called me by my name and she usually did not even know who my Dad was. The one thing she would always say was that my Uncle Francis was in a box on the wall. This scared me more than anything.

We did not visit her very often and every time we did go, Ed and Kelli and I would hold our breath because it smelled so bad in that place. Mom was motioning me to come over to her and I joined her so we could say a prayer by Grandma before they began the wake.

I honestly did not know the frail, almost mouse-like woman lying in the casket. This person did not look like the lady who was in the nursing home, or the lady in the family pictures. I felt like I was looking at a stranger and I truly was. The Mass cards had the same prayer that Grandma Coughlin's had on them and part of me thought that was not right. I knew Grandma Coughlin and that prayer was so perfect for her. She was safely home in heaven where all the pain and grief was over. The more I thought about it, Grandma Slattery was finally safe too. She had her memory again, but unfortunately I didn't have any of her.

Everyone kept saying that it was a blessing that Grandma Slattery was dead and I didn't really get that. I realize now what an absolutely awful time that must have been for my parents. Bob and Delores Slattery and their kids, Peggy, Mary Kay, Jimmy, Jeannie, and Jeff had gone through everything we had. Delores was Mom's sister and Bob was Dad's brother so the two deaths affected them as much as they did us.

Grandpa Slattery had lived alone in Kinsman for years and he was able to manage on his own. He did come and stay with us more often after Grandma died, but there was never a whole lot of love shown between my Dad and Grandpa. My mom and dad would still go out when Grandpa came for the weekend, which I thought was rude.

What I did not realize at the time was that Grandpa Slattery was the root of Dad's issues. The rough exterior was all that Dad had growing up. The words "I love you," or "I'm proud of you," were never uttered from father to son.

My dad never left the house or hung up the phone without saying how much he loved us. He was playing catch up from a childhood that centered around one goal. Tom wanted his dad's acceptance and he wanted to feel his love. Unfortunately for my dad, some goals could never be achieved.

Chapter 10

The Wolf Was at the Door

Not long after that grief filled summer, reality was setting in at the Slattery house. The bills had been piling up and the biggest bill of all was not being paid. Mom and Dad were on the verge of losing our house on Chippewa.

Dad had borrowed against the house and now with two mortgages they were sinking fast. It was no secret to anyone on either side of the family what the root of the problem was and they offered their unsolicited advise to mom every chance they could get.

In my 11-year-old eyes, our family had money. We drove a nice car, we got new clothes when we needed them, and we still took vacations every year. The only real difference was that my mom worked. My Uncle Bob and Aunt Dode seemed so together and Dode did not work outside the home. I spent quite a bit of time with them since I would stay with Jeff, my cousin. Mom's younger sister, Betty, and her husband, Elwood, really had everything. I loved to spend time out at their house off of Route 47. They had four-wheelers and motorcycles and tons of land to ride on. I loved playing with my cousin Kaye, who was the most adorable child with her beautiful white curls. We got boxes of clothes from the Pfeifer girls and it was like Christmas when they cleaned out their closets.

We usually spent one holiday a year with the entire Coughlin clan. Thanksgiving was the most anticipated holiday hands down for me. The family was so big that we rented St. Patrick's Parish Hall in Dwight and spent all day eating, playing cards and shooting baskets. If the weather cooperated, there would always be a snow football game. With 28 first cousins there was always an easy group to recruit. Add in the in-laws and friends and you had quite a party. Because we were full-blooded Irish, the adults usually participated in their fair share of drinking.

I loved seeing all the cousins. Aunt Joyce's family would drive from Ames, Iowa. Her boys would usually stay with us and Gary and Kevin would get quite a kick out of Dad's antics. These were the times everything seemed fine, but no one knew the truth. No one knew how much Mom and Dad were really struggling. I knew it was hard for mom to defend Dad at every turn, but she did it over and over again.

Mom's only brother, Bill, and oldest sister Colleen, were co-executors of Grandma and Grandpa Coughlin's estate. Each of the children would get a portion of the land that Emmett and Eileen owned in Kinsman. One seventh of that land would belong to Mom when Grandpa died. Mom and Dad had a plan that if they could get half of Mom's portion of the estate now, it could save them from losing the house.

I'll never forget the day that I came racing around the corner through Paulsen's Chevrolet on my Miss America bike. I could see a new car in our drive. I was not sure who was visiting, but I bounded up the steps two at a time to see who it was.

I heard the raised voices before I ever saw Uncle Bill's face. Mom was sitting on the couch choking on sobs and Dad was standing, his face reddened with emotion. Bill was sitting on the couch leaning forward, resting his long arms on his long legs. He was shaking his head at Mom with a sympathetic look in his eyes.

They all put on happy faces when I came into the living room, but I could tell something was really wrong. Mom told me that I should go for a long bike ride and that we would talk when I got home. That talk never happened and it was not until I was a grown woman that I realized what had happened that day. Bill was furious that Dad had put Mom in this situation. Bill's solution was for them to file bankruptcy rather than use every last bit of money that Mom was entitled to. He wanted Mom to do something for herself with the money from Grandma and Grandpa, not replenish what Dad had squandered away.

I'm sure the family all hoped that Mom could start over without Dad. Bill was gone when I got home, but he came back again when it was time for bed. This time Dad was drunk and he and Bill came very close to a fist fight. I was so mad at Uncle Bill for making Mom cry. I was so confused, but I knew from the tightness in my stomach that this would not be fixed quickly or easily. The silence told more of a story than any family talk could have. Don't talk, don't tell, don't feel. Oh, if it had only been that easy.

Mom and Dad got the money from Grandpa and were able to pay off a lot of the bills. My Mom's devotion and commitment to my Dad was never more evident. To her brother and many others, it was not devotion and commitment, but stubbornness and stupidity. When she took her vows of marriage, she took them for life. In good times and in bad she stuck with the man she loved so completely.

Chapter 11

Making a Big Splash
1977

I had my pool bag packed for two days. At 12:30 today the pool in Dwight would officially open. I had watched from the circular fence as they neared completion on what I thought was the most major addition to our town in my 11 years.

I watched in awe as they installed the high dive and low dive in the deep end. Finally we would have something to do on those hot summer days. It was much bigger than the Odell pool with its two diving boards, Olympic size lap lanes, and a kiddie pool complete with a bubbling fountain in the middle.

Everyone was going today and I could hardly wait. They were having an official ceremony this morning with a diving exhibition and several community members speaking on behalf of Bob Stevenson, whom the pool was being named after. I had a new blue and yellow Speedo and I felt its slick spandex under my t-shirt. Brenda and I would be meeting at the corner by Dr. Steineche's house.

We parked our bikes in the bike rack and joined the many Dwight residents streaming through the open gate by the concession stand. The water was crystal blue and looked so refreshing.

As usual, Brenda was totally prepared for her pool experience. She had a full bag of pool necessities including Gee Your Hair Smells Terrific shampoo and conditioner and several towels. I had packed my bag days ago, but all I had was a towel and a five dollar bill. B.Babes had three different kinds of suntan lotion and various sunscreens. I could always count on her to remember what I forgot. She also had a lock for her basket in the locker room. That was

Brenda; always prepared.

We sat on the warm concrete and watched as the divers showed off some fancy stunts from the high dive. I did not know who the diver was, but he was so lucky to get in first. We listened to the boring speeches as the time crawled towards 12:30. Mark and Mike Buss were introduced and the other lifeguards. Kelli, Jenny Miller, Vicki Vickerey, and Paula Kern were going to be some of the first lifeguards. Kerry Fogarty, Bob Bellis and Steve Szchau were also working as guards. Mr. Flott was the manager which was a perfect job for a teacher. His co-manager was Peggy Tambling.

Finally the festivities ended and we had to go and line up to come back in again. I had decided to go off the high dive first thing but Brenda would not go. I let several people go ahead of me so that we could go off the boards together. Our jumps were perfectly timed as she went off the low dive and I leaped from the high dive. We entered a new era in fun simultaneously that day.

The beginning of sixth grade brought a new friend to our twosome. Mary Krischel came from a family of ten. It seemed there was a Krischel in every grade in the school. I remember the first day I saw her in the library. Her short dark hair was flipped back with ironed curls. Her shy smile revealed her white teeth and we exchanged our first hello.

They lived in a small house by the crick and it seemed the move from Wenona was not easy for any of them. Mary's mom, Dorie worked at Fox Center so Dwight was the obvious choice. Their father had stayed on the farm in Wenona, but he was very much a part of their lives. Mary had three sisters and three brothers at home, so we became fast friends.

This was the year of Junior High dances. I had watched for two years as Kelli would decide who to go with. Brian Bossert had been her constant, but then there was Kent and Kerry too. My constants were Brenda and Mary and the goofier we acted, the more fun we had. We were in "the" group of popular girls, but we were second or third tier popular depending on the week. Janet Pokarney, Julie Scott, and Vicky Clavey held firm to the first tier of popularity.

They seemed much more mature than we were but we all got along. We were all invited to sleepovers and the boy-girl parties were just beginning.

I was able to separate myself into almost two different people. I was always the comedian, no matter who I was with. To say that this was an act was true, but I had a blast as long as I could make people laugh. The flip side of this crazy comedian was a worried, embarrassed young girl who was ashamed of her father. I worried constantly about what others thought of our family. I didn't apply myself like I could have in school and I was fine to be average. I wish I would have been pushed, but I know Mom and Dad were doing the best they could at that time.

Where I wanted to show my strength was in my athletics. I wanted to make Eddie proud of me and I wanted the boys to consider me an equal. I even tried to go out for Basketball but because of the locker room situation, I was told I could not.

This was the time that Ed and I were closer than ever. Kelli was into hair, makeup, and boys and it used to drive Eddie insane. I loved how he would ask me to play basketball and snow football with him and not Kelli. He never told me I couldn't play and he never allowed me to shoot, throw or hit like a girl. Unfortunately, I was a girl who was trying to figure out her own way in her mixed-up world.

Chapter 12

The Big Date
1978

The perfectly formed blue numbers on the overhead swam in front of me as I tried to concentrate on Algebra. My stomach felt like a wave pool as I looked down at the note Scot Banks had just passed me.

It was all set. Tonight, Mary, Brenda and I, would meet Scotty and John Ruskin at the movie. What was I thinking? Like I was ready to meet a freshman boy for a movie date.

Realizing that I was two people away from my problem in the book, I tracked my answer and focused all thoughts on $2x + 3y$. Of course my answer was wrong and confirmed by a disappointed look from Mr. Flott. I felt like he did not like me ever since the pigtail incident. Who knew that putting pigtails all over my head would cause such a distraction?

His words that day still stung when I recalled how embarrassed I was being sent to the hall.

I had touched a nerve by acting goofier than usual and I had been trying extra hard to get Mr. Flott's approval since that day. I was afraid the damage had been done. The lunch bell rang and ended another Friday Math class. Sitting at the lunch table, I showed Mary and Brenda the note and we made our plans. They would both spend the night as usual.

Brenda's mom picked us up right on time for the 7:00 showing of Donna Summer's movie, "Thank God It's Friday." This had been the favorite pool song over the summer so we were excited to see the movie. "Jason and the Argonauts" was the late show and I really did not care to see skeleton soldiers jumping off cliffs, but we would see what the boys wanted to do.

I was so nervous I could hardly speak. I had liked John since the summer and Scotty was his best friend so he helped to get him to the show. I was sure he always thought of me as a kid. He was two years older then I was, even though he was the same height.

He had been through a really rough summer. His mom and dad had just gone through a divorce and his dad was now living in Geneseo, Illinois. Dwight's rumor mill had been in full swing with John's mom and dad being the hot topic of conversation for months. His little sister Emily was five and Paula was nine, so I felt bad for all of them.

We were waiting in the front lobby of the theatre when Scot and John arrived. I felt so stupid as I avoided all eye contact and focused on my shoelaces. I managed to notice his black wavy hair sticking out of his Notre Dame hat. He was sporting a green and white Trojan letter jacket like all new freshmen. His braces shined in the lights as he said hi.

I was not ready for this scene at all. Put me on a basketball court or a baseball diamond and I was as comfortable as could be. This was just too much. Heck I did not even wear a bra yet! What would be the point of that?

We clumsily made our way into the dark theatre and Brenda and Mary left an open seat for me next to John. At least I would not have to talk. The movie started and ended without any problems other than Mary and Brenda making a large scene of walking behind our seat. They "accidentally" dropped a comb and their attempts at whispering were enough to make me want to run and scream.

"Are they holding hands?..........I can't see!" This was followed by uncontrollable fits of laughter. I was much more comfortable acting stupid than sitting next to a boy wondering where I should put my hand.

It happened during "Jason and the Argonauts." In a bold move, he grabbed my hand which I did not move for the next 40 minutes. Not that I had any choice in this. The pain the old metal seat was causing to my wrist and lower arm had rendered my fine motor skills useless anyway. I have no idea what the movie was about because I obsessed about this scandalous act until I almost threw up in my snow caps.

The contact was broken as the credits rolled and as was tradition we all walked back to my house and put in a Tombstone Pizza. This is when the real panic set in. I really just wanted them to go but Scotty, Mary, and Brenda stayed out on the porch in order to give us, the couple, some alone time. Alone time for what? I really began to hyperventilate as he put his arm around me on the couch.

This was moving way too fast for this tomboy. Before I knew what was happening, I was confronted with a mouthful of metal coming my way. His high school experience was obviously way beyond anything I had readied myself for. He actually tried to kiss me using his tongue! Oh God! It was met with the equivalent of Fort Knox on my lips. This was not fun; in fact, it was gross!

I broke away and decided to sit in my dad's chair far away from that tongue of his. He picked up a crossword puzzle book and wrote "Will you go with me?" I did not answer immediately since I thought about what would be expected on a second date. I did really like him though. He was so funny and easy to be with except tonight.

I wrote yes on the Pontiac Daily Leader tucked in the side of Dad's chair just about the time the others came in. It was going on 11:00 so they needed to go.

The next day, Eddie had talked to Scotty and had his teasing gun loaded as soon as he came in the door. That was all it took. I just wanted to be a tomboy. I did not want to go with anyone.

It took all day Saturday for me to get up my nerve to call John. I told him I changed my mind and that I just wasn't ready to go out with anyone. He seemed like he was laughing at me. What a stupid little seventh grader. I was fine to be just that.

Brenda, Mary and I spent as many afternoons as we could laughing in the booths at the Newstand uptown. We would always see Kerry the Mailman and we would eat until our stomachs hurt. Kerry was originally from Gardner, Illinois, but was a favorite in Dwight from the moment he started delivering the mail. He was just 20 years old but his youth and friendly manner were welcomed by all.

His signature laugh made you crack up even if you missed the joke. He was so good to us girls. We would ride to basketball games with him and John Pagel and usually end up causing a scene wherever we ate afterwards. Kerry didn't drink or smoke so Mom and Dad had no reason to worry.

Chapter 13

My Other Family
1980

This had been the year of graduations. Ed graduated from Dwight Township High School and I graduated from eighth grade all in the same week. Kelli had finished up her sophomore year and I would finally get to join her in High School. She had been dating Kerry Fogarty since 8th grade and they seemed pretty serious; too serious if you talked to Mom and Dad.

I had made Junior Varsity football cheerleading which I still could not believe. I was never much of a tumbler, but I did have enough spirit for several squads!

I was so nervous to move to the big school. The summer before starting High School, Brenda and I were treated to a trip to Wisconasin Dells. I should have been on Zeke and Delores' tax return since I spent more time with them than my own parents. They took me everywhere. We had traveled to all of Wayne's football and basketball games, and now they were taking me on vacation. Brenda and I got to choose our fun, so the hotel pool was a good place to plan the evening's events in the Dells.

The Tommy Bartlett Water Show was something to see according to Zeker so we planned to eat "The Best Chicken in the Dells" at the famous Shank's restaurant. Our plan was to get our seats for the show before dark.

Zeke and Delores were such easy people to be with. Delores rarely said a lot and she never got angry. Zeke on the other hand had quite the temper and I had been witness to several comical episodes with his anger. I would never forget the time he bought a file cabinet at K-Mart in Kankakee and the cashier opened the drawers to check for merchandise. His beady eyes started to dart around. His chest had puffed up with the breath he was not exhaling.

"What are you doing?" he asked the checker pointedly.

"Oh, it is standard policy sir to make sure no one is trying to shoplift." Here we go.

She might as well have called him a thief! She had no idea what she just started. Delores tried to shoo him out of the checkout lane, but he was hot by this time.

"Whyyy....You think I would hide something in the drawers? You obviously don't know how much I shop here! Whyyy.......just take it all back. I don't want to buy from people who think I am a thief. Let's go Delores." His face was beat red along with the rest of us as the checkout counter had gotten deathly quiet.

Brenda's new velour short outfit and my candle would not be purchased today as we watched Zeke huff and puff his way to the car. He had to stop and have a smoke and he continued to pace in the parking lot going on about never having someone check him for shoplifting.

"Do you believe that Duker?" he asked as we got in the Ninety Eight. He had called me Patty Duke since Kindergarten.

"Sure don't, Zeke. She picked the wrong file cabinet to peek in," I said knowing I could always make him laugh. We managed to be on our way but Zeke held onto this for a long time. I was telling the story again while we waited for our food at the chicken house. We were all laughing at the table as I imitated Zeke.

We had ordered our dinner quite a while ago and Delores seemed a bit distracted. The place was filling up fast and dusk was rapidly approaching.

"Have you seen our waitress?" Delores asked Zeke quietly. We watched as table after table received their food as we sat starving. The purple haze of night fall could be seen through the red and white checkered, curtained window. The place was really packed now and there was hardly room for the waitresses between the tables.

Delores must have seen our long lost waitress out of the

corner of her eye and just as the waitress tried to shoot past us, Delores slammed her tiny hand down on the table. She upset the napkin dispenser and sent Handi-wipes flying. The smack of her hand made all of us, including the frightened waitress, stop in our tracks.

"MAM! IS THERE A PROBLEM WITH OUR ORDER?" Delores roared. I had never heard her raise her voice before and Brenda and I looked on in utter amazement. The startled waitress answered, "Um... Well... Ah... The cook apparently lost your order." All eyes were on Delores and she shook her head in disgust. Zeke stepped into the arena before Delores could answer.

"Just tell the Son of a Bitch, Thanks," he said as we all got up. The waitress should have kept her mouth shut at this point, but she felt it was important that we know that the cook was, in fact, a woman. Zeke turned as we headed out the door and yelled, "Then tell the bitch Thanks!" With that we headed to the Tommy Bartlett Water Show.

I made some extra spending money that year as the coffee girl at the News Stand in Dwight. Frank and Elaine Beiswanger owned the News Stand and I had known them my whole life. I worked with lots of older high school girls and I loved Barb Dorsett. She helped Frank, or "Bike" as he was known, manage things. I got to know lots of the regular coffee group which my dad had been a part of for years.

There was Bob Graham, and Joe Eggenberger who were regulars at dishing out wise cracks. There was Joe Campbell and Pat Patterson who always stood at the counter rather than to grab a seat in the worn, green vinyl booths. There was the lawyer in town, Roger Gomien, who had me searching under the booths and around the counters for the source of a mysterious squeak that only occurred when he came in for his morning coffee.

The sad thing was that Dad did not sit like he used to. He shook so bad in the mornings, it was hard for him to drink a cup of coffee. I know he stopped sitting so that the guys could not see his tremors. He was just 50 years old, but the drinking was taking its toll.

Coffee girl was the perfect job for me since it started at 6:00 a.m. and ended by noon. I think I made $2.65 an hour and I know that I cost Bike more than this in ice cream alone. I got to know most of the older men in Dwight and they all gave me a hard time, but I loved every minute of it.

Kelli and Mary Clausen started the fall of 1981 as Seniors and just as they had through their last 12 years, they rode side by side in the Homecoming parade. They were up for queen along with Joan Scribner. It did not matter in the least bit that neither Kelli nor Mary got queen that year.

I had made Football Cheerleading for the second year and I was having a blast. I became friends with a girl who had moved to Dwight as a freshman. Her name was Rhonda, and I envied her tall, slim figure. Her mane of golden blond hair was always perfectly styled and she carried herself with the confidence of someone who did not worry about the thoughts of others. Once I got to know her, I realized she was as crazy as we were.

Lots of the girls in our class had boyfriends, but for those of us who piled into Debbie Birky's Suburban, it was all about fun. This car, or should I say tank, was so old, the gears were manipulated with buttons. Common protocol was to keep your ice scraper ready so that the inside of the windows stayed clear. Debbie was not a good driver, but our options were very limited. Our one goal was to keep her on the right side of the road and to keep the Suburban chugging.

That fall, Ed headed up to Grayslake, Illinois for his sophomore year. He played on the golf team at College of Lake County and this year was crucial. He wanted to transfer to a Big Ten school so he had to show his best stuff if a scholarship was in his future.

Chapter 14

Law Breaker Take 2

New Years Eve 1981

"I can't believe you forgot your records, Kim," I said as we sat at the counter in my kitchen.

"I know!" Kim said, "And my mom and Dad are already out for the evening."

Mary, Brenda, Kim Kratochvil, Jim Gschwendtner, and John Keegan had all come over to hang out for New Year's Eve. We all had new Christmas sweaters on but we were already bored and it wasn't even 8:00 o'clock yet.

I had a plan but I wasn't quite sure if we should do it. PAL sat idle in the driveway and the keys were sitting on the counter. Mom and Dad were out for the night and we could get to Kim's house and back before anyone would know we were gone. I was months from getting my permit but I was the best driver of the bunch.

I did not need to convince the girls who had their coats on before I did. The boys would wait at my house for us, so off we went in the beginning of a nasty ice storm. I was a cautious driver and the roads were starting to get slick so I took it really slow. Kim was in the front seat with me and Mary and Brenda were in the back.

We decided one quick buzz around the high school was necessary since we were already out. We headed south on Franklin Street and just as we crossed South Street, we saw familiar taillights. Kent Jensen was ahead of us so I gunned PAL a bit to catch up with Kent. I caught up to him just in time to look with horror in my rearview mirror.

The red and blue and flashing lights had to be a mistake. I

was not really being pulled over. I slowed to a stop and watched as the police car passed me and proceeded to Kent's blue Thunderbird. 'Thank God,' was all I could think. He did not want me, he wanted Kent!

Mary was already crying in the back seat and I'm not sure what possessed me to make a u-turn, but I cranked PAL around and headed north on Franklin Street. In my first moment of clarity, I realized that I was trying to outrun the cops and I did not even have a permit to drive. We were just supposed to get records! How could this have gone so wrong so fast!

The police car followed my lead and I quickly stopped in defeat. A million thoughts popped into my brain as I wondered how jail food tastes.

I turned around quickly and told Mary to shut the hell up. The police would know that we thought we were in deep trouble if he could hear her sobs. My heart was racing so fast I was sure the cop could hear it as he approached my window. I turned to see Steve Dorsett looking in my window.

"Hi Steve," I said as carefree as if we were passing on the street.

"Patti! What are you doing?"

"I'm sorry," I said as I explained that I thought he wanted to pull Kent over and I got scared and turned around.

"I was pulling both of you over. It is getting slick out and you were going way too fast," he scolded.

"I know and I am so sorry. We were picking up records at Kim's house but we are going straight home." I hoped he could not hear the quiver in my voice.

"You promise?" he asked as a smile crossed his face.

"Scouts honor!" I answered as I gave him my best salute. My heart was beginning to return to my chest. He obviously thought I had my license. I got back in the car and turned and told the girls to Thank God because we had just been saved!

Mary was still whimpering, but I managed to get us home under shaking hands. I parked PAL just were she had been in the driveway and we rehashed the events over and over. I was so thankful that I knew Steve. 'Some times it does pay to know the right people,' I thought as the phone rang.

My 'no worries' hello was answered by the same voice I had just had scold me.

"Patti?" I heard Steve say.

"Is there something you would like to tell me?" The heart racing thing was back and this time I was having a hard time finding my voice.

"Are you there, Patti?"

"Yes, Steve. I am here."

He went on to tell me how he had just gotten off his shift and when he got home he told Barb about our little encounter. Barb thought he knew that I did not have my license and she commented on how she didn't think I even had my permit yet. This was all news to Steve. The jail food came back into my mind.

"I am very sorry Steve," I said ashamed of taking advantage of him.

"What do you think I should do, Patti?" he asked. The silence hung in the phone until I tried to break the tension with a bit of humor.

"How about we forget this ever happened and I promise you that I will not drive until I'm 16."

"If you do Patti, I will make sure you don't drive until you are 18! Do you hear me?" he said with the same tone my dad used when he wanted to make a point.

"Yes sir! I understand. Thank you Steve." I hung up the phone with the same shaky hands that I thought had disappeared. The only detail we had not worked out was whether or not he was going to tell my mom and dad. This would have been an important fact to straighten out. In my heart I know he wanted me to sweat it out. All in all, I came out of the evening a very lucky 15-year-old.

Chapter 15

My Reddick Connection

I had made new friends outside of my Dwight group during my short time as a Dairy Queen employee. Tammy and Gina lived in Reddick and we became fast friends as we laughed our way through our evening shifts at the DQ. Tammy and Gina were a year older than I was. They loved cruising the Dwight scene since it was a booming metropolis compared to Reddick. Reddick was a small town just 9 miles east of Dwight. The booming population of about 250 people did not give the town's teenagers much to do.

They took me with them on crazy trips to Kankakee and introduced me to all of their Reddick friends. I met Maureen 'Moe' Kehoe and Holly Schott and I in turn introduced the Reddick girls to Brenda, Mary and Kim. We spent most of our time waiting for Holly to get ready. This gave me a chance to get to know her parents, Kim and Ruth.

I was not in to the party scene so I would usually drop the girls off and cruise the neighborhood while they checked out the party. Tammy had a mile long beige Cadillac that held seven girls easily. We laughed so much and caused such a scene most places it was a miracle we were allowed into any establishment in the county.

I never dreamed that a casual introduction would find me a friend that knew what it was like to have an alcoholic father. Moe's dad, Tim was a recovering alcoholic but she could relate to all the mixed up feelings I had about Dad. She was there when I needed her so many times and her mother Carol got to know Mom well through some of the Al Anon meetings.

Chapter 16

The Country Club Years
1982

I was so excited about my junior year. I was Junior Class President. Brenda, Debbie Birky, and Brian Severson were also class officers. We were finally upperclassmen.

The year began with the golf season. I decided since I had been playing more than ever that summer, I would try out for the team. I knew I would be the only girl, but I was used to this since very few girls played at all. I was one of the guys and John Keegan, Brian McArdle, Scott Schultz, Scot Banks and Matt Siebert made sure that I was always a part of things.

Dad had taken over running the clubhouse that spring and I worked as a waitress and ran the Pro-shop when Keegs (John Keegan) or Brian McArdle could not work. We played golf together and ran around town usually causing quite a disturbance wherever we went.

Kelli had started college at ISU and Ed had transferred from College of Lake County to the University of Illinois. He had received a full scholarship to play golf so it was odd to be the only child at home. I missed Kelli so much. I missed Ed too but he really had not been home even when he was home. He was living with John Cyborn who also transferred from CLC so he had a pretty easy transition.

Dad's new job could not have been a worse occupation for an alcoholic. Dad had easy access to any liquor he wanted and he took full advantage of this on a daily basis. He had stopped working at Maurie's Tap in Kinsman, where he ran the bar. The insane thing was that he changed jobs but kept the same surroundings. The one plus was that he did not have to drive as far after he had been drinking.

Working for him was not always easy. He was never a mean man. He never raised a hand to me or said abusive things. What he did was lay on the sentimental bullshit that would make me want to scream. He bragged about us so much and it only got worse as he got drunk.

I would usually work from 11:00 to 2:00 and he would already have that foggy look by the time I showed up. He thought his tinted glasses could hide his glazed eyes, but I knew the minute I saw him whether or not he had been drinking. He was so well liked by everyone that I had to pretend that he was the great guy that everyone thought he was. But inside I had built such a wall.

I remember hoping that he would wreck the car and kill himself without hurting anyone else. We had so many family discussions where we would confront Dad and beg him to stop. It was a regular event every Christmas. The dialogue was always the same and so was the outcome. Ed would start by telling him that we all loved him and that he needed to change something in his life. Whether it was where he was working or whatever he felt he needed to do, he had to get a handle on his drinking. We just wanted him to try to get happy. He had a great family, a great wife, a good job and great friends.

What he had that we still wrestle with today is a serious disease. Every year he would promise to get on track and for a month or two he would keep it. But the demons would not stay at bay for long and the destructive forces of the disease would take over.

I was so jealous of both Kelli and Ed that fall because they could leave him. I wanted to get away too, but I had nowhere to go. This was supposed to be the best time of my life. I finally got my license in September and since Kelli was a freshman and living in the dorm, she had to leave PAL at home.

PAL was a brown '71 Monte Carlo. I had been driving PAL since I could see over the steering wheel. Kelli and I would drive around town almost every night. I would let her smoke, if she would let me drive. This was our escape. But now it was just me who drove around to get away from my Dad.

I could not wait until Harvest Days, Dwight's fall festival that brought everyone home. Kelli was coming home. We had never gone this long without seeing each other, but she wanted to stay at school and really make a go of it on her own. I could not blame her a bit for not wanting to come home.

Home was a confusing mix of being with the two most important people in my life but wanting to change everything about the situation. Mom continued to try to justify not kicking him out, and Dad continued snoring that thick, drunken drone in his chair most afternoons and evenings.

The fall proved to be the rock bottom that all alcoholics have to hit. The latter part of the summer should have landed my Dad in jail, but he managed to keep his license and continue to drink and drive.

He took back roads and alleys home to stay out of view, but the splintered remains of a swiped telephone pole told us how scary his trips home were becoming. I spent as much time away from home as I could, but Dad was spiraling down to depths even he had not imagined.

Chapter 17

The Fight of His Life
November 1982

The time had finally come. Mom and I had talked last night and tomorrow Dad would be out of the house. His suitcase stood at the top of the stairs holding so much more than just his clothes. It sat there as a symbol of what Dad had become.

This time he was really going. He refused to get help and I had told Mom many times that it was either him or me because I just couldn't deal with the embarrassment anymore.

I got ready for school that Friday like I always did but I kept coming back to the same thought. I could not imagine my mom and dad divorced. How could he just walk out rather than to get help? He would rather drink than stay and be a dad. What I wish I could have accepted was that Dad could not control his drinking anymore than I could control my anger.

He was not the only one making decisions that Friday morning. My decision was to quit too. I was done giving him so much of myself. It was time to put him out of my heart just like that worn suitcase was being put out on the porch.

I walked downstairs and paused briefly as I saw him putting his rings on by the TV. His, "I love you, Patti," fell on an empty heart as I grabbed by Trojan bag and ran out the door.

'NO YOU DON'T,' I wanted to scream, but I let it rage inside of me as usual, festering in my deep pit of dysfunction.

Big drops landed on the sidewalk as I slammed into PAL. I guess the forecast was right since they had said we were in for quite the storm over the next few days.

I let the rain come from inside of me as I let go of my tears. The familiar smell of PAL was like a blanket. The lingering remnants of Benson and Hedges mixed with a bit of perfume and a damp mildew smell. It made me ache for Kelli.

That day was no different than any other day. I got to school and strategically applied my "everything is fine" mask and was able to act as if nothing was wrong with my life. I had done this for so long, and done it so well, it felt normal to me. I should have won the academy award that year.

That weekend brought one of the worst floods Livingston County had seen in years. Dad spent most of it holed up at the Fiesta Hotel in Pontiac trapped in his second floor room because of the rising flood waters. He truly had nowhere to go but treatment.

By Monday afternoon, Dad met Mom as soon as she came home from work. He was ready to go to treatment. Mom and Uncle Elwood took Dad to Brokaw Hospital in Bloomington, Illinois. This is where he spent the next 30 days. He was there for Thanksgiving and Christmas that year which actually came as a relief in some ways to all of us. We went through some family therapy sessions, but I was so wary of trusting him.

I watched the counselor move her paper on the overhead showing the many different roles that children of alcoholics take on. I felt my cheeks burn as she discussed the characteristics of the clown. It made me so mad. How did she know what role I took on? I shut out everything she was saying. I did not want the very thing that made me feel normal; making people laugh, to be a bad thing. I didn't want to fit into some stupid category because noone knew what it felt like. What about Ed and Kelli? Why weren't one of those roles so easily applied to them? I refused to think that I needed to get better since it was Dad who had the problem. How very wrong I was.

Tense would be the one word to describe Dad's return. I had never really tried not to talk to him. I had to remind myself to be mad at him, but before long he seemed to be OK. I slowly lifted my guard. Dad did everything he was supposed to. He went to meetings and called his sponsor when he needed a lift. He drank Pepsi and smelled good again. His eyes took on their old sparkle, but none of us could see that something still wasn't fixed. He just didn't seem very happy.

I can't imagine how hard it was for Dad and Mom to change everything in their life. He and Mom hung out with non-drinking people now. They played cards after their Friday AA meetings and even began to help those who were struggling like Dad had.

He was coming to my basketball games and we started to find some middle ground again. I had missed him so much and it made Mom so happy to see us come back together. I think Mom was just as scared as I was, but we all took it one day at a time.

Chapter 18

Spring of 1983
Can I Get a Date?

As Spring arrived, I helped Dad out at the Country Club. I always held my breath that first sober summer until I kissed Dad and saw his eyes. I think he knew I watched him out of the corner of my eye whenever he went behind the bar. Part of me thought it was not a matter of if he drank again, but when. As if the situation did not pressure him enough, now his teenage daughter was the Gustapo.

I did have plenty to keep me busy. It was all about Prom. As Class President, I had quite a bit to do. The nagging question was would I have a date after all this hard work. Mr. Kresl, our class sponsor, was just as worried and offered to take me to the Prom. This was more depressing than I can share.

One morning it happened. The skies opened up, the seas parted and I got asked to the Prom. The best part was that Tank was exactly who I wanted to go with. Mike Tambling was Tank whether he liked the nickname or not just like his brother before him had been. He was a senior and we had known each other forever. We would go just as friends, of course. God forbid if I actually had a boyfriend. That spring it actually felt like it though. We spent so much time together that everyone thought we had more of a thing. I was the one acutely aware of the fact that there was no-thing going on! We were going to double with Scott Schultz and Holly Schott so it would be a night to remember.

A memorable night it was, as my date in his high top tennis shoes stole the show. I believe his story was that his tux shoes had come in too small but I was not buying it. I was not one to be outdone and my hat turned a few heads too. We had sat with Buford (Brian Walkup) and Amy Gomien. Buford's idea of family style dining was placing the spaghetti at his place and digging in. The night was so fun and the best part was that Tank and I didn't have any expectations other than to just be ourselves. That is exactly what friends were for.

I spent the summer as a lifeguard at the pool. Brenda and I both had the perfect summer job. The pool staff was like a small family that reunited every summer. The summer was passing uneventfully until one decisive summer night. I actually went on a date that turned out as bad as any nightmare I could have imagined.

Kim Kratochvil had been dating Brian Bennett and they had tickets to see Journey. They asked Brad Johnson and I to go with them. My mom did not feel good about this at all. She rarely said no, but she was wavering on this outing.

I had just got off the phone with Brian who needed to know if I was still going. No sooner had he called, than Kim came by. She had been crying and I knew there was trouble with her and Brian. Kim was so in love with him but I did not think Brian was ready to settle down. He had begged me to go since Brad was looking so forward to it. Brian had said he was working on finding someone else to go instead of Kim. Kim was also telling me to go because Brad had finally worked up the nerve to ask me out. I did want to go with Brad so I talked Mom into letting me go.

When Brian Bennett pulled up with Patty Peach as his date, I knew the evening was going to be interesting. I really did not know her since she was a year older than us. I knew she partied quite a bit, but hopefully I could do this and get home in one piece.

We made our way through the snarl of Chicago traffic on a Friday night just in time to see Steve Perry on the gigantic screen. We were at the Rosemont Horizon in Rosemont, Illinois, west of Chicago. I had never seen such a huge arena in my life. The band was so far away. I kept thinking, 'This is what people pay all this money for?'

I had never smelled pot before, but it was all around us. It smelled like burnt leaves and the person in front of me was not doing a very good job of being discreet. I was educated far beyond my years in the small amount of time we spent in the nosebleed section that night.

If I had thought traffic was snarled on the way up to the concert, it was nothing compared to the mess leaving the Rosemont. We needed to get on Interstate 90 and head back east to get to 294 South and head home. We had sat for at least an hour waiting in the interminable line of cars.

We were finally on the highway picking up speed when traffic stopped dead. Brian tried to stop, but slammed into the car in front of us. Patty's head hit the windshield as we were all pitched forward. I waited for the impact from the car behind us but somehow the other cars avoided us.

Within minutes, a traffic officer was at our window shining a flashlight, "Everyone all right here?" he asked. Patty seemed shook up, but her head was not bleeding. I had never been in an accident with another car and my hands and legs were shaking like crazy.

Brian's silver Monte Carlos which was rarely even dirty, was now a picture of broken headlights and mangled metal. We were given a ride to the Rosemont Police Station in a squad car and the dread continued to creep up on me. I was so afraid that I smelled like pot from the concert. All I kept thinking was 'Why didn't I listen to my mom?' Here I was, not even 17 yet, and I am in the back of a squad car in Chicago with no way home.

The police took our information and I asked to use the phone. "You all need to call your parents," he said in an authoritative tone. Oh God! How long would it take me to undo this mess.

I thought of how scared Mom and Dad would be when they heard my voice on the phone. I looked at the digital clock as I dialed my number. The blaring red neon showed 12:30 a.m. I should have been home in bed, not in a cold Police Station, miles from home. How did Mom know this would not be good?

Dad's tired voice answered and I tried not to cry.

"Hey Dad, it's me! We are all fine, but we got in an accident leaving the concert. We can't drive the car so Brian has his Grandma coming to get us." I looked at Brian who was on another line calling his house.

"Let me get some clothes on and I'll get on the road," Dad said as he got his bearings.

"NO!" I said a little too fast.

"I don't want you to have to do that. Just don't worry. I'll be home as soon as I can." The tears started as I said, "I'm sorry Dad! I love you."

After hanging up, I realized that Brian had called Scotty Banks instead of his Grandma, but he could not get a hold of him. I knew who to call, but I just didn't know where to find her.

We called information and got Phil's Harvest Table on the line. Everyone ended up at Phil's after a night out. With a prayer I did not deserve, I asked God to let her be there.

"Is Kelli Slattery there by chance?" I waited for the casual no from the busy waitress as I held my breath.

God did me the biggest favor since the next voice I heard was my sister. I was crying before I even told her where I was.

"I'm coming, babe! Just let me talk to the Police Officer so I know where I am going."

The next hour crawled by as we walked outside. I focused on the big red rose painted on the water tower, as Brad sat next to me on the pavement.

Before long, I heard the familiar hum of an engine, as PAL came charging around the corner of that deserted street like the Calvary. Kelli had asked Butch Oelschlager to drive with her since he knew Chicago so well. It was a silent trip home that morning.

We dropped everyone off and as we pulled in the drive the sun was coming up. Mom was standing on the front porch in her robe and the minute she saw us she fell to her knees and wept. I knew it was going to be bad, but I never dreamed I would hurt my mom like this.

She could not talk, but her anguished tears of relief said everything as she hugged us both. I did not realize that Kelli had headed up to get me without telling Mom and Dad where she was going. They had known where I was, but when Kelli did not come home the worry doubled.

Dad came down the stairs and found all the words that Mom was not able to say.

"Do you have any idea what you have both put us through?" he roared with tears in his eyes. No punishment could have hurt the way the guilt pounded inside of me.

"This is all my fault!" I said through choked sobs. We spent the next hour explaining the nightmare that was now thankfully behind us. Note to self, 'Never again question Rita's intuition.'

Chapter 19

A Homecoming To Remember
October 1983

The coke fizzled as it spilled from the large Dairy Queen cup saturating three nights worth of letters.

"Trojans Are The A-Team!" was what it was supposed to say. Mrs. Kresl's kitchen had been transformed into float central. We were all doubled over with laughter, when Mr. Kresl came in to see what all the commotion was about.

"Let me guess, it was Patti!" he said with that grin that lit up his whole face.

"I didn't do it!" I demanded, but the guilt was coming out with every burst of new giggles. We were able to salvage most of the dripping letters and they were distributed around the dining room to dry overnight before we covered them with tin foil.

Mr. Kresl and I had worked together on many projects so he knew my antics well. He had been a science teacher at DTHS for years, but he had touched my life way beyond his science and biology lessons. Mary, Brenda, Rhonda, and I walked out the backdoor to see how the float was coming. We were the self proclaimed Trout Women. I'm still not sure why we called ourselves this. I was still not getting a mental picture of our float and we were down to the last two nights, but Mr. Kresl had faith that it would all come together.

We watched as Ron Delong and R.J. Jamieson stood the red goal posts up in place.

"Where is your dress and hat Patti?" Ron asked as he caught his side of the leaning goal post just before it fell over. He was referring to my Nerd Day costume. The whole week had been such a blast. It was hard to imagine that this was our last Homecoming.

I had been working up the nerve to call Tank all week and ask him to go to the dance with me, but it was Wednesday and I still could not do it. I had picked up the phone about twenty times, but I never got farther than the first few numbers before I panicked and hung up.

He was a freshman at Joliet Junior and he had an apartment in Joliet with another Ag major. He was playing on the football team so I figured he probably had a game. I had not told anyone that I was going to do this since Brenda planned on going with me as usual. I hated to disappoint her and if he said no than we would do the girl thing like we had for the past four years.

I just, for once, wanted to have an actual date. I wanted to get a flower that I had not bought myself, and be taken out to dinner. We had gone to Prom together and I knew he just wanted to be friends, but there was no one I wanted to go to my Homecoming with but him. Brenda nudged me back to Mr. Kresl's backyard and I realized I had not answered Ronnie's question.

"It had to be dry-cleaned after the spill I took trying to push Mr. Swartz's car!" I yelled back to him. Each lunch hour this past week had been filled with activities. It was a beautiful cool fall night and the small tree on the opposite side of the drive was losing its battle to hold on to its orange and yellow leaves. The familiar pop of the staple guns mixed with Loverboy surrounded the float builders.

I watched and laughed as Jim Gschwendtner and Harry Hoegger, each armed with a staple gun, fired away at each other. No wonder we were so far behind. It was time to pack it up for tonight so we helped Mrs. Kresl clean up and I headed home. Tomorrow was Punk Day and I already had an idea for my outfit.

I was thinking about what shoes would look best with Mom's maroon fish net nylons, as I opened the front door. I heard Jake whining and realized it was coming from upstairs. I wondered how he got up there since he was too little to climb the steps.

Jake was my cocker spaniel puppy that Dad had bought me for my 17th birthday. Dad and I had started working our way back to each other over the past year, and he certainly knew the way into my heart. Jake was jet black and hyper as can be.

I could hear his pitiful, scared cry from the top of the stairs and I took the first five steps a couple at a time until I was standing on the landing where the stairs turned.

"Ja-----". I froze to that spot as I watched my dad stagger out of the bathroom.

"This damn dog doesn't know what he wants," he slurred. I watched as he braced himself on the wall and lifted Jake with one clean sweep of his foot.

"There, now you can go down stairs!" He growled through a voice that was thick with vodka.

"Daaaad, Noooo!" I screamed, as I watched Jake's little body twist and bump down the stairs. It happened so fast that I did not have a chance to catch him. For a second, I thought Dad would follow him as he tried to get his feet back under him. Jake's whimpering snapped me into action and I picked him up as gently as I could.

"Oh, he's tough. He'll be fine," Dad mumbled from his weaving perch above me. I had never before felt so much hatred towards the man at the top of the stairs.

"You Son of a Bitch!" was all I could get out. I took Jake and was barreling out the front door, when I saw Mom pull into the drive. I couldn't breath. I could not get any air into my lungs. I was crying so hard that Mom ran to me as she got out of the car. She dropped her Al-Anon books as she rushed to me.

"What is it?" she asked as the worry ran over her face.

"I hate him so much. He is drinking again, Mom. Just like I knew he would. I knew it! God, I'm so stupid to have believed him! He just kicked Jake down the stairs!" The words tumbled out between sobs.

"I am done! I am never going to believe him again. Did you know? Did you think he was sober? He is such a liar and I am never, never going to let him back in again. He can keep his damn presents. I can't do it anymore Mom! I just can't!"

Mom took Jake from my trembling arms and we sat on the front steps.

"Oh honey! I'm so sorry." I let my ragged breath out that I had been holding and let all the tears come as Mom rocked me against her.

"I wish you would come to these meetings with me. I did suspect that he was drinking again, but I didn't want to tell you. I thought it would ruin your whole Homecoming and now it has. I don't know what happened." She put her hands to her forehead and swallowed the lump I could hear in her strained voice.

"He stopped going to his AA meetings and without that support he fell right back into the old ways. He actually slipped during Harvest Days but I kept him away from you guys so that you would be able to enjoy the weekend. He has been messing around with it ever since and they say that after a slip, they can go one of two ways. He either realizes he screwed up and gets back into his program or he starts drinking as if he never stopped and actually the drinking gets worse."

"I don't think he can get much worse," I spit out through bitter tears.

"Maybe this time it will kill him!" I said and felt the instant guilt that goes along with the wish for your own father to die! God, how I wanted to just run away. I looked up from our spot on the steps and watched the flag snap in the crisp October breeze.

"So how long do we just let him ruin our lives this time?" I was so angry and I knew it was not right to take it out on Mom but I had to get some of it out. How could she carry this whole burden? She was holding on for dear life too.

"Let me talk to him and see where his thinking is," Mom said with a heavy sigh.

"I'm done, Mom." Tonight I had shut the door for the last time. It felt so good to be able to control how I felt. For months I had waited and watched, wondering if I was wrong, wanting to be wrong about the fact that he would start again. Part of me thought it was easier to hate him than the uncertainty of the last year.

Mom shook her head sadly and with a hint of a smile she said, "Come on in and get to bed sweetie. You will be so tired tomorrow." We walked up the stairs together not knowing what tomorrow would bring.

I did go to the dance with Tank and I was able to put everything from that week away for a little while. I never shared with Tank what had happened that week with my dad. He, along with all of my friends, loved him. They couldn't wait to spend time at my house since Mom and Dad were so nice. Dad was famous for walking through the downstairs with his t-shirt and underwear on. I can still hear the roar of laughter from the guys at the sight of Tommy in his Fruit of the Looms. These were made to fit his waist perfect, but not his skinny chicken legs. The struggle for me was always there; love him one minute, hate the man he had become the next.

Chapter 20

If At First You Don't Succeed...
November 1983

"I don't want him to come, Mom!" I gripped the dishwasher as I steadied myself to tie my volleyball shoes.

"Let me just let him sleep until it is time to go and maybe he will be OK. I know he wants to be there for you, Patti." 'Bullshit!' I thought as I shook my head in disgust. Yes, he really wanted to be there for me on Senior Night. That was why he was passed out in his chair, making noises that sounded like his breathing would stop with every exhale.

Tonight was the last home game of the year and they were presenting all the seniors with a rose. Our parents were to walk with us as we were introduced. I had thought about just pretending to be sick and not going at all. But then the anger flowed through me again that because of him, I was thinking of missing my senior night. I couldn't win.

The last month had been the hardest in my life. It was getting harder and harder to pretend that everything was fine. I did my best to avoid him and not speak to him. That was the easy part. The hard part was when I would let myself realize how very much I missed him and needed him in my life.

I wanted my dad to be introduced with me, not the man that was in the living room sleeping off a fifth of vodka. I was sick of crying about him and as much as I tried, the tears came again as I stood with Mom in the kitchen.

What would I do without her? She was such a good person. She didn't seem as angry, but I know that her meetings were helping her. They kept telling her not to force him into going for treatment this time. She had to be so strong. I probably said several times a day that she should just kick him out. She did an amazing job of dealing with a brat and a very sick man, but the faith and love that she had for Dad was stronger than anyone or anything.

During this time, Ed and Kelli dealt with all of this in their own way too. Ed just simply chose to stay away. Kelli poured out her love to Dad in letters and visits home from college. I felt so guilty when I saw how much she loved him and how deeply I wanted to. She was able to see past the disease that enveloped him to the wonderful shell that remained.

Mom and I sprawled on the small single bed together with our identical, long Coughlin legs hanging over the edge. The house was quiet except for the abnormal noises coming from Mom and Dad's bedroom. Dad was snoring, but it did not sound like his breathing was regular or adequate. He gurgled every other breath and then gasped like it may be his last intake of air.

Mom and I had not seen each other too much in the past week. I watched as she wiped a tear from under her big glasses. She had taken the week off and driven to Bloomington, Illinois every day for intense family counseling for Co-dependents.

"They said I should not force him to go to treatment," she said as she took a deep breath.

"But how can I let him die? If he had cancer we would not let him wither away without getting him help." She had tried so many times to share her Al-Anon knowledge with me, but I just had such a hard time with the fact that Dad's drinking was a disease. I could not hate him as much if I thought he could not control what he was doing to us.

"It did not work last time so why should we think it will do any good now?" It had been exactly a year since his last inpatient stay. The past month he had regressed beyond his worst point a year ago. He was drinking about a fifth of vodka a day, and by the sounds coming from the bedroom, he could not go on like this much longer. He was thinner than I had ever seen him, and his tremors were fierce.

It had been months since I spoke with him or hugged him and it really did not seem to matter to him at all. In fact I don't even think he noticed. Mom had one more day of counseling and as we snuggled in together she said she would see what the weekend would bring.

God must have been with us that night in my lilac bedroom. Perhaps he was also next door with a beaten man the next morning.

Dad made it through the night and the next morning he called his best friend Donny O'Brien. They had gone to Korea together, but this time only Dad could fight this battle. He asked Donny if he would take him for help.

Mom and I read the note on the counter as we entered the kitchen that Friday night. It was written with trembling hands and a broken heart. We held each other for a long time and said silent prayers that this time God would bring back the man we both loved so much.

Chapter 21

Crash Slattery

The rest of my senior year flew by. I started dating Brad Johnson after we went to the Sweetheart dance together. He was tall and thin and he and I just seemed to fit. He was good friends with John Keegan and they both shared time on the bench during the basketball season. I really liked being with Brad and his parents Carl and Diane were great to me.

I was proving to be a bit of a hazard on the roads of Dwight. My problem was speed. I just could not seem to get places on time, especially school. PAL had taken a bit of a beating over the past year and we were now without access to the trunk since the key had slid down the defrost vent during one fast take off.

Dad was being very patient since none of my minor bumps were cause to report them to the insurance company or any of the higher authorities. I simply moved a few vehicles from their present position to a bit different angle in the parking lot. I was always honest. I told Shane Daniels the day I moved his huge Fury about two feet to the right. If you really want to know the truth, I gave it a better park job.

One of the luckiest days of my life occurred in early Spring of 1984. As usual, I was running late. I flew down Franklin Street and watched the sun glint off a brand new Park Avenue, which was stopped in front of the school in the drop off zone. I began to slow down to make the turn at the corner when the familiar feeling of nothingness came from my brakes.

'Not again,' I thought, as I felt the car begin to slide over the frost that was just now visible on the pavement. No matter how many times this happened, for the life of me, I could not remember to take my foot off the brake.

Looking straight ahead, I recognized the driver of the Park Avenue. I saw the terror on Bill Stevenson's face, as I careened toward that shiny new vehicle. I was able to get PAL turned enough that I did not hit the door panel. I did, however, clip the hell out of his bumper. By now, the final bell had rang and Miss Siebold's Math class had a front row seat to the action.

"Patti, I saw you coming but I just couldn't get out of your way fast enough," Bill said shaking his head. We both looked down at his bumper, which was holding on for dear life.

"Do you think we should call the police?" I said with a shaky voice. Dad was going to kill me.

"I tell you what, you go on to school and I'll give your dad a call," he said with about half a grin on his face. He seemed to be taking this quite well. PAL had sustained minimal damage since my bumper had been here before.

I hurried inside and got my pass to class. The abuse started immediately. At lunch, Brian Farris and Joe Call were selling chances on the date of my next accident. Someone had set a plunger outside my locker.

I finally got a chance to call Dad during second period. His first words were, "Do you have any idea how lucky you are?"

"Ahh, no," I said in a guilty voice.

"Bill Stevenson had just picked up his new car from Rubs. They damaged his bumper when they were getting it off the truck. The same bumper you hit. Rub's was going to replace the bumper, before you ran into him so we do not have to report this one." I could tell by his voice that he was not as ecstatic as I was about this news, so I continued to grovel.

"I am so sorry, Dad."

"You need to slow down, Patti Jo!" Oh the middle name, I was on my last leg here.

"I will. I promise."

I did slow down but my crashing days were not over. The summer before I left for college proved to be the most serious crash of my life. What started out as a normal evening out, ended in what could have been a tragedy.

Moe and I were heading to Essex for a wedding reception. Essex was another small country town about a half hour from Dwight. I was driving the yellow Ford and we were both dressed up and looking forward to one of our last weekends before I would leave for Western Illinois University. The summer had been really hard for her since she and Kent Jensen had broken up. This would be a girl's night out. I was able to get served at the old bar in Reddick, so we cruised around the country roads with Seagrams 7 and Mountain Dew.

The reception was at the Essex Lions Hall and proved to be a blast. There was a live band and an open bar so we stayed until the band quit and then followed the party to Reco's in South Wilmington. We had to be home by midnight since Moe's mom and dad were calling. They were away for the night and this was their way of checking on us. I was planning on staying at Moe's, so we headed home about 11:30.

I had just received a new license since I had lost my purse earlier in the summer. For some reason, during our trip home, when I should have been focusing on the road, I started freaking out that I had lost my license again. I had stopped drinking when we left the reception, but I know I should not have been driving. When I bent down to check under the seat for my license, I brought the wheel with me.

We dipped into the left ditch and I was just getting the right wheels back on the pavement when we hit something really hard. My head hit the steering wheel hard and Moe's head hit the dash even harder. Everything slowed down as if I were watching it from above. Neither one of us were wearing our seatbelts. We came to rest in the ditch and the yellow Ford was smoking from under the hood. I heard Moe's whimpering cries before I could even worry about myself.

"SSShhhh," This was all I could get out. I knew we had to get the car out of the ditch. I thought if we could get it out, I could drive it home.

I could see Moe's eye was cut and she was crying really hard.

"This is really bad, Patti!" she said in a very shaky voice.

"Is anything else hurt on you?" I asked, looking closer at the cut which just missed her eye.

"No. I am just so cold." I watched her wrap her arms around herself as her now ripped, grey and white sundress hung off of her. I grabbed a jacket out of the back seat and put it around her. I told her to get in the driver's seat and to give it gas when I told her to. I was going to push us out. Obviously Moe was not the only one in shock.

The ditch was pretty deep and all we managed to do was angle the Ford so it was now looking straight up at the stars. My knees were shaking so much and when I saw the headlights coming down the dark road I started to pray. If this was a cop, I was dead.

"Come on Moe, we have to flag this car down." I helped her out of the car and we stood in the middle of the road waving our arms. What a sight we must have been. I did not see lights on top of the car and I was more than a little relieved when a young couple pulled up and offered to give us a ride back to Moe's.

Moe's teeth were chattering by the time we got into her kitchen. I put her in her mom and dad's bed with extra covers and made my way to the basement to get out of my dress. All I could think of was what would happen if a cop came along before I could call Dad.

With shaking hands, I dialed the familiar numbers. Dad did not yell or even ask questions. He was going to send Phil Becker with his wrecker to Moe's to pick me up and we would go get the car. The problem was, I could not remember exactly where the car was. Moe always navigated me around the roads surrounding Reddick and

South Wilmington and I was not sure of the name of the road.

Phil was my angel that night since he knew the roads well. There was one straight shot from South Wilmington to Reddick and we found the yellow Ford just as we had left it. The blaring emergency lights from the wrecker illuminated Chippewa Street as they announced our arrival. Mom and Dad had obviously been watching for us and were both at the end of the driveway by the time I got down from the wrecker.

I felt sick to my stomach. The look of disappointment on Mom and Dad's face was worse than any tongue lashing I could have received. I wanted to just bawl and I did as soon as Phil pulled away. I explained as best I could, but Dad did not talk much. I could tell he was beyond disappointed. Mom just kept hugging me but I could tell she was mad too.

Later as I stared at my ceiling, I wondered if this was enough stress to make Dad start drinking again. I would never forgive myself if he did.

I called Moe early the next day and her mom and dad had come home as soon as they heard. She probably should have been seen for her eye, but her neighbor, Maureen Joyce, was a nurse and had put a butterfly stitch on it. I worked at the pool that day and just as I was pulling into the driveway on my bike, Joe Call and Billy Hooker pulled up. They had heard the news and wanted to make sure I was OK.

I did not talk to them long and as I climbed the steps to go into the house, I felt the ache of unfamiliar bones. My neck and back were really sore. I walked into the living room and felt all the life drain out of me. It only took a second to take in the scene. I saw my license first. It was displayed in the middle of the living room like a piece of evidence on the green shag carpeting. Next to it, in a perfect line, was a can of Mountain Dew. The last and most damaging piece of evidence reflected the lamp that sat beside my dad as he scowled from his big green chair. The brown bottle of Seagrams 7 from the night before stood tall showing remnants of dirt from the cornfield it had been thrown in.

"Mom and I went for a ride this afternoon to see if we could tell where you had the accident." Dad almost whispered. I could hear his words, but the pounding of my heartbeat was competing for every word.

Mom walked in and sat beside me on the couch. I felt the warm tears of guilt hit my bare, tan legs. Did I think I had gotten away with this? Part of me knew that this was coming. All day, I felt the monkey that I had placed on my back. The only thing missing was a police officer, handcuffs and Thank God an ambulance.

"You did not just go in the ditch, Patti Jo." Dad's voice was getting louder but shakier with each word.

"We followed the tracks and from where you went in the ditch. You hit a concrete culvert and the tracks show that you were airborne after you hit that culvert. People don't walk away from an accident like you had, Patti."

I was fighting to breathe between my sobs. There was nothing I could say or do. I had destroyed any trust they had ever had in me.

"You not only took your life in your hands last night, you also took Moe's. Dad and I got out to look at the tracks when we found these in the field."

Mom's voice sounded strangled as she jabbed her finger towards the floor.

I was afraid to move, afraid to speak. I just wanted to rewind the clock and do it all different. I know God did not want Moe and I to die that night. I was so lucky that I did not have the guilt of killing someone on my soul. I did kill the trust that Mom and Dad had in me, but I know they knew that the difference between me and lots of other kids my age was that I was caught by my parents; parents who were so thankful to be given the chance to teach me one of the most important lessons of my life.

Part 2
College Bound and Clueless

Chapter 22

So You Want To Be a Leatherneck?
August 1984

As I looked around the cluttered bedroom, I knew I was taking way too many clothes, but the weather was hard to judge. I knew I would be home for a weekend before the weather turned too cold.

Tomorrow was the day I was leaving for Western. I had received my dorm assignment earlier that summer and the name of my roommate. We had talked once on the phone and it was very obvious that she was black. Even though I had an open mind, I could not help feeling afraid.

I had never even had a black person in my school, let alone in my bedroom. I just kept telling myself that people are people and I just had to try to make it work.

I thought about all of this as I sat down on my lilac bedspread. I traced one of the familiar faded flowers and tried to imaging not sleeping in this room after tonight. I heard the creak of the stairs and knew instantly that someone was coming up the steps. My mom walked in with a stack of towels to be packed.

"I think we may have to buy you some new ones once we get to Macomb," she said as she held up a very thin blue bath towel.

"Those have seen better days," I said.

"You OK?" Mom asked as she joined me on the bed. I lied and said, "YES! GREAT!" as two huge tears spilled out.

Mom pulled me to her and I rested my head on her shoulder. I let the tears that had been so close to the surface all day, pour out.

"I'm afraid I'm not smart enough for college, Mom!"

"Oh honey, I wish I could make you believe in yourself as much as Dad and I do!"

"But what if I can't make it and what if I can't get along with my roommate?" I said in a strangled voice that sounded foreign even to my ears. Mom held me away from her and lifted my chin so that our eyes met.

"What have we always said? Huh? You know." Laughing and crying at the same time I nodded and said, "I know, no matter how bad it gets, I can always come home." I wiped a tear from her soft cheek just as she did the same for me.

"Now come on, we have got to get to bed. Dad says we are leaving at 7:00 a.m., so he'll be outside honking at 6:45!" I knew that for sure, so I finished up and was asleep before I could worry anymore!

The next day began with warm sunshine pouring into my bedroom. I glanced over to Kelli's bed as I had done for the past 17 years. It was stacked high with boxes and suitcases soon to be loaded in the yellow Ford. I wished so much that she was going with me. I could easily have joined her at ISU along with about 10 other people from my class, but I truly wanted to spread my wings. I wanted to go somewhere that no one knew me.

Kelli had already left for school and she was living in an apartment for the first time. For years we seemed to think the same thing at the same time. She was thinking of me just then and I ran into Mom and Dad's bedroom to grab the phone.

"Hi babe! Are you all ready?" Her excited voice made me smile.

"I think so," I said.

"I'm so proud of you for doing this Patti! I know you will love it!"

"I'll call you tonight after I get settled in the dorm!" I said.

"Is Dad in the car yet?" Kelli laughed knowing how prompt Dad was!!

"I would not be surprised! I better go, I love you, Kel."

"Love you too, Doll!" As I hung up, I put my hand to my

stomach to try to squash the butterflies. I was as excited as I was scared but there was no turning back.

It was a long three-hour drive and we stopped at the Dixie Truck Stop in McLean, Illinois, for breakfast. Dad had been very good about not rushing me, but he did not have to. We sat in a booth and I watched him as he sat across from me and eyed the truckers at the counter.   His blue eyes were as clear as the August sky. He held the worn coffee cup with both hands, but they still shook as if a small earthquake were passing through them. He looked back and caught me watching him.

"I'm as nervous as if I were starting college," he said with a chuckle. He grabbed my hand and we stayed like that until our food came. Nerves may have had something to do with it, but the real reason was because of the years of drinking. He was sober now and that was all we could focus on. ONE DAY AT A TIME!

Mom and I headed out to the car hand in hand and waited for Dad. I could feel the time I had with them slipping away, and I was holding on for dear life. I heard the familiar sound of Dad's change jingling and turned around as he approached. "This might be the most important item you take to school sweetie!" He handed me a small box with a new Timex sparkling inside. I breathed in his signature smell as I threw me hands around his neck.

The last hour and a half of the trip went quickly and I began to recognize the small college town of Macomb from our visit to the campus back in the spring. We made our way through the square and headed down Adam's Street. The street dipped down and as we stopped at the stop sign, my dorm came into view.

I was staying in Washington Hall which was on the south side of the campus. Lincoln Hall was the guys dorm and I ducked down in the back seat to take in the tall buildings through the windshield. There were cars everywhere and we parked in the closest spot we could find along Adam's Street. We had no sooner opened the trunk, when a group of students with matching shirts appeared pushing a noisy laundry cart.

"Welcome to Western!" one of the girl's said, as I read her

t-shirt. It said, SOUTH QUAD MOVE-IN CREW '84!, in big bold blue letters. They loaded my things and we made our way down the sidewalk and underneath the dorms. I was trying hard not to let my nerves ruin the sights and sounds of my new home. A loud thumping bass was blaring from opened windows, and several groups of black students were sitting around cement planters in the common area between Lincoln and Washington.

I knew my mom and dad were noticing everything. As we entered the elevator that would take us to the fourth floor, I watched them both take in the people in the lobby.

As we stepped off the elevator, I saw a short coed with fair skin, freckles and red hair. "Hi, I'm Beth, your R.A." I almost hugged her on the spot. She explained that she was sort of the mom of the floor and that she would be the one to come to if we had any questions.

She showed me my room and I met my roommate whose name was Jeanette. My roommate was a little bitty thing and she was busy moving all of her things in. I could tell she was just as apprehensive about rooming with a white girl, as I was rooming with a black girl. My mom and dad stayed and helped me put up posters and unpack my things. I needed to buy some more things for the walls and I needed to buy my books, so we headed across the street to Chapman's Book Store.

There was a Domino's Pizza and a sandwich shop right next to the book store, so we grabbed lunch and decided that after we got my books that Mom and Dad would take off. Dad had gone to get the car and Mom and I hugged for a long time in front of the bookstore. I was trying so hard not to cry because there were people everywhere.

I watched as a group of black guys crossed the street and walked by us. They all wore the same colors, purple and gold, and they were obviously part of the same fraternity. I had no idea what the letters or symbols meant.

"Please don't go out by yourself, Patti," Mom said in a worried tone as she eyed the group too.

"Don't worry, mom!" We watched Dad as he nabbed a prime parking spot in the Domino's Pizza parking lot. This was it! They had to go and I knew this, but every inch of me wanted to just jump back in the yellow Ford and go home. Some people live with their parents their whole life. Why can't I?

Dad hugged me as he always did!

"We'll see you, Bum! You be careful! We love you so much!" He choked on the last words as he turned and headed for the car. One last hug and Mom was with him. I waved and put on a brave smile as they drove away. I could see Dad watching me in the rearview mirror and he blew me a kiss. I watched the car until it made its way up the hill on Adam's Street. It took every bit of courage that I could muster not to run after them.

I stood for a long time lost in my thoughts. I was brought back to the present by the same crowd of guys that entered the bookstore. They were now leaving and heading back to the dorm. I picked up my heavy bag of books and headed for my new home, Washington Hall!

Chapter 23

I'm Your New Roommate

I settled into my new college life rather quickly. The classes were much harder than I imagined, but I also tried my hand at actually studying. I was so homesick that I was seriously considering transferring to ISU. After talking to Brenda, I knew that I was not the only one having trouble adjusting. Brenda was miserable at Northern but it sounded like she was in the geek dorm.

We talked regularly and we both were going home almost every other weekend. Every time I saw Brenda over the past few months she continued to get thinner and thinner. I was really worried that she had a problem with not eating. Eating was not my problem since it appeared the old freshman 15 was right on track.

I had met lots of nice girls and one that lived at the end of the hall, I had played basketball against. She was from Marseilles, Illinois and her roommate was transferring.

My roommate and I were getting along fine, but she had a chance to move in with another girl that she knew, so we did a switch. Lynn Bishop was my new roommate and she proved to be one of my best friends during that first year. She hardly looked like a college freshman. She weighed all of 92 lbs. and everything about her was little. Lynn went home quite often because of her boyfriend, Todd.

With more and more homework, I decided to start staying at Western rather than go home every weekend. One Friday afternoon, I was coming out of the bathroom. Chaka Khan was blaring on the other side of the hall and I smiled as I watched a tall skinny girl with long straight black hair dance out of her room.

"Hey! Are you staying here this weekend?" she yelled over the music.

"Yes, I am," I answered.

"Well get in here then!" she yelled, motioning me to her room. I walked into a happy hour in progress. There were several girls from the floor and quite a few guys that I did not know. Dori, the tall dancing girl, called out my arrival to everyone.

"What is your name?"

"Patti," I yelled. She flew around the room pointing and calling everyone by name. I noticed a small keg of beer hidden under a blanket. I looked around their room, as I helped myself to a beer. It was obvious by the pictures that both of the girls had serious boyfriends back home. I saw picture after picture of Dori's boyfriend, John. I asked her where he was and she explained that he was going to school in Chicago. She told me that they had been dating for four years and she planned to marry him after college.

Looking out the window, I wondered if I would ever get there. It had been such a crazy summer between Brad and Tank and I still had not figured out what I wanted. I had just got off the phone with Brad before I saw Dori in the hall.

Feeling the familiar guilt, I went over the past few months in my mind. I had been dating Brad for most of my senior year but over the summer everything had changed. With one kiss, everything that I thought I had figured out, went completely out the window. Just when I had given up hope that anything would ever become of the strong friendship between me and Tank, he came along and brought back all the feelings that I had for him for what seemed like forever.

We had done so much together, but it was strictly platonic much to my disappointment. I had resigned myself to let the whole thing go and I was having a great time with Brad. Things were going fine with Brad and we really had fun together. We shared graduation and it was that night that started my confusion.

Tank gave me a present at the school since he could not come to the house. It was a beautiful gold bracelet and I was shocked. I put it on right there in the gym and Brad asked about it on the ride home. I knew I could have told him the truth, but I lied and told him that my aunt and uncle gave it to me. I did not take it off from the minute I opened the box.

I looked down and touched the small heart that dangled from the chain. It seemed like from the time that I put that bracelet on, my heart was divided.

It was several weeks after graduation that I saw Tank at the Carbon Hill Homecoming. All of us girls went together and we all found different people to talk to. He was sitting on the picnic table in the beer tent and we sat there and talked for most of the night. He had come alone so he asked if he could bring me home. The girls were all having a great time so I went home with him.

When we got to my house he came in just like he had always done. Part of me thought, this night will end just like every other night. But to my delight and complete confusion he finally kissed me. I realized that it did not matter how long I had gone out with Brad or how much I would hurt him, I was with the person I wanted to be with. The rest of the summer had been spent trying to figure out what Tank wanted, instead of what I wanted.

I was brought back to reality with the sudden silence of the music stopping.

"Hey, are you alright?" Carol, Dori's roommate, asked as she nudged me.

"Yes, I'm sorry. I was just spacing out there for a minute." I did not have time to return to my boy problems since before I knew it, Dori pulled me up and had me dancing to Doctor Doctor. I twirled and bounced around to the beat losing myself in the music. Looking around, I realized I had found my friends at Western.

Chapter 24

Motorcycle Joe

The cafeteria was the social mecca for Washington and Lincoln Hall. The guys all sat by the door where the girls came in and it was a little like being at an auction. With Lynn at my side every night for dinner, the heads turned from all directions. She was cute and little and she had pretty brown shoulder length hair that she curled back to frame her face.

I, on the other hand, was round-faced with short hair. I was a good head taller than Lynn and outweighed her by about 50 lbs. I had no distinguishing waist and one could probably not find it if one tried.

My one, or should I say two attention getting features were my larger than life breasts. For some reason my boobs grew during my freshman year at an alarming rate. I hated them with a passion and did everything humanly possible to hide them. My posture began to melt forward in a lame attempt at absorbing the large melons I had to lug around. I had never been thin, but I had never worried about it; probably because I had never had a roommate that wore preteen sizes.

Needless to say, I walked in Lynn's shadow and watched in awe as the guys made fools of themselves around her. I no longer had a first name. I was Lynn's roommate (You know Lynn, the little hottie on the fourth floor!)

There was one guy that I watched every night. I had seen him driving around campus on a motorcycle and he was just a fine looking thing. I knew he was not even in my league, but I watched him just the same. He was tall and muscular. He had dark hair that he swept over his forehead with his hand all the time. He face was blessed with a perfect olive complexion. His square jaw framed a great smile. I found out his name was Joe and from then on he became Motorcycle Joe.

The girls all knew about this, so it was a nightly thing for them to point him out and embarrass me as much as possible. He just was not interested, so I just resigned myself to gawk from across the cafeteria.

The girls from the fourth floor were all fun. I really became close with a girl named Susie Weidl. She was very short, but unlike Lynn, she was round. Her chest made mine look average. She could hide hers well with her beautiful long red hair. Her nose was small and lifted slightly to show off her fair skin and endless freckles.

Susie rarely stayed at Western on the weekends, since her boyfriend, Mark, picked her up and drove her back to school from her home in Grant Park, Illinois. They seemed very serious and he was much older than Susie. When she did stay, we had a blast.

My ideas about transferring disappeared as my first year began to unfold. I had not been totally honest with Brad about everything I was feeling. We broke up and then got back together only to find that whenever Tank called I would make whatever excuse I could to be with him.

Tank turned out to be as confused as I was, but it became apparent that I was not his dream girl. I began to realize that I had settled for anything he could give me which was not healthy. We saw each other off and on all through my freshman year, but it was becoming more and more clear that Tank was not satisfied with just me.

Over Christmas break, I spent so much time picking out his present. We had made plans to exchange gifts and spend the day together, but when he came to the house, he left his car running and gave me one red rose. I realized that I wanted so much more than he could give me.

Lynn was having her own boy troubles. Her, and her

boyfriend, Todd, had decided to see other people, so the offers came flooding in. I was the phone lady and one night in the spring I answered and found myself talking to none other than the infamous Motorcycle Joe.

The only problem was that he was not calling for me. He had met Lynn at a party and wanted to ask her out. She was feeling really bad until I told her to go for it. I would finally get to see him and talk with him up close even if it was as Lynn's roommate.

They saw each other all through the spring and Lynn took him home for a wedding in Marseilles. He was a super nice guy who had not let his good looks go to his head. It was about this time that I met someone. Jim was in one of Lynn's classes. He invited Lynn and her roommate (my name is Patti!) over for beers after one of the many warm afternoons out on the lawn. Of course, I went along, but for the first time all year Lynn was not the focus. I was!

He and I talked about everything and as we talked I found it hard not to notice what an awesome body this man had. He was not too much taller than I was, but he was tan and buff and he wanted to know about me! He did mention that he had a girlfriend who was at Eastern so there went the air out of that balloon. Even so, the attention was wonderful.

The fourth floor was like a second family. I had made so many different friendships and each one was special.

One girl, Julie Jones, lived at the other end of the hall and as the year progressed we began to talk more and more. She loved Jimmy Buffett, which was enough to make her my new best friend! Joe Call, Billy, Buford and Joe Steichen, or Opie as he was affectionately called, had introduced me to Buffett. Jonesy lived in a small town just outside of Macomb, so she spent a lot of time home on the weekends. She was from a family of 10 and after several beers we would all try to go through their names which all started with J's. She would prove to be one of the few lasting friendships that my college years produced.

May arrived with large amounts of warm weather and even

larger amounts of homework and studying. The year was coming to a close and everyone had spring fever. Joe and Lynn were spending more and more time together and Jim and I were too. We would start out trying to study together for finals, but we always ended up talking about everything else.

It was very clear how close he and his girlfriend were and I never let myself believe that our relationship was anything more than friends. I kept telling myself this, but the reality was that I was falling head over heels for him.

Brad had been down to visit the last weekend in April and it had not been a real good visit. I knew why it wasn't working, but it was just so hard to end it all together. We had gone to several parties, but all I could think of all weekend was how much I wanted to be with Jim.

To make matters worse, Brad informed me that he had been accepted to Western and was going to come here next year. I didn't know how to feel about this. As selfish as it sounds, I felt like this was my school and now he was coming. I did not have room in my life to worry about any of this, so I focused on my studies even harder.

Chapter 25

Whoever Gets The Sunglasses
May 3, 1985

"Which shoes, pink or beige?" I turned to see Susie in our doorway with one of each color on her tiny feet. Her long red hair was pulled back in a headband and her freckles were out in full force after time in the sun.

In unison, Lynn and I answered, "Pink!" Susie turned to head back down to her room and we both yelled, "Hurry up, Susie!"

Five minutes later we were crossing Adam's Street and walking towards the Sigma Phi Epsilon house which was right across the street from our dorm. It was the last free Friday before finals started, so Happy Hour was going strong.

The front yard was filled with college kids; most with sunburns from the new spring sun. Looking up, I shook my head at the condition of this house. Animal House looked like a mansion compared to this barely standing structure. The front porch sagged miserably and a bent, rusted gutter was hanging on for dear life just above the broken steps. A black heart-shaped sign hung between two windows on the second story with the Greek symbols for Sigma Phi Epsilon and a skull and crossbones below it. The bushes that lined the porch had not seen a trimmer since last summer.

None of this seemed to bother anyone, as we made our way into the basement for a beer. Standing right by the beer was Jim.

"Hey, there's my girl," he said as he crushed me into a hug. My stomach lurched as I returned the hug.

"I've been waiting for you," he said, as I tried to hide the blush that crept up my neck. 'Why would he say these things if he didn't like me?' I thought. I just did not know what to think about this guy. We walked outside to stand in the sun and we sat down on the dirtiest couch I had ever seen. I had been placed under the tree in the front yard. There was a lot of traffic since the Domino's Pizza was right next door.

I looked out at the traffic and watched as Joe turned the corner on his motorcycle. He drove it around back to park and within a few minutes he was standing next to Lynn.

"Hey Joe, I want a ride on your motorcycle," I yelled over the music.

"I get to go first," Susie piped in.

"Alright, alright, girls. There is no need to fight. Whoever finds sunglasses first, wins," Joe said with a big grin!

Susie and I pretended to shove each other out of the way to go find the prize. I got talking to a guy from my Art appreciation class. His name was Jim Slattery so we shared a good Irish name. He always called me sis, so we talked about the upcoming final in Art.

Before I knew it, about a half-hour had passed. I was standing at the edge of the yard and I turned to follow the noise of a motorcycle coming down the street. I watched as Susie's red hair flew behind her in the wind. She had her arms around Joe's waist and they were both smiling. I waved and laughed as I yelled, "You won, Susie!"

There was a line of cars stopped, so Joe slowed down only for a second before swerving around the cars to pass. I held my breath as I watched the front car turn left just as Joe accelerated the bike into the pass.

My grip on my beer tightened so that beer squeezed out of the top of the plastic cup. I couldn't scream and I couldn't believe what I was seeing as I watched Joe try to stop. Everything seemed to slow down. Their bodies lurched forward as Joe tried to stop the bike. He had just enough time to turn the bike to the left, before it slammed into the driver's side of the green car. The sounds surrounded me; the awful whine of Joe's bike before they hit; the incredible thud of the impact of their bodies with the car; the screech of metal on metal, the screams that others could find as they watched on in horror.

I followed Susie's body as it flew over the car and landed under another car that was parked right by the door of Domino's. I was sure this was a bad dream and that everything would return to normal if I could just breathe. I had not realized that I was running until I reached her. All I could see was red hair. Lynn was standing there screaming.

"Don't touch her!" someone screamed. The Domino's workers were kneeling beside Susie and she was breathing.

I stood frozen not knowing what to do or where to go. I turned to see the entire party surrounding what was now the accident scene. Joe was lying on his stomach behind the car and blood was slowly dripping out of his ear and his nose. The manager from Domino's had called 911 and within minutes the ambulances arrived. We had covered them both with blankets from the Sig Ep house but no one knew where to start.

The police made everyone move back and Lynn was pushed up on the lawn of the Sig Ep house. She was standing with Joe's roommate Chris. I could see Lynn from where I stood out on the street and I felt the nausea coming as I saw Susie's little pink shoe in her hand.

There were people everywhere and I felt someone hug me from behind. It was Jim, but still I was frozen. I was closer to where they were working on Joe, but I could not look at him. I knew he was dead. I don't know how I knew, but I did. I did not take my eyes off of Susie. She was awake but she didn't seem to be able to talk. I couldn't believe what I was seeing.

I watched a paramedic cut Susie's hair because it was caught in the hub cap of the car she was thrown under. They took Susie away first, but it seemed like Joe's ambulance sat there forever. This only meant that they could not do anything for him.

I met Lynn on the steps and we rode together to the McDonough County Hospital. I was so worried about Lynn. She was shaking from head to toe. I realized much later that we were all suffering from our own versions of shock. We were some of the first people to arrive in the emergency waiting room. Joe had pledged a fraternity that spring and some of the Theta Chi's slowly filtered in.

Joe's roommate, Chris, was sitting alone in the corner. He was a wiry looking guy with curly black hair and a bad complexion. He had lived with Joe for the past two years since they were both sophomores.

There was a small clock on the wall directly across from where I was sitting. I remember focusing on the second hand. This was the only thing I could do. I couldn't cry, I couldn't talk, I just sat there, watching the second hand tick away. I kept thinking that it was only a matter of time before we would hear that they were both dead.

We arrived at 5:45 and it was going on two hours that we had been waiting for some word. I could not stop seeing the images of their bodies being thrown in the air. Every time it returned, I felt the bile work its way up my throat.

No one knew what to say or what to do for each other as we waited for some kind of news. We left the sitting area and stood in the sterile hallway simply for a change of scenery. The buzz of the fluorescent lights and the intermittent ding from the elevator were the only sounds besides our heavy sighs of anxiety. The room where Joe and Susie were being worked on was just 10 feet away but we couldn't get to them.

Finally a Doctor came out and addressed us all with the amazing news that Susie was hurt very bad, but she was going to be OK. They were going to airlift her by helicopter to Saint Francis Hospital in Peoria because she needed major reconstructive surgery to her leg. She was conscious and she had told him to tell us all hi. My tears started with relief, but as he stood there with a lost look on his face, I knew what was coming.

Everyone held their breath.

"Your friend, Joe, never regained consciousness. He suffered extensive head trauma and he passed away just a few minutes ago."

I heard Lynn's moan and I caught her limp body as she sank to the cold tile.

We held each other on that cold tile floor and I finally let go of the tears that had been frozen since this nightmare began. The Doctor came over and asked, "Are you Lynn and Patti?" We nodded.

"Susie has asked to see you before she goes but it is very important that we don't tell her about Joe yet. Do you think you can see her?" We both took deep breaths and told him yes.

We waited outside by the helicopter pad and watched as the team wheeled her stretcher out. The warm spring afternoon had disappeared and there was a chill to the breeze that blew the Doctor's lab coat. I wanted to ride with her so that she was not alone, but there was not enough room in the helicopter and I didn't think I should leave Lynn alone. They had told us that Susie's parents, Ken and Carol were going to meet them in Peoria so we did not have to go.

I thought for a moment how they were feeling. To get that dreaded call that every parent worries about.

"Hi guys!" Susie's familiar voice was husky with medication. We leaned down and gave her a quick kiss.

"Hang in there Suz! We love you!" We both choked on fresh tears as we watched them load our broken friend. From where we were standing, we could see her little thumbs-up sign as they lifted her in.

Everyone from our floor was waiting for news, but Lynn needed to get away from people for a while. I called Lynn's mom and she was on her way to get Lynn. It would take a few hours for her to get from Marseilles to Macomb, so we were taken to the Theta Chi house. Father Rickey, the chaplain from the Newman Center, was going to talk to all of us. Joe's parents had been flown down from Chicago. Joe was still alive when they left, but now they had to be told the news that they had lost their son.

"Hi Mom." This was all I could manage to get out before breaking down.

It was around three in the morning and Lynn had just gone with her mom and sister. I had come back up to the room and for the first time, I found myself alone. It was the first time I had to just sit and go over everything that had happened. I realized through everything that I had not called Mom and Dad. They knew Susie, since she had been home with me for a weekend and Mom and Dad had seen her again when they came down to Western for a weekend.

I would have given anything to be home with them. All I wanted was to crawl into their arms right then. I wanted to lie between them just like I was six again. I didn't want to be old enough to feel this pain. I wanted them to know that it could have been me, should have been me, but I couldn't get anything out once I heard Mom's voice on the phone.

"What is it, hon?" Mom asked in her hoarse, middle of the night voice.

"We're right here, Bum," I heard Dad say as he got on the other line.

"It's OK," They were both trying to get me to stop sobbing, but it was finally coming out. Every emotion that had been frozen since the accident bubbled out with each anguished cry. I managed to choke out the details as best I could and Mom and Dad were both crying with me before it was all out. They wanted to come and get me, but I needed to do so many things.

Lynn was supposed to call with Joe's funeral arrangements and I needed to talk to my professors about postponing my finals so that I could go. I wanted to see Susie and find out more about her condition. I could not even fathom studying at this point. I felt so much better just talking to Mom and Dad. The minute my head hit the pillow, I fell asleep.

To my surprise I awoke to the first signs of sun coming through our window. I was the only one up on the floor and I took the first shower to wash away the cobwebs. It was too early to call any of my professors and besides it was Saturday so the chances of taking care of anything were slim to none.

As I came out of the bathroom, I saw Beth, our R.A., standing in her doorway. Without saying a word, I walked to her and we hugged for a long time. Fresh tears fell as I tried to swallow the lump again.

"How is she?" Beth asked.

"I'm going to call right now and find out," I answered. I headed down towards my room. I stopped when I heard Beth call my name.

"Patti, are you OK?" I really could not answer because part of me felt like I would never be OK again.

I looked down at the yellow Post-it note as I hung up the phone. Reading like a grocery list instead of a list of Susie's injuries, I went over everything that Ken, her Dad, had told me. Susie had a broken back, and a broken pelvis. She had shattered her knee cap and had broken both of the major bones in her lower leg, the tibia and fibula. She had been in surgery most of the night and they had removed her spleen. They had still not told her about Joe, but they were going to sometime today. Ken asked if I could get some things of hers together and bring them. She was in St. Francis Hospital in Peoria and she would be there for quite some time.

My next call was to Lynn. Her mom said she was still sleeping, but she relayed the funeral arrangements. I decided to get out of the room for a while, so I borrowed Beth's bike and cruised around aimlessly. I was riding by the Union, when I happened to catch a glimpse of the newspaper out of the corner of my eye.

There on the front page was a picture of Joe being loaded into the ambulance. I focused on his red high tops since I could not read the article until I could get some air in my lungs. The campus was deserted at this time of morning so I sat on the bench at the top of the stairs and slowly read the details that had been replayed a million times in my mind over the past 12 hours.

Susie spent 6 months in that hospital in Peoria. She came home with a walker and a limp that would serve as a constant reminder of her struggles. I made that drive at least once a week during that summer and regularly from Macomb after my sophomore year started. Lynn never came back to Western. We stayed in touch and we often went together to see Susie.

The accident changed us all so much. It changed my life in ways that I was not aware of right away. Death slapped me in the face at a time in my life when I felt completely invincible. Twenty year old Co-ed's were not supposed to die. They were the ones who were supposed to attend their grandparent's funeral.

I wondered so many times why it had not been me on that motorcycle. God knew the plan, but I just couldn't understand it. I understand now that he had other plans for me, for Susie, and Lynn. He needed Joe more than any of us did. The hardest part was not feeling guilty for going on with my life. Although I continued to move forward with my dreams, a part of me always looked back on that day in May.

Chapter 26

Young Love

That summer brought the first wedding in our young lives. Kim Kratochvil had waited for this day for as long as she could remember. She was marrying Brian Bennett who was leaving for the Air Force. The wedding was a blast and Mary, Brenda, Missy Miller and I were the official cake cutters. We were all so worried that they were too young, but only time would tell for the two of them.

Kim and Brian had to leave home at the age of 18. What must that feel like? I had trouble staying at school for more than a few weeks without seeing Mom and Dad. I was very glad that I did not have to make the grown up decisions that were ahead for Brian and Kim. They were the picture of hope that day. Together, we knew they would find their own way.

My summer was not the same without Kelli. She had decided to go up to Lake Forest to be with her boyfriend. His mom had helped Kelli get a job at a bank and he was the manager of a Burger King. Kelli seemed happy, but the last few times we had talked she had seemed distracted. Mom and Dad were not too thrilled that Kelli had chosen to live with her boyfriend, but he had lived below her in the apartment complex at ISU and Kelli was old enough to make her own decisions.

The summer was just beginning and I had just gotten home from the pool one night in early June. I heard the phone ring and I answered it in the bathroom. I barely got hello out when I heard Kelli's choked sobs on the phone.

"Patti listen, I'm coming home. He has totally lost it. I

came home to find all of my perfume bottles broken against the wall and my clothes were all over the lawn! I just left everything and got out of there. I have been driving for a while and I don't think he is following me. I'm so scared he is going to find me!"

"Where are you? I'll come get you!" I screamed. Mom had walked in and the blood was now draining from her face. She mouthed the word 'Kelli' and I shook my head.

"No! I just have to get home. I just threw my stuff in the car and took off. Just pray I can make it home with the amount of gas I have. Don't tell Mom and Dad."

She hung up the phone before I could get anymore info out of her. I stood there, feeling Mom's intense grip on my arm wondering what to tell Mom. I yelled for Dad to get in here.

"It's bad. She is trying to get out of there. He went a little crazy over something. She just wanted us to know she is coming home tonight."

Mom sat down heavily on the toilet seat and began rocking back and forth as the worried tears came tumbling down.

"I knew this would happen. My gut has told me something wasn't right for a while now." She said placing the guilt on herself.

"Should we call the police?" Dad said.

"I don't know what to do?" I said, feeling the fear that was evident in Kelli's voice.

If we headed up there, we took the chance of missing her. None of us had been to their apartment, since she had just moved in the last month.

A memory kept creeping into my mind and I could not escape the dread that I felt. I remembered the story of Doug's visit to Kelli at the apartment at ISU last fall. Kelli and Doug had dated for a while, but Kelli had not seen Doug for four months. He finally decided to visit her. This was typical of their relationship and Kelli had been fed up with the lack of attention Doug had shown her.

They had been dating for over a year and even though Doug treated Kelli as good as I think he could, it was not good enough for Kelli. She had started seeing the guy downstairs, but she made it clear that Doug was coming that weekend. He was obviously much more serious since he broke down the door to Kelli's bedroom and assaulted Doug. He had gone to jail that night, but Kelli had felt responsible for the whole thing.

This new boyfriend was insanely jealous and I could only imagine what had set him into this crazed rage tonight. If only she would call again. Dad drove up and down Interstate 55 for the next hour hoping to see her headlights and finally they both rolled in the drive.

Kelli came out of the car and nearly collapsed from relief. As I hugged her, I could feel her shaking body.

"I'm so sorry!" she kept saying over and over.

"YOU HAVE NOTHING TO BE SORRY FOR!" Dad said in that throaty voice he used when he was very angry.

Kelli never saw him again, but the fears he instilled in her have never left her. She sees him every time a car follows her for more than a mile or two. She sees him every time the line goes dead as the unknown caller hangs up. She sees him every time she hears the Boys of Summer blaring from the radio just as it did on her answering machine on her 40th birthday. Thank God she got away from him before our fears were realized.

What a difference a year made. I went back to Western as the move-in crew my sophomore year. I had so many friends and I also had my buddy Billy Hooker across campus. He and I ate together and studied together at least a couple of times a week.

Julie Jones was back and just down the hall. She did not know it yet, but she was going to help me through Economics. She was a finance major and I knew she had that Math gene that I did not posess.

Brad was here too. He was in Lincoln Hall and I was in Washington Hall so we shared every meal in the same dining hall. Jerry Prindiville was also at Western. He had transferred from Joliet Junior College and was living in a house off campus with another guy from Mazon, Illinois. Jerry and I had grown up together since our parents had been friends for years. It was such a fun fall. Jerry was my chauffeur on the weekends. He took me to my first Rocky Horror Picture Show. He laughed hysterically when I was struck in the head by a loaf of bread! It was the craziest thing I had ever seen. We had so much fun together.

I would see Kelli again at Harvest Days. She was finishing up at ISU this year. She had been dating Gerry Miller since late in the summer. She was working so hard and she had gotten so thin.

I, on the other hand could have done a Miller Lite commercial. Not as one of those hotties, but as an example of what could happen if you drank beer and ate Domino's Pizza regularly. My boobs continued to arrive places before me, but life was good.

That fall, I met Brenda and Moe in Champaign, Illinois. We went to see Kelly Sullivan who had started at Parkland College. Parkland was just across town form the University of Illinois. U of I was famous for their Halloween weekend and we were ready to celebrate.

I had brought my new purple rain slicker and I wore my new shaker knit sweater. I had just bought a pair of those plaid pants, so my whole outfit was brand new. There were lots of Dwight people visiting that weekend. Brian McArdle was a freshman at U of I, so Brad and John Keegan were staying with him. We ran into them at our first stop. Timmy Watters, who was also from Dwight, was having a Happy Hour. The partying started off with a bang as we all played a tequila shot game.

I had never met Jose Quervo, and he had quite an affect on me. I was feeling really crazy as we left Timmy's party. He lived in an apartment complex that opened into a long hallway. As we stepped into the hall, our group paused to decide where to go next. My focus was on a Domino's Pizza delivery man.

For reasons no one knows, I took off at a dead run and before I knew what I was doing, I had tackled the skinny, startled man. My hand slammed the orange, carpeted hallway declaring my take down. "One Two Three…."

That is when the girls pulled me off of him. Gathering

change, they were able to talk the disheveled man out of calling the cops. Brenda's white Cutlass was a welcome sight for my out of focus eyes.

The girls were just getting started on the party circuit, but I used the next hour to nap in Brenda's back seat. I was dressed appropriately for the next incident, but my new purple slicker could not repel all the tequila that made its presence known again.

We rode home with the windows down and my slicker slapping wind out the Cutlass window. Betsy, Kelly's roommate, held the door opened, as I was assisted to the bathroom. She said very little, but her disapproving look said it all.

The shower felt wonderful. I was just starting to feel normal again and as I reached up to turn off the water, I lost my balance. In an act of pure self-preservation, I grabbed hold of the shower curtain. In a loud crash, I fell out of the shower and sat holding the remnants of the broken shower rod. My rescuers arrived again and this time I was put to bed before any further damage could be done.

There were two things that would never happen again after that night. The first, was that I never played with Jose Quervo again. The second, was that Betsy never invited me back to Champaign.

The rest of the fall was spent focused on school. I was getting into more of my Child Development classes and I knew I had chosen the right major. By December, I was very ready for Christmas break, and headed home for a life changing month.

Chapter 27

A New Beginning

January 1986

The cars were parked all over the front part of the lawn at Birdie's house. It was New Year's Eve and everyone was out. We had started at Kent's house, but his parents came home early so the party moved to the Sparrow's house on Waupansie Street.

As we entered the party, the floor in the entry way resembled a shoe store tornado zone. I took off my black boots and added them to the pile. I was with Moe and Brenda who were now roommates at ISU. Brenda had transferred from Northern and was looking more and more healthy everyday. She had gotten terribly thin over the past year and we had all been really worried about her.

I made my way through the dining room and said hello to Birdies mom, Sheryl. Wow did she have the patience of a saint.

"Hey Patti Jo!" I heard Kerry Fogarty's voice from behind me. Turning around I saw John Ruskin who was home on leave. He was such a riot. We had been cracking up together at Kent's about the most stupid stuff. He had been dating Vicki, but Brenda had heard that they had broken up. They had been together for a while even though he was still in the Navy and she was at ISU. I would have to get the scoop.

I continued to cruise around the party. Opie (Joe Stiechen) caught me in a big hug. I had the sweater on that Opie, Joe, Billy and Buford had gotten me for Christmas. They were my best buddies, but I had been spending more time with Opie lately. I wasn't sure if he liked me for more than a friend. I was so confused about how to handle this with one of my best friends. He could not have treated me better. He had even come to pick me up at Western a couple of times. Now that Billy was at Western they came to visit often. I just was not sure what to do with any of this.

Someone passed me a hat and I told them to hold on while I ran to the car to get my money. I slipped on the first coat I could find and a pair of loafers that fit me perfectly. I made my way back to the keg so that I could contribute to the cause.

"Hey, whose shoes are these?" I yelled feeling the beers of the evening kicking in.

"You've got my shoes on!" John said laughing hard.

"Check it out, they fit me perfect." We stood there and talked for hours. He had me laughing so hard I had spit beer twice. He was home on leave from Camp Lejeune, North Carolina. I asked him about Vicki and he said they both decided to end it. I had not seen her over break, and this probably explained why.

I had not realized how long I had talked with John. Looking at my watch, I knew I had to get home. Kerry had the green Maverick and he and John offered to give me a ride home. I never dreamed that the ride home would have my head reeling with feelings for this hilarious little guy.

John asked me to go to a show on New Year's Day and I said yes. The whole date was comedy. We ate at White Castle and went to see "Out of Africa." It had been given unbelievable reviews, but we were not sharing in Ebert's excitement. I remember how we both jumped as the screen snapped. We had both fallen asleep, but were now doubled over laughing.

Perhaps the late partying the night before was catching up with us. This guy might just help me lose weight. My stomach hurt from laughing so much. The next day was the second of January and when the doorbell rang early that afternoon I was floored. A huge bouquet of fresh flowers greeted me and for the first time I realized that maybe there was more here than just something to do over Christmas break.

We saw each other almost everyday, but within a week he had to go back to North Carolina. I had no idea what I was doing and I had hurt Vicki more than I ever thought I would. It made me question whether I had made the right decision. I had never had so much fun with a guy who actually wanted to be more than just friends. It was like slipping on the loafers that night. We just seemed to fit.

I felt so empty when he left. This was a whole new feeling. Of course it had to be with someone who had to be away from me. I went back to school and wrote more letters than I ever thought possible. We talked on the phone and as corny as it sounds, we fell in love long distance.

I avoided Brad at every turn, but I knew he knew I was seeing John. Every party I went to, he was there. Every day in the dining hall, Brad was there. He rarely talked to me and who could blame him. It was just so hard to have that much history with someone and go back to being just friends.

January brought the Super Bowl Shuffle and Super Bowl fever like Chicago and Illinois had never seen. Jonesy, Dori, John Smith, and I watched the Bears cream the Patriots in an unbelievable victory! John, Dori's boyfriend had transferred to Western. We did everything together.

I flew for the first time in March of 1986. In a move that would strain my friendship with my roommate, Julie Ohl, I headed out to North Carolina to see John instead of going to South Padre Island, Texas. We had planned our spring break trip early in the year and when I changed my plans, Julie was understandably angry.

I just had to find out if this was real with John. I was really scared about this visit since I would be staying with John. I had decided long ago that I would try as hard as I could to save myself for when I got married. I was not sure if he had decided to do the same. I made this all very clear before I came out to see him and he was totally fine with this.

The trip to North Carolina was so fun and I knew it would probably be the last time I saw John before he went on a six month deployment to the Mediterranean Sea.

It would be almost a year before we would see each other

again. That was very scary for me. To think how much I had grown and changed in the past year and to think that he would not be a part of that much of my life was something I could not even fathom. I knew that if we were meant to be together, we would be.

The only real problem was that I was bigger than John. Not just taller, but wider and I didn't think this would bother me, but it did. In every picture of the two of us, I began to slouch so that he appeared taller. Like I could hide the girls! Maybe I could try something crazy like losing weight before he returned. I knew I would have plenty of time to think about it.

Chapter 28

There's No Place Like Home
March 1986

In all the years in this house, I had never seen bare walls. Everywhere I looked the shadows of pictures hung for years were all that remained. I brushed the tears away as I washed the base boards.

Mom and Dad had made one of the hardest decisions in their life. The stairs in the house on Chippewa were proving to be too much for Mom's hip. They had put the house on the market and within weeks Joel and Barb Patten had bought it. Mom and Dad found a perfect apartment on Franklin Street.

Now came the reality of that decision. I had started to move some of my things to the new apartment, but today was the day that everything would go. I looked at my reflection in the wall of mirrors that had watched me grow into a young woman. For the last time I sat on the window seat where I had read for countless hours.

I looked out the window and down at the driveway that had held so many cars over the years; the Rambler, the blue Ninety-Eights, Ed's Nova, and PAL. As I closed my eyes, I could hear each car's distinct engine noise.

Mom had come in and caught me in my moment.

"It's sure hard to leave!" she choked out.

"I know, but this is also a new beginning for you and Dad!" I said as I swallowed my selfishness.

"Is everything out of your room?" she asked.

"I'll go up and check!" I caught my breath as I entered the only bedroom I could remember. It had been our room, mine and Kellis, for the past 20 years. The white twin beds with their gold outlines and lavender bedspreads were no longer side by side as they had been for so many years. The two nails that had held my reading light had been forgotten. They looked like little eyes wondering where everything had gone. I had read and studied under that light my entire life. Gone were the posters and bulletin boards and ceramic P's and K's.

The vanity where we had sat and done our hair and makeup was replaced with scratches and black marks on the wall. This room held our hopes, secrets, our dreams, and our nightmares, but all that remained were dust bunnies and nails in the wall.

I looked down from the window towards the driveway. How many times had I ramped up that small incline on my bike; 1000, maybe 2000 times? I thought about Barb, Joel, and Ashley Patten. Barb had been our babysitter. She had grown up just two houses down from us. Joel's childhood home was on the corner of Chippewa Street. This was now their house to build dreams in. How lucky they were.

I walked down the stairs and out the front door for the last time that day. This was not just a house to me, it was my center and my foundation. As I walked out of my house that day, I left a part of me at 123 West Chippewa Street.

Summer of 86

The spring flew by and I had to say another goodbye; this time to Dori, my first friend at Western. She was graduating and had accepted a job in Chicago. I knew I would see her often since her boyfriend, John, would return to Western.

The summer was filled with swimming lessons, parties with Mary, Brenda, Moe, Kelly Sullivan and Susie. The pool was so much fun. We car hopped on roller skates for Cruise Night and managed to teach most of Dwight's youth to swim.

Susie was using a cane now and was getting around really

well. She was sporting a cute new short hairdo and driving a brand new Grand Am. We would go back to Western together in the fall. We were going to rent an apartment just off campus on Charles Street in Macomb.

Kelli was finally happy. Her and Gerry Miller had shared the same major at ISU and they seemed like a perfect match. Gerry met all of Kelli's friends and he fit right in. They had dated for almost a year and Kelli was sure she had found the right man. They were engaged by December of 1986 and planned their wedding for November of 1987.

Ed had his first job as an Assistant Pro at Forest Hills Country Club in Rockford, Illinois. Mom and Dad were settling into the apartment nicely. Dad was trying hard to work his program. He helped himself stay sober by helping many others get and stay sober. Mom and Dad had started AA meetings in Dwight so they both worked hard at making this lifestyle change work.

Dad had bought me a new car. I was the proud owner of a Monte Carlo 442. The silver and maroon cruising vessel was quite a piece of work. It had been Craig Jensen's back in the day but that was several owners ago. The only problem was that the accelerator would stick on occasion and I had to add brake fluid once a week. But I had wheels again, so I was ready for school.

Chapter 29

Quadruple What?
September 1986

Junior year came and I was again one of the boys. I met Joe Washburn working at the cafeteria at Washington Hall. He lived off campus with a guy by the mane of John Sloan. They became my best friends as Susie pledged a sorority. Susie immersed herself in becoming a Delta Zeta and I hung out with Sloaner, Joe and a new Opie. I thought it was very odd that I would know two guys with the same nickname. David Douglas was easily the sweetest guy I had ever met. His fair skin and reddish blond hair completed his innocent charm.

Things were starting off great that fall until early September. I held the phone with a death grip the day my mom called to tell me Dad had been rushed to Springfield and would be having a quadruple bypass within the next two days. He had been hiding all of his symptoms from Mom, but he had finally been scared enough to get to the Doctor. I cruised down and met Kelli and Mom in Springfield.

Dad was at St. John's which was the leader in heart surgeries in Illinois. Dad's surgery was a success, but none of us were prepared to see Dad in recovery that day. He had tubes coming from everywhere and he looked as grey as I had ever seen him. St. John's was a wonderful Catholic hospital but we found the nuns to be a bit overwhelming. That meant well but they did not give you very much privacy.

Every time we sat down, Sister Mary Holy Water came to console us. We had just left Dad's room after seeing him for the first time following his surgery. All of us were crying in the hallway. The well meaning nun came up to us and in harmony we yelled, "Not Right Now!"

That day the nurses insisted that Dad sit up. The phlegm had built up in his lungs and he had to get this out. We watched as he hugged a pillow and maneuvered his tube infested body to the sitting position. Hours before his chest had been wide open and now he had to cough!

His face grew redder and redder and I was sure I was watching him die right in front of me.

"Cough, Dad, Cough!" we all yelled. He was gurgling and lurching forward when suddenly, he let loose with one of his career hoikes. From that point on, his recovery took off and he was home within a week. Dad came home with a new appreciation for life. He ate healthy and walked religiously everyday. He was really a new and improved man.

Chapter 30

No Pants, No Socks, No Problem

Sloaner's house became my other apartment as Susie bonded with her Delta Zeta friends. She had so many pledge requirements that we rarely saw each other. I just didn't get it, but I was busy with school and working at the cafeteria. I was now a Key Student which was quite demanding. I helped manage all the student workers in the cafeteria. The money helped out so much and I could eat for free at work so I planned my schedule around my meals. My boss was a wonderful lady. Jane was single and bored to death in Macomb so we pulled her along with us to the bars when we would all go out.

Joe W. had also been a Key Student, but he had left school in a rushed decision that none of us understood. His dad came one day with a U-Haul and he was gone. Sloaner lived in the big house alone now.

Sloaner was easily the skinniest person I had ever met. He became my best friend. I told him everything. He loved music of all kinds and introduced me to Boston; the greatest rock band of all time. He was a diverse groupie as we jammed to the Carpenters following Boston.

I would drive up to see him jamming in the big picture window with the broom most afternoons. He never wore real pants or socks. His usual attire consisted of faded sweat pants pushed up to his knees, and tennis shoes. Even on the coldest day in January, his wardrobe never wavered.

He and Opie II (David) came home with me for the weekend and my dad was fascinated by Sloaner's wardrobe. They got along perfectly since Dad could pick on him and Sloaner could give it right back. I had never met anyone who could care less about his look. He shaved his head on a whim during the winter that year. He was always full of surprises. Opie was always so good to have with us. His infectious laugh was contagious and he kept Sloaner in line most of the time.

With my John on a ship, our communication was completely cut off. I could not talk to him. With school taking off, I did not write him like I had the year before. I missed him, but I felt like maybe I wasn't missing him as much as I should be. I loved the fact that I was able to breathe a bit. This worked great until the mail came. His letters came in bundles. He wrote almost daily, but the mail did not go out regularly. I received four and five letters at a time. He was in no way ready for a break. He talked about getting out of the Navy when he got home. He wanted get his degree and marry me.

As the letters continued, I felt like I was not being honest with him. I did not want to get married right away. I didn't even know if John was the right person for me. I made a decision to write him and tell him to cool it and that I needed time to think things through. In military terms this was the dreaded Dear John letter. I had the letter for two months before I sent it. I did not want him to come back in March and expect to propose to me.

I began to wonder what was wrong with me. Why couldn't I figure out what I wanted? What was it that I was waiting for? Was it Sloaner? Did part of me wish our friendship could go somewhere? Was it still Tank who now had a steady girlfriend but still made my stomach lurch every time I saw him? Other people around me were committed. I just wasn't sure of anything.

Just after I sent the letter, a tape arrived. John had made me a special tape of songs that broke my heart. I did not know what I was doing! I remember sitting in the living room of the apartment bawling my eyes out one Saturday night.

I had no idea who was at the door when I heard a loud knock.

It was Billy and I needed him big time that night. We found a bottle of Champagne in the fridge and proceeded to drown our sorrows. He seemed to always know just when to come visit.

Chapter 31

Go Greyhound
Spring Break 1986

Jonesy was another constant. She stayed many a night with us at the apartment since she was living at home that year. She always showed up with beer and pretzels. I swear the girl never ate.

I'll never forget the day she brought me an ad from the newspaper. The ad held the answer to our spring break prayers; an $80.00 round trip ticket to Florida. Her boyfriend, Mike, lived in Florida. Jonesy's sister, June, was married to the Dodger's Pitching coach, Ron Perinowski. The Dodgers did their spring training in Vero Beach, Florida. She also had another sister, Jan, who ran a landscaping business with her husband in Vero Beach. All we had to do was get there.

We rode a Greyhound for four days. Four days of lying on cold bus terminal floors in terrible areas of numerous cities just to go where it was warm. We didn't shower or eat much but we laughed more than any person should. Once we arrived, we were treated like royalty. We met Dodger players at Bobbie's in Vero Beach. We had VIP passes to a Dodger's Spring Training game. We had the time of our lives and each of us had $13.00 combined for the trip home. June sent us on our way with bags of food and memories to last a lifetime.

John returned to Dwight as he had planned in March of 1987. He got out of the Navy and was working at R.R. Donnelley's. This was where his mom worked. I saw him off and on, but I had hurt him just like I had hurt Brad. I had no idea what to do, but I figured sooner or later I would figure out what I wanted.

As my junior year of college ended so did my time with Sloaner. He had been making major life decisions and was following his dream of becoming a pilot. He was leaving Western and had been accepted at Park University in St. Louis.

I could not imagine my day without him. Our relationship was so easy. He knew more about me than almost anyone and he still loved me. We ate together, laughed together, drank together and managed to help each other through heart aches. I loved him so much, but I was never sure that I should ever test that by going further. There is always that someone who you wonder about. Sloaner was that person for me.

I knew where his heart was. He had fallen hard for his best friend's little sister. Unfortunately for Sloaner, David's sister, Debbie, was pre-engaged to a guy from her home town.

It was so hard to say good-bye to Sloaner, because I knew how different our lives would be from that point on. I wanted to just freeze time and not go on without him. But life moved on for both of us.

Chapter 32

The Decision of a Lifetime
Fall of 1987

I would return to Western for one more semester and I could not wait to finish. I focused on my classes and sent applications all over Illinois for my internship. I had decided to do an internship in Child Life which was a program in hospitals that provided play therapy to hospitalized children. I was very excited to find out where I would be placed.

I still saw my Western Opie and we spent most weekends together. His major was Criminal Justice and he was just as anxious to finish and begin the next phase of his life.

I also did some serious soul searching. I had to make a choice about the men in my life. I realized that I did not want to marry Brad. I had messed things up with him so long ago and to try to repair that had been a constant struggle that after three years was not getting any easier. Bard had done so much to help me and we had literally grown up together. I felt that if he was truly who I should be with, I would never have treated him like I did. I did not want to cheat on him the rest of my life. He didn't deserve what I did to him. No one does. I just couldn't love him the way I should have and it was time to face this reality.

John had treated me like a queen from the minute I started dating him. I thought about him all the time and I wondered what I was waiting for.

The last time we talked he was heading down to Illinois State University to start school. He had been accepted for the fall semester, but his housing was not good. He was being placed in a dorm lounge with up to 10 other guys since the dorms were so crowded.

He had just come off a ship living like this for six months. Needless to say, he never went to ISU. He had come home and was now living in his mom's basement. He took classes at Joliet Junior College, but I don't think he was even going. I wanted him to find some sort of direction before I decided what I would do with my life.

For my 21st birthday the girls came to visit. Mary, Kelly, Brenda, Moe and Roxanne came from ISU to celebrate with me. I was living with a girl named Tracey that I had met in my Child Development classes. I only needed a semester so the dorm was the right choice.

John found his direction by going back into the Navy. The Navy gave John the anchor that home and college could not. I could no more choose his direction than I could choose where my heart led me.

John's family was growing. John, Emily, and Paula gained a baby sister in October. The long awaited arrival of Mesha Marie Ruskin finally became a reality on October 28th. She was four-months-old when she arrived in a basket at O'Hare airport from India. John's dad, Bob, and his wife, Ann, brought their new baby to Ann's parent's farm to meet the entire Ruskin/Trainor family. What a birthday present it was for Ann's dad, Bob, who was 65 that day.

Mesha was the most beautiful baby I had ever seen. Her dark skin was perfectly matched with the darkest brown eyes imaginable. Her coal black hair refused to cooperate under the tiny barrette the social worker had so lovingly placed for her amazing journey. Ann's fair skin and red hair were a perfect contrast to her new baby girl. Mesha was surrounded by love from that day on.

Kelli was also surrounded by love on her wedding day in November. The ladies in red watched her start her new life with Gerry. I was ready to start mine as well.

I finally knew at Kelli and Gerry's wedding what I wanted. John and I began to date again, but now I had the hardest decision of them all. John would be leaving soon. I knew in my heart that I didn't want him to leave alone, but I needed to finish school.

We were engaged over Christmas and planned a May wedding which would give Mom and Dad a chance to build their savings back up. Now the real adventure was about to begin. We would be apart during the five months of my internship. It was to be a perfect test for us.

Chapter 33

There Ought To Be a Handbook
January 1988

My internship began at Children's Memorial Hospital in Chicago, Illinois, on one of the coldest days ever recorded. Kelli's husband, Gerry, had grown up in Mount Prospect and his mother, Fern, was kind enough to let me stay with her. At the time, this set up was a life saver since I received 12 credit hours for my internship which would complete my degree.

The only thing I did not receive, was any sort of payment or living expenses. Fern opened her house to me and I was grateful. Kelli, on the other hand, was completely against the idea because she knew that Fern had a serious drinking problem. I could not be choosy however, so I moved in and became one of the millions that daily were called commuters.

Keeping in mind the small town girl that I was, commuting held many challenges for me. The Metra, which is a commuter train that runs into the city, departed from downtown Mount Prospect every morning and returned every evening. This part was a piece of cake.

I slowly began to recognize familiar faces each morning and I was sure that before too long I would have several people to converse with so as to make the daily grind less grinding.

One morning, as I sat next to a man that I had seen everyday for the past two weeks, I attempted to make conversation.

"I'm so glad it has finally warmed up," I said removing my gloves. He looked at me out of the corner of his eyes, but did not respond. He instead, snapped open the Tribune.

As he began reading, I glanced at the headline, "COLD SNAP FINALLY ENDS." Noticing that I was reading his paper, he folded it, and wedged himself into the corner of the seat and the window while turning the paper so it was out of my view. I could not believe it! I was obviously not going to be sharing anything with this idiot.

Unfortunately, I found this to be the pattern. If you spoke to a fellow commuter, there was something seriously wrong with you. Smiles were not returned and under no circumstances did you ever, I mean ever, look at a newspaper that was not yours. I soon started carrying a book to pass the time.

After sharing my commuter journey with the girls at Children's, I learned that Clybourn Station, which was where I was getting off the Metra, was very high on the list of scary places in the city. I should have figured this out since no one got off but me. You would think that the other commuters would have given me some sort of clue since I was a young, white female, but I guess they figured it was justice for reading their newspapers.

After this tidbit came to light, I began taking the Metra into Union Station like half a million other commuters. For those who have never experienced Union Station at rush hour, imagine a stick being carried by the current in a raging, swollen river.

The minute I stepped off the platform of the train, I was swept into a crowd of people so thick that the simple act of breathing was difficult. Upon entering the station, I had to first pass through a set of revolving doors. Because of the close proximity to the person in front of me, and behind me, this became quite a game.

I remember that first day. I was completely overwhelmed by the sheer volume of people around me. I remember thinking that Clybourn station, with all its negatives, could not be as dangerous as this crowd.

I had left the platform and was watching the person directly in front of me. I was sure I was going to be one of those statistics that is read and discarded without a thought. I could see the headlines, "Woman Trampled By Crowd, Found After Rush Hour!" I was setting my pace with the man in front of me because I was certain I would be mowed down from behind if I hesitated for a second.

Just as I looked up, the man in front of me entered the turn style of one of the revolving doors. I had followed his every footstep but what was I supposed to do now? If I dared take a step back who knew what kind of commuter etiquette I would be breaching, so I lunged forward to join the man in his turn style.

What happened in the following seconds was beyond even my imagination. I bumped him in the back from the force of my lunge and startled, he turned to face me. The man's face went completely white and his eyes showed the complete terror he was feeling.

"What the hell are you doing?" he screamed.

"I I I I I Don't Know!" was all I could manage to yell back.

The door's opened and we exploded out of the turn style. He continued to mumble to himself as he hurried through the station, while I sat down on the nearest bench. I was laughing so hard, the tears were streaming down my face. I was laughing like a lunatic. I'm sure people thought I was just another street person telling herself jokes. I laughed just as hard when I shared the story at Children's. I'm sure that poor man still has nightmares about the crazy woman who shared his turn style.

I decided about half way through my internship that I needed a different living arrangement but my options were quite limited. The only other person I knew in any surrounding suburb was Moe. She was working for Midway Airlines and lived in Palos Hills which was a far south suburb. Moe, and her roommate, Amy, were gracious enough to lend me their couch for the two months I had left in the big city.

As if I had not learned enough about commuting already, I now added several more modes of transportation to my morning trek. I now caught a bus on 95th Street and took either the El or the Metra into the city. The El was Chicago's elevated train system. Cash made the decision and most weeks it was the cheaper fare on the El which put me in a pretty scary part of the city. What I found was that everyone was in their own world.

I sat close to the front of the bus every day and watched the same nameless people take their same, cold, plastic seats. I said good morning to the same bearded bus driver who never smiled. His grey PACE nametag read 'Randy', but no one ever called him by his name. I would feed my dollar in the electronic machine every morning and watch it pull it in like a hungry animal.

One day, I watched a man hand Randy a dollar bill and he received twenty cents in change. At this time in my life twenty cents was a lot, so I asked Randy why this man got change.

In a very matter of fact voice he said, "The fare is 80 cents."

"80 cents! Why didn't you tell me?" I said in disbelief.

In that same, matter of fact voice he answered, "You never asked."

A huge smile spread across his face.

I continued to ramble on about this injustice in a light hearted way, but I realized another secret commuter rule had been uncovered.

The machine does not give change but the driver will. Who knew! This simple exchange opened the door to my first friendship with a Chicago Transit Authority Bus Driver. It also brought the other nameless riders into the morning banter as well. Without even thinking about it, we all started to sit closer together. Randy actually stopped the bus for me a few times when I was running really late. I would pull the Cruising Vessel (my 442) along side the bus at a stoplight and he would point to where I should park. The girls at Children's could not believe these stories.

I brought donuts on my last day in the big city and I laughed so hard when Randy and the rest of the gang gave me a card. It had a five dollar bill in it for all the change I didn't receive!

There should be a manual handed out to new commuters to outline the dos and don'ts, but somehow, I found them all out in my own way!

Chapter 34

My Little Stick of Dynamite
February 18th, 1988

My internship at Children's Memorial Hospital was into its second month and I was getting my daily routine fine-tuned. My mornings consisted of helping Amy set up the Pre-school Play Room for the morning group. I was surrounded by some of the sickest kids in the country, but their time in our morning play group was the bright spot in their day. It also gave the parents a much needed break.

I was becoming accustomed to the constant beeping of IV machines and the maneuvering of beds and wheelchairs. The startling baldness of a four-year-old became something of a norm and the only goal was to see a smile across those yellow jaundiced faces.

I had started seeing individual kids in the afternoon who were either too sick to come to group or needed a little extra interaction. I was meeting a new girl today and I was a little nervous because she was a 12-year-old. I had not had much experience with adolescents, but the adolescent intern had a full case load so I needed to pick up the extra cases.

Kara Chasen had been in the Intensive Care Unit since January 19th. As part of her team, I was able to review her medical record, but it was overwhelming. It was two full volumes and had quite a bit more medical terminology than my class provided last semester..

What I did gather was that when Kara was two she was diagnosed with Wilms Tumor, which is kidney cancer.. The cancer was in her right kidney and she had this kidney removed. A few months later, they found a tumor in her right lung. She had the tumor removed and received full lung radiation. A year later, another tumor was found on the right upper lobe of the same lung. This portion of her right lung was also removed. Three months later, she returned and this time a tumor was found behind her right lung on the back chest wall. She had a portion of her chest wall removed, and two ribs.

Finally the cancer was gone, but Kara's problems were not over. As the rest of her body grew, her neck, chest, and hips did not. The months and years of chemotherapy and radiation had taken their toll. She now had extensive scar tissue in her lungs.

She had been well for the past 7 years, but a bad cold had developed into pneumonia and she was in respiratory distress when she was brought in on the 19th of January. She was on 100% oxygen and the report from the nurses was that she was bored and angry.

Geez! I was not ready for this one, but after lunch I hit the game room and found some fabric paint and some pillowcases. I headed down the ominous hallway and buzzed the speaker to identify myself.

The electric doors opened and I entered a huge room with a busy nursing station in the center. There were four beds on each side of the room. I heard a woman's laugh and followed the sound with apprehension. I watched, as this woman unpacked her knitting and began to settle in to a chair next to one of the beds.

My eyes connected with the young, frail girl whose mom had just arrived. She was very thin, but the scowl on her face said everything she was feeling. She whispered something to her mom as I checked in at the nurse's station. I had not worked with older children before and I was as nervous as I could remember.

The nurse introduced us and I was instantly swept into a conversation with Kara's mom, Sheila. I tried to talk with Kara but because of her mask and the need to save her energy she used a dry erase board to communicate. Her black straight hair hung over her eyes which reflected the mistrust of someone who sees many people come and go.

I showed her what I brought and although she looked as bored as I did scared, we started working on decorating the pillow. My lack of artistic ability was instantly noticed and before long she was laughing uncontrollably at my attempt to draw a bird. I realized this was my tool to reach this amazingly strong young girl. The afternoon flew by and one of the nurses followed me out the big doors.

"She has not laughed since she has been in here," She said as she touched my arm.

"Please keep coming." I did not have to be told since Kara was as much my savior, as I was hers.

In February, she was moved to the Step Down unit which was actually a step above ICU but it was still a constant care area. We spent our afternoons making friendship bracelets, decorating t-shirts and polishing our nails. For the first two months of our time together Kara never spoke a word.

We spent most afternoons together and the nurses began to trust me. I would pull Kara in a wagon and we became a well known duo from the gift shop to the cafeteria. I stayed away from her medical issues and I know that this is what she needed. She didn't want to talk about her O2 levels or her weight.

We were just two buddies. She was preparing for her Bnot mitzvah and I was preparing for my wedding. I shared all the decisions with her from my dress down to the music we would have. I helped her study her Hebrew which was something new for this Irish lassie! We went to the zoo and celebrated Passover in the nurse's lounge. We planned on going to a Cubs game before I left, but this was not to be.

My internship ended with Kara exactly where I had met her. She was making preparations to go home but it seemed like every step brought more challenges and compromises on her fragile health.

As I bent to hug her goodbye, I felt each bone on her frail back. It was my turn to be unable to communicate. The lump in my throat would not allow even an, I love you.

"I will see you in a month," she said with more confidence than I felt! Her husky voice brought tears to my eyes as I gave her a thumbs-up. Her big day was first and we promised to be there for each other.

I kissed the top of her head and turned to go. I was leaving a part of myself with Kara. No one had touched my life like this 50 lb. stick of dynamite. I knew I would never look at life the same after my time at Children's.

Part 3
Getting Under Way

Chapter 35

The Newlyweds
May 1988

It was here; the day I had been dreading and anticipating my entire life. I was a married woman and I was leaving home for good today. I could hear the rain hitting the gutters outside of Mom and Dad's apartment. I couldn't help but think how lucky we were, since the entire weekend had been nothing short of spectacular spring weather.

Our wedding was on Saturday and had been everything I could have hoped for. Over 400 of our family and friends helped us start our new life together. It was so much fun. I wanted to do it again. We had it all on video and I was already missing those I would not see for a while.

Kara and her family were there and she was the one who caught the bouquet. She looked so cute. John had a great time too, so much so that I had to drive us to our honeymoon suite! We had received the nicest gifts and we both felt a bit of the pressure lift after Sunday.

We were heading to Key West, Florida and our only choice was to rent a van. Because it was a One-Way rental, it was going to cost $1500.00. I chuckled as I remembered the card opening ceremony. When we hit the magic number of $1500.00 you would have thought we won the lottery. I think John's mom and Larry and my parents were more relieved than we were.

I peeked out the bedroom window and saw John and my dad loading the one piece of furniture we owned into the bright yellow van. Zeke and Delores had given us a brown rocker as a wedding gift. I was also taking my dresser which had been Grandma Coughlin's.

I gathered up the last of our hanging clothes and made my way outside. We were done loading and the van was only ½ full. Pretty scary to see all of your worldly possessions and not have them fill up a van.

Birdie had just pulled up to send us off and so had Larry, John's step-dad. Mom had managed to stay very busy all morning. I knew she needed to avoid any down time to think of the impending separation.

This was it. I had to be a grown-up now. I was having trouble taking deep breaths as I watched her make her way out to the van. She had sent us off with a tune on the organ, "Please Release Me, Let Me Go."

"I think that is everything, guys!" Mom laughed as John put Opus, the stuffed animal he got me years ago, in the front seat. Mom was trying hard to keep her tone light, but I could hear the thickness in her throat.

Brenda had walked out with Mom too. Brenda had always been by my side and here she was again. We said our goodbyes and pulled out. Mom and Dad were standing arm in arm with brave smiles and watering eyes, waving and blowing kisses as we started our new life together, alone.

Most people have to leave home at some point in their lives in order to step out on their own. I felt so lucky that I knew where my home was. This town in the rear view mirror felt like the beams of support on which you build a new home. I knew every crack in the sidewalks and every bump to avoid on the small streets of Dwight. I knew the fire whistle blew at noon at the exact minute that Bozo Circus came on the air. The organ music coming from the Congregational Church meant it was time to get home for supper.

More than anything else, the people make a town what it is or isn't. It is good and safe to be where every body knows your name. The beauty of a small town like Dwight can sometimes only be seen from a distance. For me, it would always be the most beautiful place in the world.

Chapter 36

Home Sweet Home

We took our time driving to Florida. Our first stop was in Alton, Illinois to meet John's Grandma and Grandpa McDonough. Shorty and Pauline were so sweet. Shorty may have had something to do with John's height issue since he only stood about five feet tall. We had a nice visit with them, but I was getting very anxious to see our first house.

House is such a strong word for what John had secured for us. He had been in Key West since February and found us a great spot to rent while we were on the housing list.

He kept calling our spot an adult RV condominium. He told me over and over how beautifully landscaped it was and that there was a pool and a community building within the complex. It was even a gated community and he was sure I would love it.

The Keys were breathtaking. A gentle breeze moved through the Palm trees as the ocean cast the backdrop with the deepest blue I had ever seen. As we drove down US 1, I felt like I was finally living in one of Jimmy Buffett's songs. The song that kept coming back to me was the one with the line, "I'm just glad I don't live in a trailer." I could not sing this line anymore.

John pointed out the sign for the Sea Side Resort and we turned left off of US 1. We pulled up to a huge chain link gate. John inserted his card into the security system and the gate slid to the right to reveal a beautifully landscaped courtyard.

Three tall palm trees stood behind a weathered sign. The sign covered their middle and the swaying trees resembled long-legged women chatting in the sun. A shorter banana tree shaded the left side of the sign that was bordered by red plumeria bushes. Huge white rocks were positioned to the right and left of the courtyard and I read the sign as we made our way into the park. "Seaside Resort Where the Land is mostly water and world is mostly sky."

As we drove through the quiet park, my fluttering stomach began to relax. Every place we saw was well maintained and beautifully landscaped.

"Nice, huh?" John was more nervous than I was. I kept waiting for him to stop at one of these nice mobile homes, but he kept driving.

We were entering the back of the park and the beautiful landscaping was no longer apparent. There were three identical trailers at the end of the road and I really could not see past the small aluminum sheds that sat to the right of the gravel driveway. 'Please, no!' I thought!

My stomach dropped as John pulled into Trailer #2. There was a tall thin tree completely overgrown between the shed and the end of the trailer. I could see wheels peeking out above the rusted skirting. I was trying so hard not to cry and speaking was completely out of the question. John's question had hung in the air.

"What do you think, P.J.?"

I was going to be sick. We got out and made our way through the weeds growing in the neglected gravel yard. A huge blooming plumeria bush, exhausted from the heat, rested on what was a poor excuse for back stairs. The staggered cinder blocks showed the remains of an unfinished paint job by someone who either ran out of paint or energy.

There was a good 12-inch gap from the first step to a skinny door. I made a mental note not to use the back stairs. A small window to the left of the back door had not seen Windex in months. A white picnic table sat off center in the gravel.

I made my way around to the front entry which was a sliding glass door. This was obviously the only usable entry since the wooden stairs were equipped with a railing. Another window, a bit bigger than the one in the back, sat to the right of the sliding glass door. The brand name LAYTON proclaimed itself on dingy white aluminum.

The trailer sported two stripes that in their day probably gave it quite the curb appeal, but they simply looked dirty from where I stood.

I did not want to go inside, but there was my new husband, waiting at the top of the rickety wooden steps, to show me our new home. I tried not to notice the large white hitch on the front of the trailer. For God's sake, we could be hooked up to a pick-up truck and taken in the middle of the night!

I was sure the steps could not handle any carrying over the threshold, so I stepped into our living room. The heat was so intense it about knocked me down; the heat and the mustard colored 70's pattern on the furnished sofa.

There was a small kitchen table under the window to my left. The windows were neatly curtained and there were small lamps attached to beige paneled walls. A small TV set sat on a stand in the corner. I was pleasantly surprised that the inside was this nice.

The trailer's kitchen was economy sized with the oven taking up just half of the space it usually should. As we made our way back through the narrow hallway, the bathroom gave little options. Once you entered you either had to piss, shit, or get in the shower. The sink and mirror were in the hall. The back of the trailer housed the bedroom. We sure were going to be together!

We began by opening up the trailer and unloading the van. As I began to move into the drawers, I realized how dirty everything was. I reached into the silverware drawer to prepare to wash what was there.

I looked in just in time to watch an inch-long palmetto bug crawl across my hand. I was out of that trailer in seconds. I do not do bugs and after the shock of the trailer, I was ready for a hotel. It took every bit of convincing on John's part to get me back in our new home.

Chapter 37

The Other Newlyweds

We had good reason to return home after our first month in Key West. It was John's moms turn to have her special day. Larry and Shirley were married on June 25th. John gave his mom away and we all watched as Larry whisked her away on his Harley. She was ready for her first ride as Mrs. Larry Seabert with her one of a kind garter complete with Harley bloomers.

They had both been through difficult divorces and it was obvious that the second time around was definitely the charm. Emily and Paula were excited about their mom's new start. Paula was at Eastern Illinois University and Emily was a freshman at Dwight High School. Em and Larry seemed to get along really well and she would finally have a father figure at home.

Whether it was our close quarters or God's plan, I was pregnant by July. I was so excited. I could hardly stand waiting nine months. Mom and Kelli were our first visitors and then Mom and Dad came out for Thanksgiving. I thought the hide a bed would kill Dad before the visit was over.

I got my first job as a Pre-Kindergarten teacher at Mary Immaculate Star of the Sea School in Key West. I had 24 four-year-olds and earned every bit of my $16,000 teacher salary. We got our military housing on Sigsbee Island in January of 1989 just in time to welcome our new addition.

The reality of living thousands of miles away from friends and family was beginning to set in. We did not have enough money to fly home for every big event and I can't explain the feeling of helplessness that this caused. I never imagined I would not be with one of my best friend's on her wedding day, but it happened. Mary and Jim were married on March 3rd and even if I could have figured out a way to travel, the Doctor told me not to fly since my due date was so close.

Mary and Jim had been together since they were sophomores in high school and they were true sweethearts. The pictures would have to do since John and I had our own special day to look forward to.

Chapter 38

Pregnant Woman Walking
March 17, 1989

I was sure that today would be the day that I would have my baby. As I rolled my huge stomach over, I heard John downstairs just leaving for work. Looking out the bedroom window, I could see the clear blue sky. It was going to be a beautiful Friday morning in Key West.

Swinging my legs off the mattress, I completed the learned ritual of getting out of bed. Sitting for a minute, I glanced toward the closet which John had left open.

The full-length mirror returned my reflection. Some days, like today, I couldn't believe what I saw staring back from the mirror. I felt so huge even though I knew I had carried my weight pretty well.

Standing up, I felt no different than any of the other days that seemed to have run together over the past nine months. I had actually never felt more healthy. I had gained exactly what Dr. Morse and Helen wanted me to. The extra 28 pounds were beginning to feel a lot heavier as my due date approached.

I was not actually due until the 25th of March, but with every fiber of my being, I was going to try to make this baby a leprechaun. What a party little Erin or Bobby would have when they got older.

I descended the stairs and put in my pregnancy workout tape. A half- hour later, I munched down my Total cereal and began my walking. As I locked the door of our townhouse on Batfish Court, I remembered that I had to call Vicki Miller.

We had become fast friends over the past year. Vicki had just delivered her little boy in January. Things had not gone so well for little Kevin from the beginning. He had an irregular heart beat, so he was flown to Miami just an hour after he was born.

He had come home within a week with a heart monitor and was doing fine. Vicki's husband, Drake, worked with John as a Corpsman and the four of us were practically inseparable.

I felt the sweat run down my back, as I walked with a determined stride around the Sigsbee RV Park. The water was at high tide and I could smell the familiar scent of seaweed as the tide washed it up on the embankment.

It was funny how certain smells could make me turn instantly green, but this pungent odor hardly phased me. I passed a trailer being pulled by a four-wheel drive truck. It was the exact size of the trailer that we had lived in out at the Sea Side Resort.

There were times when I actually missed our first home. I wondered if someday we would return to our little honeymoon island. It had been our beginning and it would soon be the birthplace of our first child.

I sat down on a picnic table to rest my cramping legs. It sure did not feel like St. Patrick's Day. I had worn my favorite green jumper with the pockets in front to stay festive. The pockets were hardly visible now under my big belly.

As I sat and caught my breath, I watched an older couple preparing for their breakfast. Their picnic table was set for two and I could not help but notice how contented they looked with each other. They looked to be the same age as Tommy and Rita. I had been thinking about them so much lately. I was sure it had to do with the fact that I was about to become a part of their elite group; a parent.

As the phone bills could attest, I had talked endlessly to Mom about her pregnancies and I wished more than anything that I could be with her.

I swallowed the lump that always seemed to form when I thought of them. Maybe it was my crazy hormones, or maybe it was the fact that I had never been more than three hours away from my family until now.

Mom and Dad were coming down in April and were staying for ten days. Larry and Shirley were coming down just before my parents, so we would have lots of help. I could not wait to see everyone. I felt the butterflies in my stomach with the realization that I would be a mommy by then.

I knew I better get walking if anything was going to happen today, so I got up and continued on my way. There was a warm breeze blowing off the water and it kept me cool as I continued to push myself. I ignored the pain and pressure I was feeling below.

It was two hours later that John heard the familiar ring of the phone in the Pediatric clinic. He had picked up on the first ring. He was just as anxious as I was to get this baby here.

"Honey, I have problem," I said embarrassed to be calling him in the middle of the morning.

"Are you in labor?" John was quick to ask.

"I wish. I started walking and I went too far. I am just too exhausted to get home." His concern was evident as he asked, "Where are you?"

"I'm over in Officer housing and this lady was nice enough to let me use her phone."

Trying to hide a laugh, John told me he was getting ready to give a shot. He would be there as soon as he could.

Hours later, John and I sat across from each other on the worn picnic tables. The sun was going down and another day was passing without any baby. The huge orange sun was beginning its beautiful descent into the ocean. The sparkling line of its rays moved toward us on the constant movement of the waves.

Staring out into the postcard setting, I could not help but think it a bit unreal. It sure did not seem like any St. Patrick's Day I could remember. I said as much to John who was checking out the oyster shucker. Since it was one of the last Fridays of Lent, we had decided to go out to eat.

John was hoping that this would cheer me up. My wish to have the baby today was not going to come true. We had gone to the Half Shell Raw Bar which was one of our favorite restaurants. It was the hot spot for locals and tourists alike and tonight was no exception. The familiar sounds of James Taylor could be heard above the dinner crowd.

I got John's attention by pointing out to a fishing boat that had just docked. A very suntanned Captain was holding up a huge mahi-mahi fish much to the delight of the diners. Just across the parking lot was Turtle Kralls, which was another favorite tourist trap. John had finally got me to stop taking my camera everywhere.

"For Heaven's sake Patti, we live here now! We have to stop looking like tourists!" he scolded me before we had left that night. As hard as I tried I could not think of this crazy little island as home. It was the farthest thing from anything familiar.

I laughed as the boat captain turned so the people could take his picture.

"Told you I should have brought my camera!" I kidded as I squeezed John's hand. Our dinner arrived and after dinner we strolled around the fishing docks for a while. After my long walk earlier in the day, I did not have too much energy left. We were home before 8:00. As I crawled into bed, John rubbed my tummy.

"Guess you just did not want to be a leprechaun after all," he whispered as he kissed the baby that he and I would be meeting very soon.

Chapter 39

A Love Like I Had Never Known
March 23, 1989

The hospital had that familiar smell that all medical facilities share. A mixture of antiseptic, bleach, and medicine wafted towards us as the electric doors of the Emergency Room announced our arrival. It was just after 8:00 p.m. and my pains had been regular, but mild all day.

As I sat in the only vacant chair in the waiting room, I realized now just how sore I was from walking all day. I had started walking just after my Doctor's appointment that morning, since they were sure I was in labor. Things had gone really slow all day.

I had taken Helen's advice to walk, since as a mid wife, Helen had been through this birth thing a lot more than me. John was at the desk checking us in and as I watched him, I had to laugh. He had his Notre Dame hat on and his favorite, red, Chuck Taylor tennis shoes. He had found these at a Buffett concert. He looked no more ready to be a dad than half of the young people in the waiting room.

Looking around, I could definitely tell it was spring break in Key West. Trying to find a comfortable spot, I fidgeted in the uncomfortable plastic chair. My elbow bumped the young college guy sitting next to me. His red swollen feet were the size of watermelons and the blisters were just beginning. He saw my eyes fixed on his feet and volunteered his reason for visiting the Emergency Room.

"Got a little too much sun today, he said more than a little embarrassed.

"Do you think you are going to have your baby tonight?"

he asked.

"I sure hope so!" I answered as I breathed through another contraction. I laughed as the young man just shook his head and stared at my belly.

"That is so wild!"

I felt a lot of the same amazement, but I also felt about a hundred years old compared to this kid. As John turned around, I read the t-shirt he was wearing. "Eat it raw at Theo's, It'll put more thud in your pucker!" I got that t-shirt exactly one year ago.

Had it only been a year ago since I had been one of the million Spring Breakers to hit the Florida beaches? This time last year, Jonesy and I had been enjoying what would be our last trip together as college seniors. I still laughed out loud when I thought of Jonesy and I on that Greyhound for four days.

"What is so funny?" John asked, as he returned with what looked to be at least a half-hours' worth of paperwork.

"I was just thinking of our trip to Florida last year," I said. My thoughts were returned to the present by the tightening in my belly.

"You think all you want while you sign your life away babe," John said as he handed me the stack and a pen.

An hour later I was aone in my room. They had just broken my water with what was surely some old woman's crotchet needle. John had gone to the car to get my suitcase that had been packed and repacked at least twenty times over the past month.

Every book I had read mentioned two or three items different than the last book. So I had brought it all just in case. There was the tennis ball container to help massage my back. There were at least three different kinds of lip balm for my chapped lips. There was OPUS, my focal point. I had two or three pair of footies in case my feet were cold. There was a deck of cards, a Danielle Steele book, and the address box with everyone's phone number in case labor took a while.

I had every base covered and then some. I looked down on my protruding belly and silently wondered if I would ever look good again. It had been my biggest worry throughout the whole pregnancy.

It had been the driving force for the daily ritual of smothering my body with olive oil. I had read that Christie Brinkley did this and it worked miracles for her, so I was on a mission. It had also been the reason for my nightly walks around the housing area.

I was startled from my thoughts by the activity on the monitor next to me. I was connected to a machine that monitored my contractions and it was more than a little uncomfortable around the largest part of my mammoth, veined stomach.

As I watched the needle begin to bounce I was taken by surprise with the intensity of the next contraction. Whoa! I guess this was what I had waited for all day. Before I could catch my breath, another pain came with a vengeance.

As John walked in the room, I grabbed him by the shirt and whispered, "Don't leave again!"

I was able to stand the pain and was adamant about not taking any medication. It was almost time to start pushing and Helen asked if we wanted the Doctor present. This was not thought necessary since things were going so smoothly. The decision was made to deliver the baby right in the labor room instead of transporting me to the delivery room.

As I strained with each push, Helen advised me to tuck my chin to my neck, instead of letting my head fall backwards. Before I could lift my head to follow Helen's directions, my head was unexpectedly slammed forward. Looking up at the source of this move, I glared into my coaches eyes.

"I was planning on doing that myself!" I grunted.

John, being the ultimate Coach that he was, had got caught up in the moment.

"Sorry," he said sheepishly hiding a grin. Helen, stifling a laugh, saved him by beckoning him to the other end of the bed. The look I gave him spoke volumes. Helen was wonderful. Knowing that John had a medical background, she asked him to pull the baby out.

"NOW?" screamed an anxious new dad.

"YES, NOW!" I screamed, from the other end of the bed. The pink and slimy infant was quickly wrapped and placed on my belly. At almost the same time, John and I both screamed, "What it is? A boy or a girl?"

Unwrapping the screaming infant, we were both beside ourselves when we saw our new little girl all red-faced and messy. Within minutes, John and I were staring down at our new baby girl. There was no question that Erin Eileen Ruskin would be loved more than either one of us could imagine.

Chapter 40

A Month of Visitors

We had so much support after we brought Erin home. Bob, John's dad, and Ann, were our first visitors. They brought Mesha, Emily and Paula so the new aunts could be the first to see Erin.

The timing worked out perfect for their spring break, but I was not the best hostess. I cried almost everyday for no apparent reason and struggled with breast feeding Erin. Being a tour guide was not high on my priority list.

Ann did all the laundry for me and she cooked for the whole gang too. She spent hours pushing Mesha on the swing. Emily and Paula worked on their tropical tan.

Our next visitors were my mom and dad. Their visit could not have been better timed. I needed some serious help with this new motherhood thing. Mom rarely put Erin down, so I was able to get some much needed rest.

The visit started out a bit shaky with Mom and Dad's luggage being lost. We managed to give them clothes for their first two days before their luggage finally found them.

Dad went to work on the front yard. He decided to plant marigolds and got right to work. I was worried about him working in the heat and my worst fears were realized the afternoon he ran in the house red faced and soaking wet.

I was sure he was suffering from a heart attack, but he insisted he was fine.

"I have a slight problem in the front yard," he reported.

I opened the front door and heard the problem before I saw it. It was a gushing geyser of water shooting straight into the air at least 10 feet.

"Holy shit, Dad!"

I guess it was way too late for the "Call Before You Dig" speech! We were not the favorite neighbors that day as the entire cul-de-sac went without water while public works replaced the broken pipe.

Dad managed to stay out of trouble until the end of the week. Mom and I were working on controlling the flow of breast milk that seemed to stream out of me like a faucet. Erin was getting enough milk from me, but the damn things did not seem to have an off switch. I was ready to stop leaking and have some control over my body.

One afternoon, Dad had gone for a walk and Mom and I were wrapping up the girls with ace bandages. We had just commented on how long Dad had been gone, when the doorbell rang. I told her to just wait and we would get them strapped down as soon as I answered the door.

Thinking it was one of my female neighbors, I did not bother to put a bra on. I threw on my pink Jimmy Buffett t-shirt and hurried downstairs. To my surprise and alarm, a Security officer was standing at the door.

I did my best to cover my t-shirt, as I asked him if everything was OK. In a very official tone he barked his question.

"Ma'am, do you know a Thomas James Slattery?" He read the name from a slip of paper in his hand.

Oh God! I thought about the heat and how selfish I had been to be worried about my boobs!

"Is he hurt?" I asked frantically.

"No Ma'am! He tried to gain access to the base without proper identification. He did not have your phone number so he is in the back of the squad car."

I watched the young man motion for Dad to get out with a very impatient wave of his hand.

"That is my father. He is not used to the whole military thing! Sorry!"

The officer turned back to me, "No problem...."

He stopped mid sentence and his gaze landed on my shirt. I felt it before I looked down and knew what I would see. My entire shirt had become saturated with milk! The light pink t-shirt was now a dark round patch.

"OK then. You have a great day! Dad get in here!" I yelled completely horrified! I might as well have been a Holstein for God's sake.

"Rita, get the bandages!" I yelled, but was laughing hysterically. My breastfeeding career lasted all of 3 weeks which was long enough for me.

Larry and Shirley were the next in line to spoil Erin. It was so great to have them visit because we actually got quality time together with out anyone to interrupt. I was still getting to know them as my in-laws.

Larry had been my neighbor on Chippewa Street for years before he and his wife divorced. Shirley had been my softball coach several years in a row so we had common pasts to bring us together.

We had a great visit. I was now able to wear normal clothes and I was over the baby blues. They bought me my first two piece swimming suit ever! My weight was really coming off and I was thrilled. We went all over the Keys including Bahia Honda National Park.

Larry and Shirley did their own thing too. The day before they were to depart, they headed down to Duval Street one last time. They found several Harley friends and Shirley went for a quick ride with a lawyer that Larry had talked with most of the afternoon.

The ride ended a great vacation and began a painful week of recovery. The guy had laid the bike down trying to turn around and Shirl's shorts were no match for the gravel. Larry drove her home and we got her out to the clinic at Boca Chica Naval Air Station, where John was standing duty.

John spent the next hour meticulously removing the gravel that was now a part of Shirley's hip and thigh. She had a painful plane ride home, but Shirley was quite thankful to have a Corpsman in the family!

Kelli and Gerry needed practice with a new baby since Kelli was due in November. They arrived just as John departed for Air Crew School in Pensacola, Florida. He would return as a Search and Rescue Corpsman and he would join Drake Miller, his good friend, who steered him toward this new career.

I flew back with Kelli and Gerry for Erin's first trip home. Mom had just had hip replacement surgery so we tried to help out as much as we could. We all anxiously awaited the arrival of Erin's first cousin.

Chapter 41

I Didn't Get To Say Goodbye

Once all of our visitors had come and gone, John and I settled into life with a baby. We shared most weekends with Drake and Vicki and their baby Kevin. I loved being home with Erin and I felt like everything was just as it should be.

That is why the phone call that came that May knocked me to my knees for the next couple of months. I knew when I heard Kara's fathers' voice that morning on the phone, that there had to be a reason he was calling at 6:00 a.m.

I was not prepared to hear his news. Kara was gone. She had passed away the night before. She had grown weaker and weaker over the past few months and she just could not keep fighting. I sobbed that morning, kicking myself for not seeing her during our trip home in December. We were supposed to have gone bowling, but we just could not get all the way up to Chicago with all the family commitments we had.

Now I would never see her again. I watched my wedding video over and over to relive that magical day that she shared with me. Those are the images that I have of Kara; that smile that was bigger than her face; the raspy voice that did not match her frail frame; the beautiful eyes that spoke more than words ever could. I have an angel with me and I feel like maybe part of Kara lives through Erin since one spirit was born, and one died in the same year.

Chapter 42

What A Year!

Looking back on that first year, I find myself almost amazed that I remember so little. Sure, the traditional firsts that new babies experience are all with me, but it seems so long ago to me now. I was just 22 years old when I became a mom, but I was certain that this was what I was destined to master.

I can look back now and know that Erin saved me at a time when I felt so lost. I knew long before we were ever engaged that if I made the decision to marry John, it would be a decision that would force me to leave the security of Illinois and the security of my family.

I knew this would be true in the symbolic sense but also in the literal sense. No matter how hard I prayed, there was just no need for a Navy base in Dwight, Illinois.

Now I knew what it felt like to love another human being so completely. This new feeling was almost suffocating, but it put everything my parents had done for me into perspective.

Chapter 43

Politicians Kiss 'Em, Jimmy Signs 'Em!

What started out as a fun Saturday on Duval Street, turned into one of my life dreams. Key West is known for its Halloween celebration called Fantasy Fest. This crazy weekend brings people of all kinds down to the strip of restaurants, bars and shops that make up the one and only Duval Street. Drake and Vicki and John and I decided to load up our strollers and check it out before dark since it is known to get real crazy after the beautiful sun sets off of Mallory Square.

People both in and out of costumes (literally) crowded the street which was closed for the onslaught of the thousands of revelers expected. As we approached the east end of Duval Street, we noticed a line of people that actually curved around the corner of Fast Buck Freddies. We walked on to find the line stopping at the door of Jimmy Buffett's Margaritaville store.

This was it. This was what I had waited for all these months. He was here. A man in line confirmed my hopes and related that Jimmy Buffett was signing copies of his new book, "Tales From Margaritaville."

As if reading my thoughts, John turned Erin around and we waited in the long line until it was our turn. We left the stroller outside and as soon as we entered the store, I could finally see him.

He was sitting on a stool on the far side of the counter. He had dark aviator sunglasses on, his tan evident next to his white polo shirt. Buffett's long forehead and receding hairline stretched above his sunglasses. Grey curls framed his face ending just above his collar.

His colorful beaded necklace added just enough color as he joked with his many fans. With new books stacked to his right, he quickly added his signature again and again as we waited for our turn.

I was having trouble breathing. John kept looking at me and asking if I was alright. I did feel a bit faint, but I was just so excited I could hardly keep quiet. Thank God I had the camera and as we approached, he chuckled and said, "Let me tell you something, politicians kiss 'em, I just sign 'em."

With that, he took his permanent marker and signed the butt of Erin's play suit. I thought I was going to hyperventilate. Drake was ready with the camera and Jimmy extended his arms to take Erin. Jimmy Buffett was holding my baby! John and I got in the photo just as they were closing the doors.

We paid for the book and headed outside. It was not until then that I realized he had not signed the copy of his book, so I snuck back in quickly and got to see him one more time. John says they had to pull me off of him but he embellishes quite a bit. I simply kissed him on the cheek and then was escorted out!

Our Christmas card photo was easy to choose that year and Erin's purple play suit was never worn again.

We had met the new woman in Ed's life last Christmas and again in September. Her name was Maria and she attended Marquette University. She was very nice and seemed to fit into this crazy bunch just fine.

Patrick Russell Miller was born on November 1st, 1989. His stubborn entrance made for a very rough time for Kelli, but he was worth every bit of struggle. He didn't have an easy start as he was hospitalized with pneumonia at just 2 months. We got to be home for the holidays and what fun it was with two babies.

Chapter 44

Tug of Love

I was always so very excited to come home and I never passed up a chance to see my family. What I was not prepared for and what every new couple has to juggle, is how to spend time with everyone. This juggling act multiplies when there is a baby in the family. We usually planned to be home for two weeks and each and every day was filled with visiting.

Shirley and Larry dealt with all of this very well. As hard as it was, she never showed how disappointed she was when we would stay at my mom and dad's. Shirley and Larry had to share us with Bob and Ann too. Erin became a very sociable baby since she was lugged all over to be shown off.

The game of tug of love had only just begun.

Chapter 45

Gone to Carolina

March 1990

John always jokes that I can't say we did not have a honeymoon since our first two years were spent in paradise. After two years in Key West, our next duty station would be on the east coast of North Carolina.

Cherry Point Marine Corps Air Station was located in Havelock, North Carolina and we arrived with a walking one-year-old. Havelock was just 30 minutes from the coast of North Carolina and had all the traditional imprints of a military town. We were placed on the housing list and had rented an apartment until we could get a house on base. John was an E-4 which meant he had been promoted three times since entering the Navy.

The Carolina's were beautiful with their tall, stately, pine trees and blooming azaleas. It was much colder than we were used to so another wardrobe adjustment was needed. We were in the South now and we went with the times; listening to country music and learning about the area.

I began the job search again. I tried the YMCA in New Bern, North Carolina, which was a 30-minute drive west on Highway 70. I did not want to work, but we did not have enough money to live on one income. Many military families did it, but I did not understand how.

The YMCA did not pan out, but I was referred to the Neuse Mental Health Center. They provided Mental Retardation, and Mental Health services to a four-county area. I was hired as a

Case Manager for developmentally disabled children. The MR/DD division of Neuse Center was staffed with several amazing women; all who were born and raised in North Carolina.

To all of them, I talked funny and I just did not speak the Carolina lingo. They don't turn lights on in North Carolina, they cut them on! Knee walking, knuckle draggin' meant you were so drunk you could not stand up. Nabs were cheese crackers and everyone drank sweet tea whether you liked it or not.

People I did not even know would abuse me for my accent. Lori, Elizabeth, Sylvia, Marsha and Joanne all gave me a crash course in Carolina living.

They became my best friends. They brought John and I to parties and introduced us to all of their friends. They made me into an East Carolina University fan. We had many girls' nights at Elizabeth's house since it was just her and her cats.

They were the kind of friends I never thought I would find after leaving Dwight. I became very good at what I did because of Lori's guidance and training. She had been a Case Manager and a Respite Coordinator so her knowledge of services was invaluable. We shared an office and a Case Manager Supervisor named Kay. Kay took a huge chance hiring me since my only MR/DD experience was back in the seventh grade as a volunteer at Fox Center in Dwight.

John was taking classes to complete his Bachelors degree in Health Care Administration. Southern Illinois University had a satellite program on the weekends, so John and I had very little time together. Working long hours, I did not share much of John's Navy life at all.

John had tons of friends at the Aviation and Physiology Training Unit where he worked. I had my friends and he had his. We were making great money, but not saving a dime. I flew home as often as I could, and traveled quite a bit to different conferences through work. Sometimes, I honestly could not wait to get away. I hoped this was just a stage that all couples went through. We weren't fighting or mad at each other at all, we were just on very different paths.

Dori and John, my friends from Western, were married in Chicago in October and I was in the wedding. I was able to see lots of college friends like Sloaner and Opie and it was just like old times.

Things were not going well for Kelli and Gerry. I was really beginning to worry about Kelli. I knew how unhappy she was. Patrick was just 7 months younger than Erin and I knew she had hoped that once Patrick was born everything would work itself out between her and Gerry.

Instead, things had deteriorated rapidly. She had a very demanding job and it just so happened, that Gerry had the same job, with the same company.

They could never escape each other or the gulf that was forming in their marriage. Kelli had to keep up such a brave face, but the toll this façade was taking was noticeable to all of those who were closest to her. I wondered how long she could go on pretending.

Chapter 46

He Didn't Marry Me For My Cooking

My cooking was not improving with practice. I was amazed when people shared how much they enjoyed their time in the kitchen. I actually heard that it relieved stress for some people.

It had become the single most stress inducing activity in my life. I hated the thought of it. I had all these appliances and all these cookbooks that just glared at me when I opened my cupboards. I tried to follow the recipes, but the people who put these recipes in really assumed a lot.

I recall the fiasco of the chicken tetrazzinni. I was cruising through the preparations, when it came time to make the white sauce. The recipe specifically said to blend the milk and butter and to slowly add flour. When it was not becoming thick, I called for back up.

My mom was used to these calls and she asked the usual questions.

"Do you have a fire extinguisher handy?" and "Did anyone get sick from eating yet?"

Getting right to the point, she asked how long I had been heating the white sauce. My answer seemed so obvious to me.

"Duh, mom! It is a bit hard to heat the white sauce when it is in the blender!"

I thought our connection had been cut off, but it was just her gasping for air between fits of laughter.

"You have it in the blender?" she managed to choke out. I was being ridiculed for following instructions. I had this handy dandy new blender that had never been used and finally a recipe called for its use. Say what you mean and mean what you say. We ordered yet another pizza, since I was completely frustrated and I was out of cream.

The country was entering a very scary time with the tension in Iraq. All around us, Marines and Sailors were being sent to Saudi Arabia. President Bush was preparing to use force against Saddam Hussein if he refused to leave Kuwait.

I thanked God every day that John was not pulled to go. I could think back to the day in my office when John called with a thick voice telling me they had just called the hangar and needed an 8294.

This was it. This was the code for a SAR Corpsman and John was first to go. He headed over to manpower after our phone call and they looked confused. It was then they realized they had asked for the wrong code. They needed a SEAL Corpsman which had a code of 8492. He called back with relief that so many others were not given. We were given a very special gift that Christmas which was the simple fact that we were together.

Our holiday trip home was as busy as ever, but it was a whole new level of fun with Patrick and Erin. Shirley had found her niche, which was shopping for her granddaughter. Erin had more clothes than a thirteen-year-old. Uncle Ed was having a great time with his niece and nephew. We were finding out that children really do make the holidays.

1991 was crazy year. I actually was promoted to Case Manager Supervisor and was now distributing cases to nine Case Managers. I felt at times like I was sinking fast. I was trying to juggle motherhood and working. The 30-minute drive to New Bern each day should have helped me focus my thoughts, but I still felt like I was running on a treadmill that kept getting faster and faster.

We were in a great spot for visitors and we counted the days until more friends and family came to town. Brenda had come to

North Carolina on business and came the extra miles to see us. My parents were able to drive to see us, just like the old days. Larry and Shirley rode the Harley's all the way to the Carolina coast over the summer. They even brought Papa's Harley friends, Maynard and Eugene who managed to fix everything that was broken in our Rowell Circle duplex.

One of John's best friends in North Carolina was Jimmy Taylor. Like John, he was a Search and Rescue Corpsman, and was attending Southern Illinois University. He loved Jimmy Buffett and the water and he spent many crazy times with us. On a whim, the boys went to Key West for a week. They took Mike Evermann who was male model material, so I asked very few questions of that trip. My mom always told Kelli and I to remember that we were mothers, so this was the only advice I gave to John.

"Remember, you are a father!"

Beaufort, North Carolina was one of my favorite places. This historic coastal town housed beautiful yachts and ships from all over the country. We ate at Clausen's restaurant, and spent many weekends checking out the shops along the beach front. Atlantic Beach was just down the road and as many times as we could talk John into it, we headed to the ocean.

Just when I was beginning to worry about preparing Thanksgiving dinner, Shirley paid us a visit. Her and Aunt Emily came for a long weekend. Grandma She She as Erin called her, got to make pies with her little sweetie and she cooked for Nimmo, Evermann, and Carlos. These guys all worked with John and they were truly our NC family. A good cook was welcomed with open arms at the Ruskin house.

Chapter 47

You're All a Bunch of Freakin' Psychos

We had our first Christmas on our own in 1991. I had never been away from home, but we were planning a special trip for New Year's. Erin got her first tape player with a microphone and it became apparent that she was a singer.

Ed had arranged a condo in Fort Meyers, Florida for a winter vacation and asked the whole family to join him. He knew the family that owned the condo and it was more than enough room for all of us.

John and I would come from North Carolina and meet up with Mom, Dad, Kelli, Gerry and Patrick. Ed had just stopped seeing Maria so our hopes of a sister-in-law would have to wait.

I knew this trip was just one more part of the role Kelli was playing. I honestly think she was holding on because it had been planned so far in advance. Patrick and Erin were our entertainment the entire trip. Erin would be three in March and Patrick had just turned two.

We spent long sun filled days on the beach in front of the Launi Ki hotel. When things were fun, all was well, but the slightest change in Kelli's mood meant the problems had not been left in Pontiac.

It all came to a head one night at dinner. We had been living under one roof for four days and the tension was beginning to show. Patrick would not sit in his seat. Our food had just arrived, but Patrick got under the table and refused to come out. Before we could get him out from under the table, a glass of water crashed and sent water on several entrees.

Ed was not used to children and he had been with two toddlers for a solid week. His patience was wearing thin too. Kelli's frustration with Gerry was palpable and all the emotions she had pushed down and hidden came bubbling out.   She was in tears, as she yanked Patrick up and stormed out of the restaurant.

"You are all bunch of freakin' psychos," was all Ed had to say as he sat back from the table. I told Ed to go talk to Kelli. He needed to know what she had been going through this last year. Part of me felt so sorry for Gerry because he just didn't know what to do.

That night's dinner set a course in motion for Kelli. She couldn't keep pretending and now she didn't have to. She realized she had to make a change in her life sooner rather than later.

Chapter 48

Our Crash Course in Gender Selection

1992

John and I had also set a course in motion after our Florida vacation. We were officially done with birth control and we were going to start trying for baby number two. John had done extensive research on how to conceive a boy.

The most fool proof method began with John slamming a can of Mountain Dew. Within minutes we were to be in the throes of passion while standing in the shower. John is 5' 5" and I am 5' 7" with legs up to my neck.

The shower has never been a particularly successful place for us, but for the love of science, I did what I was told. The final step was that I had to lie down for 30 minutes following this highly romantic encounter.

All of this had to be perfectly timed to occur at 2:00 p.m. on a Saturday afternoon. Talk about pressure! By February, I was pregnant, but only time would tell if the freak show worked.

My pregnancy was going just fine but the doctors were concerned that I was not gaining enough weight. We had several ultrasounds because of this and there was no denying that the freak show was a success.

We would either have a Bobby, a Kevin, or a Joe and from the kicking and turning this child was doing, he was going to be an active boy. I could recline on the couch and watch my belly contort as this growing baby rolled over.

Making one of the most difficult decisions of my professional life, I had switched jobs and was now a Qualified Mental Retardation Professional (QMRP) at a facility in New Bern. I just could not take the pressure as the Case Manager Supervisor. I was still working long hours and hated the time I was away from Erin. I could not wait to have the baby so I could be home with Erin for at least a few months.

The trip home that summer found Kelli and Patrick in an apartment in Pontiac, Illinois. She had made the biggest decision of her life and she struggled with the reality of it everyday. Kelli was judged by people daily and many gave her their unsolicited advice on how much she had screwed up. Only Kelli and Gerry needed to know the reasons.

Almost every person she thought she could count on, had turned their back on Kelli. She didn't fit anywhere anymore and I remember meeting her new friends that summer. Like everyone else, I passed judgment and told her to stop hanging around with these people. I felt they were bringing her down. Her tearful reply made me regret my words.

"They are the only ones who are real, Patti!" I wanted to bring her back with me so she could start over, but her life was in Pontiac. I just wish I could have made it easier for her.

I was able to see Kelly, Brenda, Mary and Moe almost every visit home. That summer we had a blast at the Cubs game. This was becoming a tradition for us. Mom did give me the speech again.

"Remember , you are a mother." That wasn't the only reason to behave. The fact that I was six months pregnant helped us all get on the right train home. These times renewed our bond and helped us hang on until our next girl's day out.

Chapter 49

We Have Our Joe

October 21, 1992

A week before my due date, they ran a test to determine the amount of amniotic fluid surrounding the baby. The bad news was that I had only one small pocket of fluid which was not good for the baby. I was immediately induced and after three easy hours of medication free labor, our baby boy brightened our lives.

John asked the nurse and Doctor whether he was a Kevin, a Bobby, or a Joe. I can still remember the unanimous chorus from everyone.

"Joe, definitely, Joe!" We had our boy and now our family was complete.

Erin was an instant Mom. She read to him, fed him, changed his diapers, and sang him to sleep. Again, we had lots of support. Both John's mom, and Kelli, came out just after I brought Joe home. Mom and Dad were there for us too.

I loved being home and I dreaded leaving two babies now. I also needed to find a new babysitter since the woman who watched Erin was done with child care. God lead us to Skinny. Skinny's real name was Eloise Davis. She was an amazing woman who had dedicated her life to taking care of kids. She couldn't wait to have a baby in her house again. She made it easy for me to dive back into work, and dive I did. Most days I would not get home with the kids until 6:30 or 7:00. This left just enough time for a quick dinner, which I rarely cooked, baths, and bedtime. Each day played out like the last with me losing serious points in the "Mother of the Year" category.

It seemed after I had Joe, John and I drifted into our own paths again. He would come home from work around 4:00 and often have the guys over for beers. He did not have too many demands since I would not get home for several hours.

I was exhausted and frustrated with having the full responsibility of the kids on my shoulders. I was making good money, but was it really worth all of this hassle? I was so thankful that I had a great boss. John Meads was a Vietnam Veteran. He had been a Navy brat who understood my life like few could. We talked for hours and I valued his advice.

Without even realizing it, we became the party people with our group of friends. It started with St. Patrick's Day. John felt the need to be in full Leprechaun garb for our party and greeted each guest waving his shill alee. Just to clarify, this was a green plastic stick that came with the costume.

It just happened that the night of our party brought one of the worst Nor'Easters the coast had seen in years. The entire staff of the Aviation and Physiology Unit came and partied like they were born in the old country. We had raffles and games and green beer so from then on no one else tried to compete with our party coordinating.

We also organized the summer Buffett trip. The Tail Hook scandal was still exposing many high ranking, Navy officials that summer. We felt it was important to keep with the theme of the times. Our convention was called the Navy Parrot Hook Convention. The Crabtree Marriott in Raleigh, North Carolina, was never the same after our invasion. We made sure Buffett knew that Parrot Heads were alive and well in North Carolina.

Chapter 50

The Politician

Big things were happening in the political arena of Dwight, Illinois. My dad had decided to run for Village Clerk of Dwight. This was an elected position so he had been on the campaign trail for the past few months. He had a good job as an Addictions Counselor at Ottawa Hospital. Mom really did not want him to run, but once Dad made up his mind, he could not be dissuaded.

Dwight is a majority Republican town, but Dad surprised everyone by winning as a Democrat! It was a true dream of Dad's to win an election. Now came the hard part. Dad had to quit his job in Ottawa, and begin the process of learning a brand new career at age 62.

He needed to learn the computer and the all the intricacies of a village government system. Needless to say, this was much more challenging than he had anticipated. The staff knew who they wanted in the position of Village Clerk and it was not Tom Slattery.

The staff did as little as possible to help Dad's transition. This stressful situation came to a head in June. I got the call at work and I knew it was bad when both Kelli and Mom were on the phone.

Dad had suffered a major stroke only a month after taking over as Village Clerk. The kids and I were on the next plane home, but what Dad needed we could not give him in a week long visit. He underwent stringent physical therapy for his facial muscles and his left arm.

What the stroke did was take the real Dad away from us. The

Dad that remained after the stroke was not the same. His thinking was off and so many times we would wonder where the old Tom was.

It was hell for my mom. No one truly knows what a spouse endures when they become the caregiver. Dad had trouble with incontinence, confusion, and continuous headaches. The worst part was he continued to have TIA's, which were small stroke type attacks on his brain.

He was in and out of the hospital so much that Mom got to the point where she did not even tell anyone that Dad was in the hospital. We all wondered if we would ever get the real Dad back.

Chapter 51

Be Careful What You Wish For

We did have some great news to celebrate in the Slattery family. Ed was getting married. He was marrying Sue Gehlsen and we were all in the wedding. It would be in November, but just thinking that far ahead made my stomach lurch.

We had orders to San Diego, California, and were due to leave in December. I couldn't even think about San Diego. I had done my best to ignore the welcome aboard package that stayed unopened on the counter. I truly believed that if I did not prepare for a move, than we would not have to go.

Our deal was that we would pick duty stations that were two fingers from Illinois on our map. San Diego was almost three fingers! It was also so expensive to fly home that I knew my visiting would be limited to twice a year. It made to sick to think about it, so I didn't. I spent our last Carolina Fall, going through the motions, all the while building up a deep resentment towards John.

One day as I sat at my desk at Howell's, my phone rang.

"Hi honey!" I could tell by John's voice that something was wrong. He never called at this time of day.

"What's wrong?" I asked fearing the worst. Had he heard something about Dad? I held my breath as he blurted out the news.

"My orders to San Diego got cancelled."

"YESSSSS!" was all I could yell!

"See honey, I just knew that wasn't where we were supposed to go. Oh I can't believe it!" I said with tears of relief welling up in my eyes.

John was very quiet on the other end.

"John?" I asked concerned with the silence.

"Honey, the only billet the detailer is offering me now is Guam." It was now my turn to remain silent. My first thought was, 'Where in the hell is GUAM?'

"Are you there, Patti?" I could not even talk. This is what I got for being a brat. How was I going to tell my Mom and Dad I was moving half way around the world? So many thoughts were racing through my brain I could not think.

"So what do we do?" I asked bewildered.

"We need to take these, honey. This will be a good tour for me and the Cavins are going too." He was trying so hard.

"Whatever, Whatever. It sounds like we have no choice." I said with a defeated sigh. I couldn't breathe. The lump had wedged itself in my throat as I tried to swallow. What did I just agree to?

"It will be fine sweetie, I promise!" John said excitedly.

I hung up the phone and put my head on the desk. The sobs took all my strength. I was sure I was going to be sick. Just as I was getting control, John Meads, my boss, came to my office.

"What the hell is wrong?" he asked with a concerned look. The sobs started all over again.

That week was one of the hardest of my marriage. So many decisions were running through my mind; decisions that would have far reaching effects.

For the first time I thought about not going with John. There was no part of me that wanted to go to Guam. John was so sure of everything, and I wasn't sure of anything! In an eerie coincidence, I lost John's wedding ring. He had received a claddaugh ring for Christmas so I had worn his band on my right finger. It must have slipped off when I was helping with a patient.

I had not told him I had lost it in hopes that it would be found at the Center.

It was Thursday night and I had just gotten home from work. It had been one of the longest and hardest weeks of my life, but I had made the decision to go. John came into the kitchen with a present. I started to cry before I even opened the small velvet box.

"I don't deserve this!" I bawled.

"I lost your wedding ring this week, but I was too afraid to tell you!" He crushed me in a hug and slipped a beautiful emerald on my finger. As he hugged me, he whispered, "Thank you for coming with me, Patti. I promise it will be OK."

November brought reason to celebrate as we welcomed a new sister into the family. Ed and Sue were married on a frigid day in Rockford, Illinois. Their reception was held at Forest Hills Country Club and it was a blast. Dad was a trooper but he was not feeling too well. Joe stayed with Bob and Ann close by in Belvidere. It was a perfect time to see the whole family before our biggest adventure yet.

Chapter 52

It's Time To Fly

January 1994

The cold air hit my face with the force of a blow as I lugged the overstuffed suitcase out of the back of the van. The temperature outside matched the temperature of my heart degree for degree. I felt my throat tighten, and the tears begin as I hugged Shirley goodbye. I clung a little too long and as I let go she whispered, "You will be fine."

I did not feel fine at all. Hugging Shirley goodbye only brought my farewell with my own mom, and Kelli, the night before to mind. It was finally here, the day we would leave for Guam. All the packing was done and all the goodbyes had been said, so now there was nothing left, but the long flight.

The airport was uncharacteristically quiet since the sun had not even come up yet in this frozen city. I tried with no success to swallow the dread I felt inside.

"You look so sad, Mommy!" Erin said as she twirled in circles while we waited to check our heap of luggage. I watched her new little Guess dress move around her four-year-old body and said, "I'm fine, Sweetie."

I said it again more quietly to reassure her as much as to reassure myself. I listened as the ticket agent told John that the flight to Los Angeles left in less than an hour. The ticket agent looked at our luggage with a weary sigh.

"All of this goes?"

"You got it," John said as he shot me a look of encouragement. Poor thing! He had been battling diarrhea for a good two weeks now. Whenever we could not find him, we knew he was probably in the bathroom. I wish I could have relieved some of my stress that easy!

I looked down at Joe, who was getting settled for a quick nap in his stroller. What did he think was going on? I grabbed a tissue and wiped his nose, which seemed to run endlessly. He had just turned one and was able to get anywhere and everywhere.

As I put the Kleenex away, I checked again for the Dimetapp. Medication and sedation were going to play huge roles in this 24-hour trip half way around the world.

"Let's hit it guys!" John said. My stomach turned over again with the thought that I may never get back here again. Why did I feel like I was seeing things and doing things for the last time? Guam is just an Island in Micronesia for God's sake not a death sentence. I tried to put a skip in my step but it just wasn't there.

Our wait was short at the gate and the kids were asleep before we took off. We were greeted in Los Angeles with a beautiful, sunny day. We had already been up since 3 a.m. so fatigue was setting in.

As we walked up to the gate for our flight to Hawaii, I could not help but notice the excited travelers waiting for their trip to paradise. We settled in to wait for the Cavin family who had spent the night in L.A.

They, too, were going to Guam. Steve was a Search and Rescue Corpsman with John. His wife, Mary, and I, had become very close in the past several months. She and Steve had spent the past month with family in Tennessee just as John and I had done in Illinois. Mary was six months pregnant so she would deliver in Guam. Their daughter, Emily, was a year younger than Erin. We each started this journey with a friend

We watched as anxious vacationers filtered into the gate area. A young couple sat down across from us and I watched as they got out their hotel brochure. They were probably around the same age as John and I, but looking at them I felt a hundred years old. They were so excited and here I sat so miserable that I felt like I had a vice around my chest.

I looked over at John who was asleep in what looked like the most uncomfortable position imaginable. Erin had her head on his lap and Joe was sprawled out in his stroller sleeping soundly. Feeling the tears come, I got up and started to walk.

I found myself at the phones, dialing the number that was as familiar as my own.

"Hi, this is Kelli," I heard a voice say. It was as close to hearing my own as I could get.

"Hey, sis!" I squeaked trying to sound up.

"Where are you?"

"L.A. I just needed to hear your voice."

"It's going to be OK, Pat! Just hang in there."

I wanted to believe her. Her words were almost a carbon copy of what she had been telling me for the past month.

"Remember our song babe? Come on, sing with me." I took as deep a breath as I could muster and started to sing the Cowboy Junkies song she had found.

".....To live is to fly, low and high, so shake the dust off of your wings and the sleep out of your eyes. It's goodbye to all my friends. It's time to go again......"

As I hung up the phone, I was reminded again of how lucky I am to have a built in best friend. I know she had to have been feeling a lot of the same things I was, just on the other end. She always she kept me strong.

Feeling better, I wandered back to my sleeping bunch and found that the Cavin family had arrived. Mary, God love her, was excited and ready for their new adventure. She had been ready from the day they accepted orders. I wondered what made me so different from other Navy wives that I resented this so much. I knew I was being a bitch, but for the life of me I could not get over it.

Mary had cut her hair in a cute bob while they were on leave and her tummy had expanded quite a bit.

Before long, it was time to board the largest plane I had ever flown on. The Cavins' seats were several rows in front of ours and we settled in for the five-hour flight. I was actually feeling a little better. Maybe it was just knowing that they were with us or maybe it was getting harder to not get excited.

I watched as we headed out over the Pacific Ocean. This was the first time in my 28 years that I had ever been on the West Coast. 'Maybe someday we'll get to vacation here,' I thought as I gave Joseph a dose of Tylenol. He was being very good considering the fact that he had a fever.

We were beginning to show the wear of traveling with munchkins. For one thing, we were dressed for the dead of winter. There is no easy way to go from -5 to 82 degrees and stay fresh.

We had all gone for the layered look although my layers were beginning to feel quite damp. The inner layer due to my sweat and the outer due to Joe's spit-up. I felt more than a little sorry for the man sitting next to me.

I had watched his face as he approached our row. He looked at his ticket and then at the numbers on the rows as he made his way to his seat. His eyes went first from me, to Joe, then back to me, where he focused on the large amount of spit up on my sweatshirt. He was wearing a Chief's uniform and he did the smart thing before ever sitting down, by taking off his jacket. Luckily, the flight was uneventful and we all got some sleep.

The minute we stepped off the plane in Honolulu, the humidity hit us like a ton of bricks. I had pictured a true Hawaiian welcome with a pretty girl in a grass skirt with leis for all of us. Much to my disappointment (and to John's) there was no hula girl. It was just HOT!

The airport was open to the elements and the sweet smell of flowers filled the air. Blooming plants lined the concrete wall that framed the scenic view. Our first stop was to the bathroom to change the kids into cooler outfits. Our plane did not leave for two hours and by my watch it was 8:00 p.m. It was about lunch time in Hawaii but who the hell knew when to eat.

Joe was ready to run, and run he did until the time we boarded our last and longest flight. His fever was returning every few hours and to add to our stress, Erin had a bad cough. She was now running a fever as well. Sickness is inevitable when your body is thrown from one season to another in a matter of hours and the Ruskin family would not be spared.

Let the games begin! We were on board and took off for Guam around 9:30 p.m. Illinois time. As I reached to fasten my seat belt, I could not fathom being in this same seat eight hours from now. We were sitting in the front row, so the movie screen was directly in front of us. The screen showed a map of the Hawaiian Islands and Guam.

As our flight progressed, we watched our plane on the screen slowly make its way towards the small dot that was to be our new home. I rested my head on the seat and closed my eyes. I allowed myself to begin to think of how different my life would be once we got settled. Without even considering the fact that we would be living on an island 8000 miles from home, my life and my roles in that life were what was about to do a 180 degree turn.

Opening my eyes, I waited for them to focus. I watched the screen and realized that with every little advance that plane made, I was moving farther away from anything familiar. I had left my job as a Qualified Mental Retardation Professional. I had left good friends that had become so very important to me. I was leaving my family and was, in my mind, not even able to get home if I needed to.

I was now going to be a "True Navy Wife" whatever the hell that was supposed to be.   I said a silent prayer for God to please help me not be so angry. In my heart I knew that this was the right thing to do. Shirley had told me on the phone when I told her that I might stay with Kelli until John got us a house.

"You need to go, Patti. The two of you will not make it through this if you don't."

I knew everything she was saying was true, but I wanted to scream and say "But what about me? What about what I want?"

Truly, I didn't know much about the Navy. I had my career and John had his, but from now on the Navy would be my life.   I was so excited about being home with the kids. They had spent so much time at Skinny's since I was working so hard before we left.

Oh, how Skinny had cried when we left. Her house wasn't always the cleanest and it was usually so full of kids, you had to step over them, but there was so much love and so much warmth, that I never worried about the kids for a minute. Looking over the seat to see Erin behind me, I silently wondered if I would be a better mom in Guam. I guess we would all find out soon enough.

Chapter 53

P. I. C. Windsurfer.......

"P.I.C. WINDSURFER STAY BETWEEN THE YELLOW BUOYS". This had become our mantra while we enjoyed the beautiful Pacific Island Club Resort as our new home for the first three weeks in Guam. The first week was a bit tense with both Joe and Erin suffering from the change in climate and time. Instead of checking out our beautiful surroundings, John found the Emergency Room at the Naval Hospital. Joe had a double ear infection and Erin had strep throat.

It had hardly slowed Joe down. He was all boy at 15- months. He was sleeping in a port-a-crib that he managed to shake violently when he was ready to get up. John and I had become masters at not moving an inch when we heard him stir. Unfortunately, he knew we were right there. To say he was sleeping in his crib was a stretch. We had seen 3:00 a.m. for the past week, but we were slowly getting our body clocks switched around.

After a week of antibiotics, we were finally out of the room. Sitting poolside, I scanned the huge kidney shaped swimming pool and I felt the lurch in my stomach that had taken up permanent residence there. The brick wall at the far end of the children's pool held three stone fish. A constant spray of water protruded from their open mouths.

Palm trees bordered the lush grounds and tiki huts were tucked under huge shade trees. The shocking blue sky met the Pacific Ocean so far in the distance it was impossible to see where one ended and the other began.

Looking out to sea, I was able to put scenery to my feelings. I fixed my gaze on the blond, tanned lifeguard. She had no idea how connected I felt to her when I heard her speak to her friend. We were the only Americans at the hotel except for these young kids with cool summer jobs. Every where we went, there were Japanese tourists. They were fascinated with Joe and Erin. Maybe it was the freckles or the fair skin, but they were snapping photos faster than I have ever seen.

I watched Joe assume his favorite stance. His little pudgy legs were bent at the knees and stayed perfectly balanced above his fat play-dough feet. He watched a little Japanese girl fill his bucket.

"You have a friend Joe, Joe!" I said as I watched him confirm the universal goodness in children by petting the beautiful little Asian girl on the head.

Before I could grab my camera, the Japanese paparazzi descended on the kiddy pool. Joe was eating this up. Not to be left out, Erin arrived on the scene just in time to get in on the photo shoot. Erin's freckles were out in full force and the two of them looked like a commercial from where I sat. They were something.

We were still with the Cavin family, who had just gone up for an afternoon rest. We were inching our way on the housing list, but with the Navy footing our bill, we were finally enjoying our time. We were learning how terribly expensive things were in Guam.

Erin and I found this out the hard way one afternoon. I ordered a pina colada and Erin ordered an orange juice. I began to hyperventilate when the waitress asked for $14.00.

"No, we just had two drinks," I told the waitress. Her frustration with the stupid American was evident as she repeated the total with a tone this time.

"Yes, it is $14.00!" I gave her my cash and sipped on my coconut delight. Just as I was getting ready to tell Erin she better drink every last bit and eat the ice, I heard a familiar sound. I watched helplessly as her foot kicked a bright orange river onto the pebbled deck.

I had to fight every instinct not to use her straw to collect what I could of the $6.00 Orange Juice! I thought of sending her to the car like Dad always did when I spilled. I realized, we did not even have a car! It was still on the boat on the way over here! We packed a cooler from that day on.

I'm not sure whether it was a mind game or truly a cultural difference, but everything had a weird smell in Guam. John kept telling me it was in my head, but nothing seemed to taste the same either, including my beloved Diet Pepsi. How could this be? It is a universal product. The milk was another item of contention. It was absolutely horrid, but Joe seemed to like it so who was I to judge. The only thing that tasted normal were the Pringles I ate from the selection in the room. The bill for the compact size of Pringles was $7.00. We needed to find the commissary fast.

Chapter 54

Hafia Adai Bro

Before too long, we got our house on the Naval Air Station in Barrigada, Guam. We were right in the heart of Guam and we had an awesome view of the downtown area and Tumon Bay. Other than the Easter egg blue stucco, our house was the best military housing we had lived in.

The high, white, cinder-blocked walls met beautiful brown tile throughout the house. We had two bathrooms and room for the kids to drive the jeep and ride the tricycles down the hallway to the bedrooms. We arrived during the rainy season and it did not disappoint. 10 straight days of rain had me ready for a rubber room. The kids made forts, we did crafts, we made tapes for Grandma and Grandpa, and still it rained.

When the sun did shine, the thermometer climbed above 90 degrees before noon. As the weather improved, we spent the sweltering days at the pool and fit right in with the other Search and Rescue wives. Todd and Tonya Gonterman lived just down the street from us. They had one little girl, Shelby, who Joe and Erin loved to play with. We saw Mary and Steve and Emily quite a bit too.

Most weekends were spent touring our beautiful new island home. Guam was an island of contrasts, from the southern, aging Naval Station, to the rural mountains with old worn down caribou tied up on the side of the road, to the glitzy commercialized hotel row on Tumon Bay. Chammoros were usually quite friendly and accepting of all the Americans on their island. Hafia-adai meant hello and how are you, so we tried to be as friendly as possible wherever we went.

We found Jeff's Pirate's Cove on one adventure. It looked like it had just been plucked out of Key West with its open-air bar and outdoor eating areas. The island sounds of Mackie Ferry in the background made the setting perfect as the view rivaled any postcard.

Waves could be seen crashing over the barrier reef as the clouds appeared to rest their weary heads on the mountains to the west. Yellow buoys served a new purpose as they outlined the sand volleyball court. An official's chair sat perched on an old tree. Its branch, the constant arm that held the net in place. There were times when I would look out at the beauty and have to pinch myself.

We worked ourselves into a routine and before too long the spring brought Mary and Steve a new baby boy. In April, Ryan Cavin joined the fun.

In May, John's sister, Paula was marrying Joe Krischel in Dwight. We had decided that there was no way we could all afford to go and Joe and I would stay in Guam. As it got closer, I realized this was John's sister and we all needed to be there for her. With a little help on the plane tickets, we all made the long trip for a quick week home.

Joe and Paula had dated for a few years and they made such a cute couple. We all had quite a scare with Paula's accident the previous winter. A car had pulled in front of her as she was heading to work in Streator. Thank God her only injury was a broken ankle.

All of that was forgotten on her magical day. John, Em and Erin were in the wedding and Shirley was the bell of the ball in her black dress and matching hat. She always looked just right for every occasion. The reception was a blast, complete with Shirl, and one of her best friends, Hal Leonard, dancing on the tables!

I really hated to go back to Guam. Everything familiar was right here. The milk tasted normal. My chocolate doughnuts were just as I remembered. My mom and dad and Kelli were here. No matter how much I wanted a life in Illinois, the reality was that my life was now in Guam.

Chapter 55

The Trip from Hell!
July 1994

I stared at the calendar with hopelessness as I realized how much we were missing this month. My ten-year class reunion and my cousin, Kathy Pfeifer's wedding were both on the 16th of July and it looked like I would miss both of them.

Feeling miserably sorry for myself, I dialed the Military Airlift Command's flight recording and listened to the flights going out this week. I knew it was a bit crazy, but just knowing that there were flights heading in the right direction made me feel some comfort. I knew how stupid the thought of going home was.

We had just been home in May for Johns' sister's wedding. It had been so fun but it was such a fast trip that I really did not even feel like it was a visit. Paula had been so beautiful and it was such fun to focus on the Ruskin family rather than just my family. We had flown commercial which put $2000.00 on our once paid off credit card. The check book was becoming a constant challenge. Every sign pointed to accepting the fact that I could not get home for these two events, but I let my father's words take over.

"Live for today because you can't take it with you." I had met another woman at the pool who was planning a trip back to the states in the next few weeks and she planned on taking the military flights from Anderson Air Force Base to Travis Air Force Base near San Francisco. The problem was that during the summer, a lot of families tried to get home from Japan and Korea. This is where many of the flights heading to the States originated.

Many times there were very few seats available by the time

they got through the different categories. Military families traveling without their sponsor were the second to last category. The last category was the retirees. I had done my homework and none of it was good news.

Even with all these obstacles against me, I set my mind to going. I talked it over with John and he cautioned me over and over on how unpredictable the flights were. He did not want me to go and I remember his resigned look as I cried in the kitchen.

He knew how hard this was for me, but I was not making it any easier for him. I hated to be told that I could not do something. He wasn't saying no, but he certainly was not excited about his wife and two kids taking military flights half-way around the world. With the words, 'Happy Wife, Happy Life' ringing in his ears, he took my leave papers to the MAC terminal at midnight in order to be one of the first to sign up for the next available flight.

That Tuesday began with the Ruskin family arriving at the terminal at 3:30 in the morning. A C-5 was leaving for Travis via Hawaii. A C-5 would be the best for us since this was such a huge plane. John felt like we would have no problem getting on this since there were so many seats. We checked in at the Anderson terminal with bags in hand and two very full activity bags.

I remember rubbing Joe's back as he slept on the seat while the terminal slowly filled up with traveling families. Almost all of them had their husbands traveling with them. I was the first person in my category so I held my breath as they started the process of filling the plane. The people on emergency orders were called first, followed by the people who were traveling on official orders. Then came the EML categories.

Environmental and Morale Leave was where I fell into this system. Unfortunately, so did the entire terminal. They never even got to my category which was EML traveling without their sponsor. After three hours, we were back at home but not giving up.

Wednesday's flight was a smaller plane, but with nothing to lose we headed to the MAC terminal. We were all packed, totally checked in, and again, they never got to our category. I had one more shot on Thursday and this was the day Kelly and her boys were trying too. I had met Kelly at the pool earlier that summer.

The type of plane leaving on Thursday was a C-130. None of this meant anything to me since I just wanted to get home. A plane is a plane. John was with us again and the terminal was very quiet. This should have been a sign. As our number was called we checked in and were given three seats. Finally! We were heading home! Kelly and her boys got on too so we said our goodbyes to John and waited to board.

Joe was the youngest child on the flight and I should have been concerned when the young crewman asked if I would need help getting on the plane.

"I will be fine," I said with confidence and thought how nice that was. As we were unloaded from the bus, my stomach dropped. Sitting on the tarmac was a transport plane with two tiers of portable steps leading up to a small door.

The stairs were narrow and angled at an impossible slope. How in the hell was I going to get Joe, Erin, and the two large activity bags up those suckers? Have I mentioned that I am afraid of heights? Like an angel, the young air crewman returned just in time to carry Joe and an activity bag. I asked if he would walk behind me so as to catch me when, not if, I fell. White knuckled and sweating profusely, I made it to the top as Miss Erin nonchalantly skipped up the last step.

As I searched for oxygen, I entered the plane. Being a Navy wife and world traveler, I thought I could predict what the inside of a plane would look like. Nothing prepared me for what I saw.

Our "seats" were army type cots placed end to end. The "seats" had no backs, just yellow netting that appeared to serve absolutely no purpose for a passenger. The smell of fuel overwhelmed me as we were handed ear plugs by the crew. 'This is what I get,' I kept thinking. 'I had to go home.' The "aisle" was a treacherous pair of steel rollers on the metal floor of the plane, obviously used to move heavy objects easier.

"We have never been on a plane like this Mom," Erin said

with wide eyes.

"You can say that again darling!" I answered in disbelief of my surroundings. The pilot came on and I listened intently.

"Good Afternoon Ladies and Gentleman. As you can see, we have a full house today. We do have a bathroom on board. Just be sure to pull the curtain so we know it is in use. (What?) We will be refueling at Midway Island and we should make pretty good time today since the weather is clear. We expect our flying time to Midway Island to be about six hours. Once we fuel up and get back under way we have about five more to Honolulu. (Oh my God!) Please use the ear plugs since the C-130 is not the most silent of aircraft. If we can do anything for you, please see one of one of the crewman."

He no sooner got off the intercom when the roar of the plane's engines startled all of us. Communication was going to be at a minimum. The whine of the large propellers increased rapidly as we prepared for take off. All of this scared Joe and I could see his fear, but I could not here him at all. Erin huddled in close too as I began to pray.

I began to run down some of the damage this trip would cause. 1) Permanent hearing loss for myself and the children. (Joe had just thrown his ear plugs and they landed deeply embedded in the rollers on the floor.) 2) Permanent fear of public toilets. (Kelly had just returned from using the facilities and had drawn a toilet seat over a bucket on Erin's Etch a Sketch.) I was sure the list would grow as the trip progressed.

We spent most of the trip back by the bathroom looking out the only window in the plane. Joe would not sit still so we continued to move as much as our surroundings would allow. Our luggage was piled in a small mound under a tarp which gave those brave souls using the bathroom a bit of privacy.

Our box lunch had been a cold chicken sandwich that none of us could swallow. I had packed lots of snacks but I knew how hungry I was, so the kids had to have been starving too. What a treat it was to get out at Midway. Joe and Erin ran sprints around that small airport terminal.

Midway was like a forgotten uncle in a nursing home. It was this beautiful gem in the sea, but it served very little purpose from its busy World War II days. It was basically an airstrip inhabited by those who kept the airstrip running, but it was sure good to get out of that plane.

We did manage to get some sleep during the rest of the trip, but the temperature in the plane kept dropping. Thank God I had warm clothes for the kids. I was using all of Joe's baby blankets to keep warm while he slept on my lap. We finally arrived around midnight Honolulu time. Once off the C-130, several red-eyed, exhausted passengers were given the worst blow of the trip. The crew had decided to lay over in Hawaii for two days. I just sat there in disbelief letting the reality of this layover sink in.

After all that and now I wouldn't even make it home by Saturday. We were on their schedule which was exactly what John tried to tell me. All I knew was that I needed sleep. Kelly and I both punched our EML orders for our trip back to Guam and headed out. Kelly, whose husband was a supply officer in the Navy, asked if I wanted to share a cab to the Bachelor Officer Quarters. John was a Second Class Petty Officer and enlisted were not allowed to stay in Officer's quarters.

John was promoted that night to Lieutenant Commander. The desk clerk asked for my ID which would have blown my cover.

"You really don't need to see it, do you sir?" I asked half pleading for some type of break here.

"Your rooms are just down the hall on the right," he said with a knowing smile.

We all slept like rocks and felt renewed by the bright Hawaiian sun streaming through the window of our room. It was Saturday in Hawaii and I had to make a decision. I had purchased flexible round trip tickets from California to Chicago so once we did arrive we were to be put on the next commercial flight. I knew I should not even be thinking about other options, but waiting for the C-130 crew meant missing everything I was going home for in the first place.

The Continental ticket agent confirmed my plan when she

told me there was a direct flight to O'Hare leaving at 1:00 p.m. that day. This was going to be one of the most expensive summer trips ever. I had to laugh at Erin's comment as we boarded the 747 to Chicago. As she ran her had over the fabric she exclaimed, "Mommy look, this plane has seats!"

We were home by 7:00 am Saturday morning and met by my sister Kelli and her new boyfriend, Mark.

The two weeks home were exactly what we needed. I was able to attend my cousin Kathy's wedding and my class reunion. Reluctantly, I began to plan my trip back around the MAC flights leaving Travis Air Force Base in California. We flew out the day before the flight to Guam and I was able to get a room at the Bachelor Enlisted Quarters this time.

We boarded a Coach bus which shuttled military members from the airport to the base. I had talked to John and he was so excited we were coming home. I missed him and I knew I should have listened to his experienced words of advice. I dreaded the MAC flight, but I knew it would be the last time I did this alone.

The digital alarm clock showed that it was after 10:00 p.m. when we finally got to our room. It wasn't a room at all, but more like an apartment with two small bedrooms and a living room. The bathroom was huge with a blue tile floor.

I got the kids to bed right next to me and struggled to get my rings off my swollen fingers. Like always, I put all my jewelry in my billfold, safely zipped in the change pocket. We were on a second floor apartment and it was stifling in the bedroom. I managed to open the window, but the night noises were enough to have me jumping every two minutes.

Needless to say, I did not sleep much at all. The grip of worry crept in and made its home in my gut. Joe had been so fussy all day and I prayed he would sleep all night. The kids did sleep but were up early. We were up in plenty of time to make the 9:00 a.m. show time for the flight to Guam.

I got Joe and Erin ready first and put on cartoons while I got myself ready. Joe was finally in a good mood and he was quite the busy beaver. I let him mess with the toilet as I tried to remedy my puffy, blood-shot eyes with make-up. I really did not care what he did, as long as he was not whining.

Trying to relax, I walked out to the living room to get my purse and saw a dollar bill on the floor. A nagging panic began as I allowed my eyes to follow the change that was not far from the dollar. The top to my lipstick was on the couch and I caught the first glimpse of my diamond ring on the cushion of the couch.

I could not catch my breath, as I frantically searched for the contents of my billfold.

"Mommy purse spilled," Joe said in his innocent two-year-old voice.

"Errrrin!" I screamed, as panic took over.

"Help me!" She dutifully picked up the money and Joe turned to go back into the bathroom.

"Oh God! He has flushed them all!" I roared.

The toilet tinkled with the sound of fresh water refilling the tank after a morning of flushes. The toilet bowl glistened white and empty. Running back to the living room, I managed to find my wedding band under the couch and my emerald under the coffee table. Still missing were two small band rings: one emerald and one ruby and my claddaugh.

I looked at the time and realized I had not called the cab to get us to the MAC terminal and it was already 8:30. I was crying and screaming at Joe who just kept saying, "Mommy purse spilled." I wanted to flush him at that point. I was shaking and wringing with sweat as I moved furniture and tipped over chairs. The three rings were gone; forever a part of the Travis Air Force Base Sewer System.

By the time we got to the terminal, it was standing room only. I made it in time to check in and felt the tears build for the second time that day as our flight to Guam, our free trip home, filled up before even getting to our category. The next MAC flight was two days away and I had $40.00.

With a defeated sigh, I found the commercial ticket counter along with the retirees. After a very long half-hour in line, it was finally my turn. I put Joe down and asked Erin to watch him. The line was cordoned off with fancy blue velvet ropes. The ropes were attached to heavy silver stands anchored by a round silver base.

I was in such a fog that I barely heard the figures the ticket agent was throwing out. At this point we would need to sell Joseph in order to pay off this damn credit card. As I was handing my now worn Visa over to the ticket agent, I heard a hellacious crash.

Knowing without a doubt that it was my children, I turned to see Joseph lying on his stomach pinned down by one of the heavy stands. The rope had come off its hook but not before bringing several stands down. Erin was trying to lift it off her brother with very little success. Several bystanders had seen the crash and came over to assist. Another stand had been brought down in the commotion and was now separating the line in half.

Joe was not crying, he was yelling when I got to him. His chin was all broke out and he had a new red bump forming on his forehead. The kid was going to kill us all before this trip ended.

"Long day?" asked one of the ladies helping me to restore order to the waiting area.

"You have no idea!" I said with a weary sigh. This had been some adventure.

Chapter 56

Don't Unpack Yet
October 1994

I was just fine to stay on Guam after that horrendous trip in July. Just about the time we got settled in our house and got Erin used to her new Kindergarten class, John delivered the news that the Helicopter Squadron, HC-5, was moving up to Anderson Air Force Base.

I knew putting curtains up was a mistake. We had heard rumors about the Naval Air Station being turned over to the Government of Guam and it was now becoming a reality. Once again we set up our pack out dates and headed up to the Northern point of Guam.

What a different world the Air Force lived in. The Air Force certainly knew how to take care of their people. We received a three bedroom house on a corner lot just inside the back gate. The best part was that Upi School was just outside the back gate of the base and we had a short walk up the hill to get Erin to school every day.

Erin had more American children in her new class and she had her second American teacher. Joe and I stayed very busy cruising around the base on our bike. We planned our day around Erin's lunch. We had a standing date to eat with her every day.

Joe was getting so independent. The only problem was trying to get him potty trained. I did not potty train Erin so this was all pretty new. Whenever he disappeared I knew he was somewhere pooping. I caught on quickly to his red faced, squatting posture. I finally bought two potty chairs and strategically placed one behind the couch and one under the kitchen table. This was his personal favorite grunting zone.

Erin had made fast friends with the little girl next door, and she and Stacey were inseparable.

As the holidays approached, my home sickness increased. Ed and Sue had just had their first child and I hated that I had only seen him in pictures. Sean Edward Slattery was born on October 5th that year. It was hard enough to get into the Christmas spirit when it was 85 degrees, but knowing that we would not be home, made it doubly hard.

Chapter 57

Christmas on Guam

We received the best present possible when Shirley arrived on Christmas Eve. She even brought chocolate doughnuts from the Country Mansion in Dwight. Although they were one large melted clump, I dove in with both hands.

We showed her every part of the island including the P.I.C., Jeff's Pirate's Cove, complete with several Navy Seals playing volleyball on the beach, and a true Chamorro Fiesta. It made me realize how many new and exciting things we took for granted.

Erin was very busy with T-Ball and Daisy's. The Cavin family made the move up to Anderson Air Force Base as well and Mary and I took turns hosting Bunko night. Anderson Air Force base had a beautiful golf course which was the scene of many lessons for Mary. Joe and I took advantage of Ladies day every Tuesday. Ladies day meant nine holes and a cart for $8.00.

Mary and Steve had run into some problems since the move up to Anderson. Steve had been caught drinking and driving as he tried to get on base after a Hash run. He lost his driving privileges for a year on all military bases which put quite a strain on Mary. He was very lucky it did not happen off base or the penalties would have been much more severe.

I was so glad that I had her. Even though we had both found other friends, we knew the friendship we had could not be broken. We helped welcome the newest SAR Corpsman, John Bullman to the island. He was newly married, but his wife and three daughters would not come for several months.

John was from North Carolina and he was pure country. He loved to golf and actually was better than any of us. Todd G. and John Bullman became permanent fixtures at our house since they were both geographical bachelors. This was another Navy term for married Sailors who were stationed without their wives and families.

I was still trying to get used to the fact that Todd had decided to get out of the Navy. He and Tonya had made this decision while they were back in the states for the summer. Tonya decided to stay with Todd's mom while Todd returned alone to finish his tour. I was so sad. I would miss her and Shelby and their new little guy Mason. The goodbyes seemed to never end.

The boys had to endure many mystery meals at our house. My cooking had not improved much but they never let on that it was anything but scrumptious.

Chapter 58

A New Family
June 1995

Our summer trip home was highlighted by Kelli and Mark's wedding. They had purchased a new home and chose their back yard as the site of their new beginning. Mark married Kelli and Patrick on a gorgeous day in June with their family and friends by their side. Mary Clausen flew in from Virginia to be by Kelli's side.

Chapter 59

Where Did He Go?

This trip was probably one of the hardest for me. It had been almost a year since I had been home and I had no idea how different Dad was. It was as if he had taken a leave of absence from the man I knew. The physical effects of the stroke had improved, but he was not well. His thinking was not right. This was never more evident than when he started smoking again.

I caught him in the kitchen the day of Kelli's wedding drinking from a bottle of vodka. I felt like I was 16 again. The rage was right back but this time I was not mad for my own sake. This was Kelli and Mark's day and I hoped he would not ruin any memories for them. He was wearing those tinted glasses again and his attempted smile showed a shell of the man whose face used to light up when he laughed.

This man, who was the most meticulous dresser, now wore things that made us all cringe. He had chosen a child's size shamrock tie to wear with his suit in honor of our Irish heritage. Mark loved him and accepted him for the piece of work he was. Dad had become sneaky again so Mom was back to her old ways of watching him around liquor. Unfortunately, the vicious cycle of his addictive personality continued.

We were home for the arrival of Mason Matthew Krischel. Paula and Joe were so happy to meet their first baby and we got to see him before we headed back to end our time on Guam.

Chapter 60

How About a Mai Tai?

Mary and I had made a pact that if we could, we would leave Guam just as we came, together. We did just that. The Cavin's next duty station was LeMoore, California. We were heading to Fallon, Nevada. I hated to start all over again, but it was time to move on. Just before we left we got a chance to welcome John Bullman's family.

Janice and her three girls were new to this military life but we did all we could to help them settle in before we headed out. Shannon, Hannah, and Angie had never been outside of North Carolina, but in the short time we were with them, we knew they would adapt just fine.

Looking back on our time in Guam, it is hard to believe how fast the time went by. I now know that God sent us those orders. He knew the path that John and I were on in North Carolina was not a good one for us as husband and wife, nor was it good for us as a family.

I needed to be reminded of what was truly important in my life. Although I went kicking and screaming inside, it was only my attitude that needed to change. Every gift in my life was right there. I became a true Navy wife and I now know what the hell that is.

It means sacrificing and scraping and supporting your husband. It means learning what all the initials stand for. It means being there when he can't be and not resenting him for it. It means sponsoring new families who will go through everything you have and finding best friends along the way. It means understanding his job so that he can be better at it.

Guam gave us a kick start in our relationship just when we needed it the most! It also gave John his Bachelor's degree and the promotion to First Class Petty Officer. He was on his way.

Chapter 61

Spring 1996
What is the Navy Doing in the Desert?

Fallon, Nevada felt like paradise to me. Its beautiful rural setting and small town atmosphere were the perfect welcome back to the states. We spent the first six weeks in the Bachelor Enlisted Quarters on base. We knew we would get a house, but we just had to be patient.

Erin flowed right into school and we made several new friends in the Search and Rescue group. Vince and Michelle Wade were from Alabama and we became instant friends. They had a son named Andy, who Joe loved to play with.

Everything was familiar again. Every where we went people looked like my mom and dad. There were cornfields and farms with cows and horses again. There were squirrels and rabbits and trains. Who would have thought that I would miss these mundane things? These were the small parts of our world that we had left behind when we went to Guam.

John was busy training with the Longhorn Search and Rescue team. I remember how impressed he was with the unit. Everyone had told him this would be the most high tech flying he would do.

Joe was having a hard time adjusting to the clothing requirements. It was February and we were so thankful for the new winter coats Grandma Shirley had sent for Christmas. Joe, however, would not keep his coat on. As soon as we got in the car, off came his shoes, socks and coat. In the grocery store, off came the shoes, socks, and the coat. He just wasn't grasping the concept of winter.

One night, as we sat amid Pizza Hut boxes watching the

Reno news, the SAR beeper went off. John was still in his Flight suit since he had flown that morning. He had just started working on his re-qualifications which were necessary at each new command. His first flight had been cut short because the crew had been called out on a search for two people missing on snow-mobiles.

They dropped him off and headed up to the mountains. The look on his face made my heart stop.

"What?" I asked with fear creeping into my voice.

"It's all ones." This meant a military aircraft had gone down.

"Do you think it is part of the Carrier Air Group?" He did not have time to answer before we heard pounding on the door to our room. John Warfield, another SAR Corpsman, was out of breath as he shared the terrible news.

"The SAR helicopter went down. Everyone's at the hangar."

John grabbed his coat and was gone with a quick kiss. As I walked around to sit down and try to absorb what was happening, the broken images of the orange and white helicopter filled the TV screen. I heard the reporter say,

"The extent of the injuries are unknown at this time." I tried not to focus on the huge tree that had split the helicopter open between the front and middle. The startling ring of the phone had me jumping off the couch.

"Please tell me your husband is sitting next to you?" It was Ken Brown, a friend of Papa Larry's who lived here in Fallon. He had been our official tour guide and welcome committee.

"He just left to go to the hangar."

"Are you OK?" he asked. I really did not know this man, but the tears came as I let go of the breath I had been holding.

"John flew for the first time this morning," I told him. We talked for a while and I told him I would have John call as soon as we knew something. When John returned, he shared the injury list. Thank God no one was killed, but all had suffered extensive broken bones.

Fallon, Nevada felt like paradise to me. Its beautiful rural setting and small town atmosphere were the perfect welcome back to the states. We spent the first 6 weeks in the Bachelor Enlisted Quarters on base. We knew we would get a house, but we just had to be patient.

Erin flowed right into school and we made several new friends in the Search And Rescue group. Vince and Michelle Wade were from Alabama and we became instant friends. They had a son named Andy, who Joe loved to play with.

Everything was familiar again. Every where we went people looked like my mom and dad. There were cornfields and farms with cows and horses again. There were squirrels and rabbits and trains. Who would have thought that I would miss these mundane things but these were the small parts of our world that we had left behind when we went to Guam.

John was busy training with the Longhorn Search and Rescue team. I remember how impressed he was with the unit. Everyone had told him this would be the most high tech flying he would do.

Joe was having a hard time adjusting to the clothing requirement. It was February and we were so thankful for the new winter coats Grandma Shirley had sent for Christmas. Joe, however, would not keep his coat on. As soon as we got in the car, off came his shoes, socks and coat. In the grocery store, off came the shoes, socks and the coat. He just wasn't grasping the concept of winter.

One night, as we sat amid Pizza Hut boxes watching the Reno news, the SAR beeper went off. John was still in his Flight suit since he had flown that morning. He had just started working on his requalifications which were necessary at each new command. His first flight had been cut short because the crew had been called out on a search for two missing snow-mobilers.

They dropped him off and headed up to the mountains. The look on his face made my heart stop.

"What?" I asked with fear creeping into my voice.

"It's all ones." This meant a military aircraft had gone down.

"Do you think it is part of the Carrier Air Group?" He did not have time to answer before we heard pounding on the door to our room. John Warfield, another SAR corpsman, was out of breath as he shared the terrible news.

"The SAR helo went down. Everyone's at the hangar."

John grabbed his coat and was gone with a quick kiss. As I walked around to sit down and try to absorb what was happening, the broken images of the orange and white helicopter filled the TV screen. I heard the reporter say,

"The extent of the injuries are unknown at this time." I tried not to focus on the huge tree that had split the helicopter open between the front and middle. The startling ring of the phone had me jumping off the couch.

"Please tell me your husband is sitting next to you?" It was Ken Brown, a friend of Papa Larry's who lived here in Fallon. He had been our official tour guide and welcome committee.

"He just left to go to the hangar."

"Are you OK?" He asked. I really did not know this man, but the tears came as I let go of the breath I had been holding.

"John flew for the first time this morning." I told him. We talked for a while and I told him I would have John call as soon as we knew something. When John returned, he shared the injury list. Thank God no one was killed, but all had suffered extensive broken bones.

The most serious injury was to the Pilot. They were not sure if he would ever walk again. The SAR Corpsman, Ken May had treated each of the crewmembers as best he could with his one working arm. The other had been broken in the crash. What a scary way to begin our new tour in Fallon.

Chapter 62

The Freaked out Camper

The SAR group grew closer through the tragic accident and the annual camping trip to Lake Lahontan brought some much needed rest and relaxation. The culminating event would be the pig roast on Saturday and we were all looking forward to getting away for a bit.

We had moved into our house on Cottonwood Drive in March and made good on our promise to get the kids a dog. We were now the proud owners of a basset hound puppy named Rockne.

His tri-colored coat was well represented on his face with a distinctive white stripe running from his black nose up to the top of his head. His sad eyes were bordered with black and his cheeks sagged with lots of extra light brown jowls. His legs and paws were white but could barely be seen behind his long droopy black ears.

We knew he was meant to be our dog when we received his birth certificate. He was born on St. Patrick's Day! The kids had both survived the chicken pox in the past month so a weekend trip was very needed.

The tents were lined up on the far side of the parking lot. There were at least eight or nine tents and some campers as the SAR bunch set up for a weekend with nature. We laid a large piece of Astroturf in front of our tent. This was bordered by coolers and big Rubbermaid tubs holding all of our essentials.

The kids had gone to sleep in the tent that first night and were snug as could be. John and I walked back over to the campfire to join the rest of the gang for some late night beers. I was still trying to get everyone's name right. There was Ken and Jodi, Pat and Lynne, Vince and Michelle, Doug and Becky, Marty and Alex and several single guys from the clinic.

We stumbled back to our tent much later and tried to get some sleep. I remember my worried thoughts about the children and the lake as I drifted off to sleep.

Not long after, I sat straight up, afraid to move or breathe so as to hear. The scared call of "Mommy!" came again. I knew it was Joe calling me, but it sounded so far away. I tore out of the tent and ran along the backs of the other campsites yelling at the top of my lungs.

"Joe!"

I heard him call again, but this time it was back in the other direction, so I ran full speed back to our tent. I was frantic and I could not understand why I was the only one searching for him.

I cut through between the May's tent and ours at a full sprint. My shins were the first to make contact with the coolers lining our area. I hit them going full throttle and flipped myself over the barriers. My knees skidded on the Astroturf and I felt the gravel embed itself in my palms. My hip started to ache immediately as it connected with the once taut rope holding our tent.

It was then that the zipper to our tent slowly opened. John stuck his head out and in the calmest voice said,

"Before you jump in the lake you should know that Joe is lying right next to me."

I needed a Doctor. I was scraped and bruised from my sleep walking adventure. I was the talk of the camp at breakfast and everyone had a good laugh. I, on the other hand, could barely walk but at least they knew what they were dealing with. Perhaps I needed to work on relaxing a bit!

Chapter 63

He Can't Come to the Phone Right Now

John and I had a difficult decision to make. We had jokingly given the kids the choice of a new puppy or a new baby. To my relief, they chose a puppy. I really felt like we were perfect just the way we were. We had been blessed with two beautiful, healthy children. I was 30 years old and very content with two children.

The deciding factor came, or should I say didn't come, just after we got settled. I had missed a period and I was sure I was pregnant. I did not want to be but I prayed that whatever I found out I would accept it as God's big plan for us. My fear was for nothing since it was just my body getting back on track after a stressful couple of months.

This made us ask ourselves some hard questions and we made the appointment for John to have a vasectomy. It would be done right there at the Branch Medical Clinic where John worked. He picked the entire team and he entertained them all with his loud rendition of the Notre Dame fight song while under the influence of narcotics.

Pain medicine was a necessary thing and we got him home and settled with an ice pack. Joe was in charge of the phone, as I headed to the store and back to the pharmacy for John's prescription. We had told Joe that he could not sit on Daddy's lap for a while because he was sore.

I left the two of them with Joe at the table coloring, and Daddy sprawled in the Lazy Boy adjusting his ice pack as needed. I had not been gone ten minutes when the phone rang. Joe had been well trained on the phone and John listened to Joe's reply which started out just like we had taught him.

"No. My Daddy can't come to the phone right now…..he's playing with his wiener."

John's scream came immediately as he struggled to get to his feet. Terrible thoughts were running through his head. What had just happened? Who could this be? All John could think of were the possible people on the other end….School Nurse (Oh Please God, No), The Commanding Officer of the clinic. Every possibility was worse than the last. When he got to the phone, he heard nothing but short gasps of air followed by howling laughter.

"This is John Ruskin." He said in an official sounding voice. It was way too late for that. It was one of the guys from the Administration Department at the clinic just calling to check on John. It took a good fifteen minutes for him to regain his composure and talk to John.

By the time I showed up at the clinic to pick up his prescription, the place was up for grabs.

Poor Joe was just being honest. To his 3 ½-year-old eyes, Daddy was doing a lot of playing.

Chapter 64

I Need a Job
Spring 1996

Joe and I spent many afternoons filling out applications and handing out resumes. I was trying to make John's paycheck stretch as far as it would go. We had come to the decision that I had to work.

I wanted something to give us quick money, so I headed out to the Fallon Golf Course to see if they needed any help as a waitress or bartender. I had no idea how fancy a place this was and memories of my stint at the Macomb Country Club began to enter my mind. But I had nothing to lose.

As I walked in, I was relieved to see it was not overly formal and the owner's, Lorraine and Bob, were very nice people. It was a quick decision by Lorraine since she was shorthanded and the weather was beginning to warm up.

She told me I had nice, trusting eyes and to be back that Friday night. I would be doing a little bartending and I would have a few tables. I began yet another attempt in the food service business.

Friday came and I was right on time. As I walked in, I noticed a tall blond haired woman behind the bar. She finished making the drink she was working on and looked me over as I stood at the end of the bar.

"Hi, I'm Patti. I'm supposed to start working tonight," I said with as much confidence as I could muster.

"Lorraine is in the kitchen," she said with a nod in that direction. I was not exactly getting a warm, fuzzy feeling from my new co-worker, but I put a smile on just the same. I found Lorraine and she introduced me to LeeAnn and told LeeAnn to show me where things were and to let me have a few tables as the dinner crowd started.

It became very apparent as my first night proceeded that I was a definite threat to LeeAnn. Every group that came in just happened to be her "regulars" so she did not give me one table until Lorraine asked how it was going.

She made some excuse that LeeAnn has been doing this for seven years and she gets in her working mode. Lorraine said she did not mean to be rude. I took one table and made five dollars in tips. So much for making the big bucks!

Things were starting out the same way on Saturday night until Lorraine asked me to tend bar at a function they were catering at the Fallon Convention Center. I felt really good after this and was looking forward to the next weekend. Again, I worked a special wedding that they were catering and did not have to work with LeeAnn even though I know she missed me.

I was to call Lorraine in the middle of the week to find out when I would work again, so I called on Wednesday. Lorraine told me they had hired another girl and she was working out really well so she would let me know if she got shorthanded again. Just like that. I was crushed.

Obviously LeeAnn had quite a say in the hiring and firing and I had just been replaced. So it was back to beating the pavement. I put all of my energy into getting a job at the Child Development center on base. There was going to be an opening in July so I began the process. The job title was Curriculum Specialist and it started at $31,000. This would be the answer to our financial problems.

We were almost ten thousand dollars in debt between the credit card, the van, and the computer so I was desperate. I had also applied for several positions with the State of Nevada, but I kept running into roadblocks at every turn.

By the end of June, I had still not heard anything, so we took our summer trip to Illinois even though we really had no business going on vacation.

Chapter 65

Brenda gets her man

June 29th was one of the happiest days of my life. A day I had hoped for, finally came. Brenda had found the love she had waited for and was married on a beautiful day in Dwight, Illinois. Brenda chose Mary, Kelly, Moe and I to be by her side. Erin was her flower girl and stole the hearts of many that day including Zeke.

I'll never forget the frenzied hour before the ceremony. Pictures were at Zeke and Delores', and Wayne, Brenda's brother, was staying true to his reputation with his late arrival from the golf course. Zeke had been left to his own devices all day and had called to get John's help with transporting hundreds of balloons to the church. Zeke's plan was for John to drive the big blue truck with the balloons, while Zeke followed in the smaller van.

With what could be called a questionable decision, they decided to leave the back door of the big blue truck partly open. It took one bad bump mixed with an afternoon breeze and John lost well over half his cargo. The balloons, which were filled with helium earlier that day, were sucked out of the van faster than Zeke could scream 'Lucky!'

By the time John got Big Blue stopped, over 200 balloons were now beautifully lodged in Mr. Kresl's tree on Waupansie Street.

"I guess we should have shut the door, Lucky!" was all Zeke could say between fits of laughing and coughing.

What a day. I remember how nervous Zeker looked standing in the living room with his tux on and his tie in hand.

"Can somebody help me with this tie?" he asked for the

second time with a note of panic in his voice. No one was paying any attention to him at all. The bridesmaids were busy carefully placing their bouquets on the train of Brenda's dress for a picture.

He felt a tug on his pants and looked down to see Erin.

"Here, Mr. Zeke, I'll help you!" she had said, not knowing she was melting his heart.

The photographer captured the moment and the tender photo shows the hint of a tear in Zeke's eye. He told that story all night at the reception. I wrote Brenda a poem and read it to her that night. That poem made me seriously think about telling my story.

Chapter 66

The Most Important Men In Our Lives

We were all a bit shocked and very worried to see Em, John's sister, during our trip home. My heart ached for her. She had gotten so thin and she looked so unhappy. It was obvious that something was really wrong.

We had all wondered when Em would come to terms with her issues and it appeared she was struggling miserably. John had filled the shoes of his father in Em's eyes for all these years and he knew what he had to do. He had called her one morning before she headed to work.

"Take the day off today!" he had said knowing what he would confront her with on their day together. We had talked about this and Emily needed to know that nothing she could do would ever change our love for her. They spent the day together and for the first time in Em's life it was out in the open.

She would not have to hide who she was to us any longer. The road ahead for her would be filled with people who did not agree with her identity, but she was facing that tough road with her big brother by her side.

The most important man in my life although I wished it was my husband, was still my Dad. Our up and down relationship dominated every trip home and every visit. I pushed the hurt away when we were not home but the scab remained and was pulled off each time he let me down. Kelli lived close and she did not seem to struggle like I did. She just accepted him for who he was. I allowed his behavior to control mine.

Mom and Dad had driven back with us that summer to spend a couple of weeks. We were able to spend Mom's birthday together. We had decided to take off for Lake Tahoe on a beautiful summer day. We stopped at a restaurant for lunch and John, Mom, and the kids sat down while I went to the bathroom. I saw Dad at the bar as I was coming around the corner and my blood began to boil.

As he approached our table several minutes later, he sat down with the clearest 'coke' ever made. I was livid that he would do this to Mom on her birthday. Mom was used to this after 40 years. Birthdays and holidays were not occasions where you held high expectations.

Unable to hold my temper I railed at him through tear filled eyes.

"What are you doing?" I yelled louder than I should have in a public place.

"Don't you ever think of Mom?" Mom came out a lot easier than the word me, but the selfish little girl was just under the surface of this tirade.

His reply was always the same. Nothing. No excuse, no fight, no reason. He sat there in his lonely lost way that I had seen so many times. I still wanted to punch him in that big nose of his.

Looking back on that day, Dad did not ruin Mom's birthday, I did. I gave him all the control without even realizing it. I'm the one who made a scene and I was getting so very tired of being so angry.

Chapter 67

The Wedding Coordinator
July 96

After our summer trip home, I was back to trying to balance the checkbook. As I sat doing the bills that Wednesday, I bawled like a baby. I was robbing Peter to pay Paul and there was nothing left. We had definitely overspent and the reality was staring me in the face.

The phone rang and I swallowed my tears and answered it.

"Hi, This is DeeDee Ferguson. You don't know me, but I got your name from Lorraine at the Fallon Golf Course. My daughter, Courtney, is getting married next week, and I have had people lined up for months to help me cater this. I am doing all the cooking myself and the reception will be at our house, but just this week everyone that I had lined up, has backed out. I need at least two people to set up, bus the tables and possibly tend bar. I am desperate for help. Would you be interested in helping me?"

It took me about two seconds to answer!

"SURE!"

At this point, I would dig ditches and this sounded like fun. It was on Saturday, the 27th of July, and I needed to be there at 4:00. She said that she had one other person lined up and that her friends were all helping out too. She told me to ask for Carol, who was the Wedding Coordinator, when I got to the house since DeeDee and her husband would already be at the church.

I could not believe my luck. She said she would pay me $5.oo an hour and any tips. Saturday could not get here fast enough. Saturday arrived as a typical July day in Nevada. It was extremely hot and by the afternoon, the dry air was beginning to be moved around by the familiar Nevada wind.

I left a little early since I did not know where I was going. I found the house, which was a sprawling brick ranch. The yard was impeccably landscaped and as I pulled into the driveway that wound behind the house, a small shiver of panic ran up my back. A huge white tent came into view. The tent had windows!

This was not going to be a small wedding to say the least. Ahead of me, I saw lights strung across the driveway from tree to tree marking the occasion. A massive wood dance floor had been set up and tall speakers stood watch silently in the corners in front of the huge tent.

I parked the van and as I got out, I heard running water and noticed a beautiful fountain surrounded by floating candles in the middle of a swimming pool. Spotless patio furniture added to the beauty of pool..

I did not see anyone in the yard, so I walked around the pool to the back door. Just as I was about to knock, the door opened.

"Hi," I said,

"I'm Patti. I was one of the girls that DeeDee hired to help."

The small woman standing in the doorway smiled and shook my hand. She wore jeans and a freshly starched red blouse. Her black hair, which was beginning to show some grey, was permed and ended just above her collar.

"Oh, you are right on time. I'm Carol, and I was just starting to set up the tables."

She showed me into the kitchen, which looked like something out of a Better Home's and Garden magazine. It was decorated in a country theme, and it was obvious that DeeDee was a serious cook. There were two huge Viking ovens covered with food. Every countertop including the island was covered with food.

I followed Carol's instructions and started carrying out tablecloths and candles to decorate the tables under the tent. The tent was lit with the same type of lights that were strung through the trees in the driveway. It looked like something out of a "Dallas" episode. The Ewing's had nothing on these folks!

When we finished, we walked over to one of the two sheds across the driveway. Obviously, DeeDee's husband had to relocate his tools since this was Wedding Central today. There were instructions up on the walls and every utensil, every bowl, and every napkin had an instruction as to where it was to be used.

Carol was pointing to a timetable on the wall that showed what needed to be done and what time to have things ready. The wedding was at 5:00 and guests should start to arrive around 6:00. We were right on schedule. According to the instructions, the steam tables needed to be lit and the head table needed to be decorated.

I casually asked Carol how many people they were expecting and without so much as turning around she answered "600!" At this point my knees were visibly shaking, but I followed her lead. Just as we were heading back to the tents, the other woman arrived.

She was about twenty minutes late and her color was not good; in fact, she looked almost green. She was a very tall lady and she introduced herself as Cathy. I showed her the shed with all of the instructions. She had also worked at the Golf Course, although I had never met her. She said she did not feel well and had almost called to say she could not make it. Green or not, I was glad to see her.

There were more tables to decorate on the far side of the dance floor so Cathy and I got to work. There were several other people around now including an employee of Ray and DeeDee's. His name was Steve Phillips, and his wife and daughters were also here to help. I introduced myself and went about my duties.

The Phillips family was setting up the bar and icing the kegs of beer. Carol had dressed both the buffet tables and was lighting the first steam table. The wind was proving to be a pain as I noticed several of the tablecloths being blown around. I walked back under the tent to see if I could secure the tablecloths.

Carol was crouched down near the end of the buffet table trying to light the second steam table. I could hear the hiss of the gas, and just as I turned to tell her to be careful, I saw a huge fire ball and I watched in horror as Carol was thrown back into the air.

Her hair was on fire as I ran to her. I grabbed an extra tablecloth and put her hair out. She was visibly burned on her face and the steam table was in flames. I helped her outside of the tent and we made our way to the shed.

The flames were at least three feet above the steam table and dangerously close to the ceiling of the tent. All I could think of was that it was going to blow up. If the tent caught on fire the whole thing could go up in flames with the wind blowing like it was.

Steve and his wife ran to us, as I sat Carol down. No one else seemed to know what to do, so I called 911. I did not even know where I was, let alone to try to tell the emergency medical team how to get there.

The Ferguson's were very well known in Fallon, so we heard sirens within minutes. My co-worker Cathy had turned a new shade of green. She was not the trauma nurse that I was hoping for. Steve's wife covered Carol with a blanket and he and I both tried to pull hoses over to where the fire was, but they did not even make it half way.

As I was struggling with the garden hose to fight this fire, the thought crossed my mind that I could very easily be blown up trying to save a tent for people that I did not even know! I heard the fire trucks approaching and as I looked up all I could do was scream.

"THE LIGHTS!" I ran around to the front of the house to stop the trucks, just as Steve yelled that the fire had burned itself out. I could see him by the table and he was able to turn off the gas. The ambulance was able to make it under the lights and they treated Carol for her burns and for shock.

I will never forget the stark contrast her dark hair made with her ghostly white face. Wedding Central now smelled like charred hair. They loaded Carol in the ambulance and before they shut the doors, I realized that Carol was the only person who knew what the hell to do to prepare for the 600 guests that would be arriving very soon!!!

"Carol," I said, "would there be any last instructions you would like to share before they take you to the hospital?"

"Just follow the time line Patti, and you will be fine!" I was sure that I should have been treated for shock at that point. Hell, I was fired from the position that recommended me for this job! Now it would appear that I am the Wedding Coordinator!

Cathy was sitting down with her face in her hands and even though I really did not care, I asked if she was alright.

"I have never worked in such an unorganized environment in my life. I'm really sick and I don't want to be here." The dread was creeping up on me as I told her, "Do what you think is best, Cathy."

I did not have time to discuss her problems so I made my way to the time line and realized that by my watch we were 45 minutes away from 600 guests. I began to take deep cleansing breaths so that I did not hyperventilate.

In through the nose, out through the mouth. We were almost a half-hour behind our timeline. I grabbed more table clothes and started out of the shed just as Cathy gathered up her purse.

"I'm going to go."

I could not believe it, but there was no time to worry about her lack of loyalty. I began to panic as several cars came down the driveway. They can't be here already! I was praying that this family was Catholic. I needed a good hour long wedding mass, which would give me until at least 6:15.

Three ladies got out of their cars and came over to where I was.

"Is everyone alright?" one of the ladies asked.

They told me that several volunteer firemen were at the wedding and their beepers went off with the Ferguson's address. Just the kind of the thing the mother of the bride needed to hear on her daughter's special day!

The ladies stayed and helped me set up the buffet line. The entire buffet tablecloth and part of the table had burned so I just chucked all of it out in the field behind the tent. They probably found it around October!

Steve had called the caterer in Reno where the steam table had been rented and they were on their way with another one. The ladies were ready to help and kept asking me for instructions. It finally dawned on me that they actually thought I knew what I was doing.

One of my dad's favorite quotes came into my mind.

"If you can't dazzle them with brilliance, then baffle them with bullshit!"

It seemed I was making a career out of this tonight! Steve and his wife were also ready to do anything that needed to be done and amazingly we were somewhat ready when the mile long line of cars began to fill the parking area. We lit all of the candles on the tables even though the thought of fire made me want to turn and run.

There were tiki lamps all along the border of the tent but I was not about to light those. It looked absolutely beautiful under the tent. Everywhere I went all that people were talking about was the explosion and fire. I felt like maybe I had overreacted but I really had no idea if the tent was going to go up in flames or not.

I had placed several people in charge of being food runners and I was the prime rib cutter at the end of the buffet line. The food was unbelievable and there were at least 600 people. DeeDee had arranged for two separate food tables so everyone was fed remarkably fast.

I spent the next hour bussing the tables and it was at that point that I felt someone touch me on the shoulder. I was quite a sight by this time between the sweat and prime rib juice. My once crisp, white shirt was now clinging to me as the humidity took hold of the night.

As I turned around, DeeDee held out her arms and gave me a big hug. She was beautiful in her pale pink gown, and all she could do was thank me. She asked where the other girl had gone and I gave her the news of Cathy's desertion.

As I was tearing down both the buffet lines, I finally saw the bride and groom. They looked so young. They were glowing as they danced under the stars. There was a lot of left-over food so I spent the next hour in Wedding Central.

"Here, you have earned this tonight."

I turned to see a glass of beer being offered by my fellow firefighter, Steve. I sat down for the first time in about six hours and let the cold beer quench my thirst. There had not even been time to eat, but I had not even thought about it. We sat and talked for a bit and as he got up to leave, he shook my hand.

"It was a pleasure working with you."

"You too!" I said.

I realized how absolutely beat I was. I finished up as fast as I could and loaded all of the food in a cart. Heading for the house, I bumped the cart along on the gravel. The party was going strong now and the music could be heard for miles. I left the cart outside the backdoor by the pool. As I was unloading the last of the chicken wings from the cart, my greasy fingers lost their grip and I watched an entire roaster pan full of wings splatter the beautiful cobblestone sidewalk.

There was no one around to hear my frustrated scream of "SHIIIIT!" I ran inside to try to find something to clean up the mess. I had to hurry because the sidewalk angled towards the pool and since I was the only food service worker for 10 miles, I could not blame this on anyone else.

All I could picture was brown, greasy water spewing from the beautiful fountain. The only thing I could find was DeeDee's kitchen garbage can and I spent the next hour knee deep in marinated chicken wings. I was able to contain the spill. What remained was a huge grease spot right in front of the door.

I thought of finding a rug to place over it, but I knew that with the light of day I would be found out. I was so exhausted, but I thought I should let them know I was leaving. It was close to midnight and there was not much else that I could do.

I wound my way back to the party and through the crowd which was a very easy task since I smelled like a goat. People were parting like the red seas to let me through. I found DeeDee, and her husband, Ray. I let them know that I was leaving and I also told them about the new design I created on their cobblestone patio.

They looked exactly as they should have, like they were having the time of their life. They thanked me and told me to call on Monday. I ended up getting $10.00 an hour and quite a hefty tip from DeeDee and her husband. I also walked away with another job title; Wedding Coordinator Extraordinaire!

Chapter 68

Back in My Element

I enrolled Joe in Pre-school at St. John's Child Care Center in Fallon and decided it would be a perfect part-time job for me. The pay was minimal, but even $6.00 an hour was better than nothing. We would start after the holidays and we were both excited.

I headed home in November for another fun wedding. This time it was Moe and Tim's turn to tie the knot. The fun weekends were always the same; too much drinking, not near enough sleep, and non-stop laughing.

John was so good to let me go home as much as he did. We could not afford it, but I had missed so much that I refused to miss their big days. I was the Master of Ceremonies at the reception so I had the privilege of introducing the wedding party.

I had written a poem for Moe. We had led such similar lives that we were an instant match from the minute we met back in High School. Brenda, Mary, and Kelly were all at her side along with her sister Colleen. I had lost my voice completely by the time I returned from that wild weekend.

My job as a teacher at St. John's got me back in my element. I loved teaching. I had the four-year-old group and they were a blast.

I remember watching this one particular mom each morning. She had two darling girls. Each morning I watched her sign the girls in and silently wondered how early her days started in order to get their pony tails so perfectly combed.

Each day they had a different dress on with matching socks

and shoes. Cristina, the older girl, was in my group and she stayed very quiet the first few weeks. Briana was in the younger group and she seemed to be a little more rough and tumble out on the playground. Cristina had some issues with another girl in my group named Kinsey and that was when I saw Cristina lose her composure. I actually talked to her mom about it and that was when I first met Ceci.

I remember her first sentence.

"So you are Miss Patti! My girls fight over who gets to be Miss Patti when they are playing school," she told me during one of our first chats in the parking lot.

I learned that they were a Navy family and her husband was a Chief. I met their son, Stevie, who shared the dark hair and beautiful eyes like his sisters. I got to meet their dad, Ray, at the Kindergarten graduation and I couldn't wait to get John and Ray together.

The Slattery family continued to grow in Rockford, Illinois. Sue and Ed added to their family and much to Erin's disappointment, they had another boy. Kyle Austin was born on April 10th. As far as cousins were concerned, Erin was out-numbered four to one.

A pregnant Kelli and Patrick came to visit us in April and we had some much needed time together. She was due in June and was feeling great.

We timed our summer trip perfectly since Kelli delivered Samuel Tomas Trainor on June19th.

Mom and Dad had moved from their apartment and were now renting a beautiful duplex in the Scott subdivision. It was great to be home, but Dad and I seemed to be struggling again. I found fault with everything he did. He was now getting around on a Scooter which he called his mule. He spent most days cruising around Dwight unsupervised. I knew he drank and I let his behavior control my behavior each visit home. Understandably, he got the hell out of dodge during most of our time home. I'm sure I made him a nervous wreck.

Chapter 69

Chief Ruskin
July 1997

In July, we anxiously awaited the results of the Chief Board. John had passed the test and his record now went before a board of his peers. It was his first time up for Chief Petty Officer and it was not uncommon for it to take several attempts to make Chief. What he lacked in sea time, he made up for with a Bachelor's degree.

"I'm a Chief!" was all he said when I answered the phone that Friday afternoon. Finally he had been given the recognition he deserved. Maybe this was the course that God had waited for. Six times he had put in for the Medical Service Corps Program which required the candidates to be within two years of a degree. That program would have made John a Commissioned Officer, but six times he was denied.

All of that was forgotten now. I could hear the excitement in his voice. I could hardly wait to tell Ceci. The rest of the Search and Rescue group was equally excited since one of their own was promoted.

As John went through initiation, we got to know the Carrillo family even better. Ray was a teddy bear of a man who looked extremely intense until his smile told you he was all bark.

We were realizing just how small the Navy was. The Bullman's had accepted orders to Fallon and again we welcomed them to their new home. Shannon, Hannah, and Angie had grown so much but it was like having family down the street. Janice, John's wife, and I finally had time to get to know each other. John Bullman had not changed a bit and it was so fun to have them here.

It was not a real fun time for John, since one did not just become a Chief in the Navy. It was a process much like pledging a fraternity. Initiation season lasted 9½ weeks and it was both physically and emotionally exhausting. There were four others in John's initiation class from other commands on the base. He spent more time with Ron, Brian, Lora and Reggie than his own family during that time.

It was all worth it the day he was pinned. The pinning ceremony is as symbolic as any Navy tradition. The new Chief chooses the people to pin their first set of anchors on their collar. The look on John's tear stained face as his mom, Shirley, stepped out to pin him was priceless. She had made a surprise visit that he knew nothing about. Erin and Joe pinned on Daddy's other anchor. John, or Jack, as he was known to his Chief buddies, was chosen to address the entire Chief's mess at the Khaki ball and he rose to the challenge. We were now a part of a great group of people who seemed to share our ideas and values.

Chapter 70

Hey Bartender

I got to use my MC talents one more time at Kelly Sullivan's wedding in August of 1997. It is a good thing I did not have too many more friends getting married or we would be broke. Kelly asked Mary and I to be readers at her and Tony's beautiful outdoor wedding at Cog Hill Country Club. Kelly's unique style was everywhere that day and she sparkled like the sunflowers in her bouquet.

Kelly and I were the best kind of friends. We shared something that only a select group of people can understand. We had best friends in our sisters. Her little sister, Kerry, was everything to her, as much as my Kelli was to me. Kelly and I did not have to talk often to rekindle our bond. She was just always there when I needed her.

My work at the Child Care center ended in November of 97, but not before I made a great friend. I had taken over for another teacher who was on maternity leave. When Shannon returned, she taught along side me. I admired her spirit and her great sense of humor. We had very similar teaching styles and I learned so much from watching her interact with children. She knew Fallon, Nevada like I knew Dwight, Illinois. It had been her home since she was in grade school. She was married to a man that worked for the maintenance contractor on the base so we knew a lot of the same people. With three children, she stayed very busy. We shared so many great talks and our true bonding experience was our trip to Michigan with the other staff members.

I was on the substitute list for the Churchill County School District, but I was not getting called as much as I would have liked. We just weren't making any headway on the bills. I had started watching another Chief's son who was a year older than Joe. Bub, as he was called, was a very easy kid and he and Joe kept each other busy most afternoons.

We became good friends with his mom and dad, Mike and Faith Esposito. Faith had been a Sea Bee in the Navy, but was currently in the Reserves. She did finishing work for a contractor and was amazing at what she did. Mike was a Senior Chief and they lived just around the corner in housing.

As we started hanging out at the Chief's Club on base, I enviously watched the bartender and her overflowing tip jar. I knew I could do what she did and I felt like this would possibly solve our problems quicker than the $80.00 a day I was making subbing. I let the Chief in charge of the club know that I was interested and I waited until the timing was right. As luck would have it, she was waiting for a reason to go home to the Philippines.

This opened the door for me to start, yet another career. My motto was simple, I was nice. You truly do not have to be good to tend bar, you just have to be nice. The bar itself was set up in a small square so getting to everyone was easy enough.

I will never forget my first night. It was early March and Becca, who had tended bar for years, told me to join her Monday night since she knew there would not be a huge crowd.

When I walked in, there were about a handful of people, mostly men. A few were back in the pool room, some were sitting off to the side and a few were at the bar. I nervously got behind the bar and listened as she explained where things were. I had never seen any of the people in the bar and I took a minute to look around.

I took a double take when I looked at the table in the attached room. There sat Roy Clark with the Commanding Officer of the base. THE Roy Clark was in our Chief's Club! Becca asked if I wanted to take them another drink, so with shaking hands I headed over.

"Hey, it looks like we have some new help here?" Captain Ronnie said.

I actually set their beers down without spilling, and I even got Roy Clark's autograph. He and his band were performing in Reno, Nevada, and they had come to the base to give a free concert in appreciation of the Military.

Gaining confidence, I made several drinks while Becca took a break. Roy's band members were enjoying a night off and I met a few of them who were sitting at the bar. The fiddle player ordered something called a red snapper. With his coaching, I made my first fancy drink and reached to hand it to him across the bar. The now bright red glass caught the edge of the bar just as I let go of his drink. I watched in horror, as the red liquid poured out and doused his beige Dockers.

The real Patti had arrived. In his attempt to avoid the spill he had jumped back and tipped over his chair. Captain Ronnie and Roy were now checking out the commotion. I rushed around the bar, hoping no one had been injured, however I could not really help much since the damage had been done. I could not apologize enough, but they were all good sports, especially the fiddle player with the red crotch.

John had the honor of being on duty the day the SAR crew took Roy for a ride.

While bartending was not the best mom job, it proved to be the most fun I had ever had. I think I made it pretty fun for most of the Chief's and their spouses as well. I only worked a few days a week, but we had made fast friends with Al, who had been the Master Chief on the base, and his wife Stella.

Al had retired, but he was now working on the base at Public Works, so he stopped in for a beer when I was working. He knew I was not the best bartender and I proved it to him one day when it was just he and I and my boss in the club.

Al had ordered a beer and paid me. There were only two people to choose from but still I turned and gave his change to my boss. He laughed so hard I thought he would pass out. This was just one of the times I made a mistake.

Balancing the register was a real problem since the club would get very busy. In most Senior Enlisted and Officer Clubs there is a bell. This bell serves several purposes. One purpose is to alert all of those around the bar that the ringer will buy a round. The other purpose is to alert the bar that someone has entered the coveted space covered, which in lay terms means wearing a hat. Wearing a hat in a Chief's Club is a very expensive mistake, especially if the bar is full. Entering covered means you buy the house a round.

These traditions are great when you are a patron on the drinking side of the bar, but they become extremely stressful situations when you are the tar bender. There is usually just one bell, but the industrious/lazy Chiefs at Fallon decided that they did not want to have to get up from their bar stools to ring the bell, so they rigged the bell to a rope that ran around the square bar.

Sea Bees can do anything and they did not disappoint using small gold hooks to keep it neatly in place and within arms reach of all patrons. It became quite a game. They would ring it once and watch me go into a tail spin. Before I even got chips passed out for the first round, someone else would ring it. I had the register so screwed up even my boss could not figure out how much we were supposed to have. My motto became, "Stop ringing the damn bell!"

The Chief Petty Officer Association was a wild group and we used our party skills to plan quite a few fun outings. We took a bus to Reno for Valentine's Day and had a great time.

John, who was known as Jack to everyone, felt the need, once again, to dress up like Cupid. We called on the sewing prowess of my friend, Shannon, who did not disappoint us. The blond wig was a bit much and I know he frightened people in the lobby of the Peppermill, but we had a blast.

We were able to pay off $9000.00 in credit card debt in less than 6 months. Bartending was without a doubt, the best job I had ever had. Imagine how much money I could have made if I actually knew how to make drinks!

We took the kids on the long awaited trip to Disneyland in the spring of '98. We were so blessed to have such good friends in Vince and Michelle Wade. We loaded up our conversion van and managed to cram more activities into our short four-day trip than even we thought possible. Their baby, Tanner was just eight-months-old, but he was quite the trooper. Andy and Joe were good buddies before our trip, but the best part was that we were all still friends when we returned!

Chapter 71

Our Northside Kids
August 1998

Our babies were both going to school. Joe started Kindergarten with his big sister, Erin, just down the hall. His teacher was a wonderful, caring woman named Mrs. Roberson. Joe was more than ready and he was doing great. Erin had Mr. and Mrs. Hansen for fourth grade. This husband and wife team were remarkable teachers. I spent a lot of time at Northside either helping, or subbing. We were so lucky to be in such a great district.

Both of our extended families were growing. Paula added another boy, Joshua Keith in July. We were so thankful he was healthy. Sue made Erin's dream come true when she gave Erin her first girl cousin. Jessica was born in August and I was her Godmother.

The month of March added a pet to the Ruskin family household. Caramel was a cute little hamster that Erin loved. Michele and Renee, my friends, had given Erin the whole set up for her birthday. All was going well with Caramel until the day that I was cleaning Erin's room. I had set Caramel's cage on the bed and fired up the vacuum. As I turned to vacuum under the bed, I had to look twice at the hamster. Obviously, the vacuum had initiated labor in our little Caramel who was now spewing out one red, mass after another.

My scream had John and Erin running. Erin was overjoyed at the thought of having baby hamsters, but I was about to be sick. Thank goodness we were able to give them away quickly.

Chapter 72

Doc Kutz
March 1999

John was now the Administration Department Head at the clinic in Fallon. He had six young Corpsman working for him and the last six months had proven to be some of the hardest of his career. He was the only Chief serving in the position of Department Head and he was watched very closely.

Shahn Kutz oozed personality. His round baby face always showed a smile and although his small stature could not be ignored, he made his presence known wherever he went. Unfortunately, Shahn's presence was usually found at Flippers bar in downtown Fallon.

Shahn had been sent home on a Monday morning for showing up drunk. John did not report this and felt his ass chewing was enough to get through to Shahn. Shahn had been accepted for Submarine Independent Duty Corpsman "C" School and he was flirting with disaster.

The phone call that came to the hangar a few weeks later proved that Shahn had a serious problem with alcohol and John had a decision to make. John had duty that day, but almost everyone in the clinic knew that Shahn was under the influence when he showed up for work.

All eyes were on John and he knew that he had to report Shahn. Shahn went to Captain's Mast, which is the Navy's version of court. His sentence was exactly what John had feared. He lost his "C" School, and was ordered to go for intensive outpatient treatment.

John questioned himself over and over after this decision.

What John did was give Shahn a chance to save his life, but all John could see was that he had taken away the one thing that Shahn wanted. The vicious arm of alcoholism was reaching out once again in our lives.

Shahn surprised everyone by his commitment to his program. He went to meetings and threw himself into his work. Shahn reconnected with his mom and John was so relieved when he spent his Christmas leave traveling with her.

John and I took rides into town regularly just to make sure he was not going to the bars. That is why I was so shocked to see the clinic van in the driveway that Monday, and to see John sitting at the counter.

"Shahn did not show up for work today and no one knows where he is," John said with one hand over the phone receiver.

He turned away as he spoke to the owner of Flippers. Sean's best friends, Dave Baker and Mike Loesch, had not seen him all weekend. They also worked for John and they spent the rest of the day searching Fallon, but they came up empty. Shahn was officially listed as UA which stands for unauthorized absence.

That night, John called Shahn's mom in Las Vegas with the hope that he had just lost his head and went home. His resigned sigh as he hung up the phone said more than his words. She had not seen or heard from her only son.

Tuesday came, and when his desk sat empty for the second day, John called the Sheriff's Department and filed a missing person's report. Now that the authorities were involved, they were able to get a key to his apartment from his landlord. There, on the coffee table, sat a bottle of whiskey with just a quarter left.

We talked that night and for the first time John put words to what had been on everyone's mind. With every passing hour, the chances of Shahn coming back got slimmer and slimmer.

"If he would just call, I could tell him it is OK to come home. Everyone messes up. He just has to start over, that's all!"

I knew John's optimism was a show. I knew and he knew that they would probably not find Shahn alive.

By Friday night, with still no word, we realized we may never get answers. We were just getting ready to leave for Al and Stella's when the doorbell rang. As I turned from the hallway, my heart sank. The Sheriff stood on the other side of the screen door.

"Is Chief Ruskin home?" the young Sheriff said officially. I invited him in, as John met me in the hall. I made sure the kids were in the back and snuck back up the hallway to watch John closely. I could hear the Sheriff's words, but their reality had my head spinning.

They had found his Jeep first, and then his body, near a small lake. Shahn was dead and I heard John's strained voice ask the hardest question of his life. I was sure he knew the answer before he ever asked the question.

"Did he kill himself?" I could tell John was holding his breath.

"Yes sir, it appears that is what happened."

The guilt seemed to weight John down as he made his way to the phone. He had to deliver the news to his best friends that they would never see Shahn again.

The next few hours were a blur. With one quick call to Ceci, the kids were taken care of. John's Officer in Charge was an incredible man and he showed his true character that weekend. Things were so hectic as they made the arrangements to have Shahn's services on the base. I watched John go into over drive. He was there for everybody that weekend. Bake, Loescher, and Shahn's mom all felt his support.

It was not until Sunday morning that I woke to feel the bed shaking. It was finally John's time. He let go of all the tears that were brimming just underneath his calm, organized exterior.

He knew in his heart that he had not caused this, but I know he wanted another chance to tell Shahn that he was not a failure. Shahn did not see anyway out and no one knew what private hell he was going through. This terrible disease had grabbed a hold of him and wouldn't let go. It just should not have taken a man so young.

Chapter 73

The Best of Friends
July 1999

It was time to choose our next home and Vince and Michelle Wade had it all picked out for us. They had lived in Guantanamo Bay, Cuba and loved it. There just so happened to be an opening for a Search and Rescue Corpsman and we committed to a 30-month tour.

We were to leave in July, but decided to stay long enough to be with Ray as he retired from the Navy. So many of our friends had become like family and the thought of leaving all of them broke my heart.

Leaving the Carrillo's hurt worst of all. I loved each of their children like my own. Ceci had fed my family more than I had in the past year. When I asked Joe what his favorite food was, he answered Ceci's ham!

Just after we started to do things together, Ceci called one Sunday.

"Did you guys have supper?" she asked in that sweet voice of hers.

"Oh, we just had macaroni and cheese and the kiddos had some cereal so don't worry about us." John had perked up in the chair.

"I have major leftovers so I am bringing them over if that is OK?" John was in the driveway waiting for her. He began to look forward to Sundays from then on and it became a standing date.

We were there the day Ray graduated with his Bachelors degree. What an accomplishment for a father of three! We had watched each other's kids and were there to cheer them on from the stands. We became each other's extended family. I had spilled on Mr. Ray more times in the short time we had known them, than I had spilled on my husband.

Ceci introduced us to homemade tortillas, tamales, carnesada, chorizo, grilled jalapenos, and many other amazing Hispanic dishes. Ray and Mr. Jack put away large amounts of bacardi as they solved the world's problems at their dining room table.

As we planned for our summer move, John and I knew there was no way we were going to miss Ray's important day. Logistically, it was a bit of a nightmare but we packed out and headed back to Illinois for three weeks. We then flew back to Nevada for a long weekend with the Carrillo family.

The depth of their friendship was evident when they volunteered to keep Rockne, our basset hound, during our time in Illinois. This was pure love! We spent one last weekend in Lake Tahoe together and prepared to begin another crazy adventure! This time we were headed to our first duty station on Communist soil. Gitmo, here we come!

Chapter 74

We Don't Care If He Dies
July 1999

We left the Carrillo's with a blessing from Ceci's mom, Grandma Valencia, and a howling basset hound.

We had arranged to fly from Reno, Nevada to Dallas, Texas, through the night in order to get Rockne on the flight. We would connect to our flight to Jacksonville in the early morning hours. The temperature needed to be below 80 degrees in order for the airlines to place a pet on the plane.

Rockne was so loud as we checked him through baggage. I could not wait to walk away so people would not know he was our dog.

The longer we waited, the more panicked we became about making our connecting flight to Jacksonville. There were other flights, but they were in the heat of the day and they were forecasting low 90's for the Dallas/Fort Worth area. I thought flying with small children was a headache! Add in a slobbering, howling dog and you better pack sedatives for the parental units.

John was beginning to hold his breath, which was never a good sign. When his stress level reached a certain point, he had a tendency to forget the whole exhale part of the breathing exchange! We finally boarded around 3:00 a.m. and were thankful once the engines roared and drowned out Rockne.

We arrived in time to get Rockne and the rest of our luggage. We prepared to get checked in on our Delta flight. The terminal was packed with summer travelers, but above all the hustle and bustle, one sound could be heard. Although he was beginning to become hoarse, Rockne's bark was relentless.

John had just exited the bathroom, and from his greenish grey complexion, he was not at his best. Every move affected him the same way. This trip was obviously not about to ruin that track record.

As we approached the counter, I remember the concerned look on the young agent's face as she said,

"You are not planning on traveling with your dog are you?"

John confirmed this with a quick intake of air as he squeaked out his reply.

"Yes Ma'am, we are."

She got a sort of half smile, 'gosh I feel bad for you,' look as said landed the blow.

"Sir, we no longer transport animals due to the risk involved. Your dog will have to stay here in Dallas."

"Well Ma'am, we were told your policy was to fly animals as long as the temperature did not reach 80 degrees or above."

John managed to blurt out while his face turned a reddish purple hue. The man was not breathing. He needed oxygen!

The patient agent shook her head in agreement as she prepared to administer the next blow.

"We have changed our policy due to several deaths of pets in the past few weeks during this heat spell."

As serious as a heart attack John responded, "We don't care if he dies Ma'am! We just need to get him on the plane with us!"

Erin was now in tears. Rockne, who now was emitting quite a funk, must have known that we were talking about him because he started this pitiful whine. The line was at least 30 people deep and none of them looked sympathetic.

"What you are going to need to do is leave him with a family member here in Dallas or arrange a kennel until you come home," she said in a very obvious tone. This woman had never moved across the damn street let alone across the continent! We had no home! What she could see was our home. Eight suitcases and a pain in the ass dog! We did not plan on returning to Dallas ever! We had no family here!

As we explained this to her, she did what all agents in a crisis do; they call a Supervisor. Upon the Supervisor's arrival, we had to recount every detail of our dilemma. We must have caught her early in her shift or she decided that a dead dog was better than an angry mob at the ticket counter.

Within minutes, we signed 19 forms that said we would not hold Delta responsible if Rockne did not make it through the trip.

We were finally on our way to Florida. Unfortunately, Rockne made it through the trip just fine. Once we landed, we had to take a minivan/taxi to our hotel in Jacksonville. A regular cab was no match for our luggage.

I wish I had a Polaroid of the business man who had to share our taxi ride. Rockne probably smelled the best out of all of us at that point in the trip. Needless to say, we all slept, including Rockne, from the minute we hit our hotel room until our alarm clock woke us that Friday morning.

Chapter 75

It Don't Gitmo Better

The flights to Cuba were Tuesdays and Fridays and even though I swore I would never do the MAC thing again after Guam, but there was only one route to our new home. The good night's sleep left me feeling fresh again and I had my new bib overalls and my new tennis shoes on for our adventure.

The terminal was filling up quickly. As I had done so many times before, I sat and watched the travelers greet each other with a neighborly familiarity that I could not share. Here it was again. I was so tired of this hollow feeling. No matter how many times we moved, the loneliness always returned with a vengeance.

I heard Erin's laughter and watched her share her braiding ability with two girls around her age. Her hands worked masterfully interweaving the three pastel colored strings for a friendship bracelet. She was amazing. She never met a stranger.

"Mom, they are moving to Cuba too!"

"Great!" I said a bit too cheerful for even me.

I pretended to read my book while I watched a couple who seemed to know everyone. Her red hair was freshly cut and stopped just short of rows of gold necklaces. Her full figure fit perfectly in the jean jumper she was wearing. Her husband was shorter than she was and his coal black hair was sticking up at the part. A mustache covered his upper lip and I couldn't help but notice that he resembled John in many ways.

I looked down at my Danielle Steel book, but I found myself staring again, as I turned toward the most obnoxious laugh I had ever heard. The husband of the couple I had been watching was cracking up while he used one hand to tell his story. The other hand was tucked under his arm resting on his small belly. The raspy laugh made me smile despite my nervousness. I noticed them looking at me and hoped they were not laughing at me.

We all boarded the plane and the short flight had us touching down in Guantanamo Bay by early afternoon. It was very hot and very windy as we got off the plane and walked to the terminal. The runway was surrounded by the blue Caribbean Sea, but the tropical paradise that I pictured was no where to be found. It was replaced by dry coral rocks and burnt yellow grassy areas. Mangrove forests hugged the shore and a few sparse palm trees were visible.

As we went through customs, we were met by our sponsor, Butch Houston. He was a tall, thin man who seemed very happy with island life. Guantanamo Bay had a Leeward side and a Windward Side. The air strip was on Leeward but the rest of the base was on the Windward side. Windward was across the bay so a Ferry took travelers back and forth.

We got a ride to the ferry in an ambulance since Rockne's big kennel would not fit on the other mode of transportation used to shuttle passengers. The other passengers took an old rickety bus that had seen better days. Butch informed us that they had just shut down the ferry due to high winds.

My first thought was 'Great! What now?' The doors to the ambulance opened and the woman I recognized from the terminal stuck her head in.

"Hey y'all! I did not know you were the new Chief at the Hospital. My name is Dorothy Buckman and I work at the Hospital. My husband is a Senior Chief so WELCOME! You need to come on and get on this next boat. They are putting us on a Mike boat because of the winds."

She was gone before I could say anything. Man did she talk fast and with that accent I only got about half of what she said. I wanted to know what a Mike boat was. I was freaking out about the high winds. As we got out, I saw our Mike boat. It was the "Saving

Private Ryan" boat where the front drops down. This looked safe, even if we did not get to sit down.

Erin and Joe were in awe. Butch helped John with the dog while I carried the video camera and as many of the suitcases as I could handle. People just started grabbing our stuff for us which I thought was awfully nice.

As we boarded the boat, Rockne began his howling again. He had been pretty quiet up until now, but the boat was very crowded and there were people standing all around his kennel. My knees were shaking after seeing the waves and white caps on the water we were about to set sail on.

The dark walls of the Mike boat were at least six feet high and made of strong steel. I made Joe and Erin hold my hand. I figured if we went down, we would go together. I really thought we should have lifejackets but you would think this was a carnival cruise line the way people were laughing and carrying on. Maybe they knew something I didn't.

We were tossed around a bit as the boat tried to maneuver in the rough bay. Before long, the boat had picked up speed and I could hear the waves crashing against the steel sides. Before I knew what happened, a huge wave crashed over the side of the boat drenching us.

The cold water was a shock and the salt was stinging my eyes as I scrambled to get the video camera somewhere dry but it was no use. Before I could even wipe the salt out of my eyes, another wave soaked us. I thought this was some kind of a joke because everyone was just laughing. I found no humor in the fact that everything I owned was getting soaked. The water was over my new tennis shoes. Rockne was not liking this at all.

I kept trying to get John to do something, but he just kept telling me to relax. Relax! My lips hurt they were pursed so much. The kids were laughing so hard, but I was so uptight I thought I was going to throw up. If I didn't know better I would think this Boat Captain was trying to get us wet. I had mascara running down my face and my eyes were burning.

I was not sure how much more I could take. I felt the boat turn slightly and I could see land in the distance. We finally pulled into Ferry Landing and with a new tinge of green to our complexion, we loaded our dripping dog and dripping luggage into Butch's car and headed to our new home.

We lived in a housing area called Knob Hill. This was on the far north west side of the base. Our house was big and beautiful and we even had a fenced in yard for Rockne.

Chapter 76

Our New Island Home

It was two weeks later that we found the kids a fun Friday night at the Youth Center. John and I had been given a tour of the bay by one of his Corpsman who worked at the Marina. The sunset was breathtaking as it sank below the mountains in the distance.

It was hard to believe that there was another life just beyond the mountains. We could see the lights of communist Cuba in the distance and this stirred such a strange feeling in me. What kind of life were they leading over there? Were they watching us? It seemed so close but yet so very far away.

The turquoise water was so clear you could see the underwater life all around you. Chris, our tour guide, showed us Hospital Cay, which was an island of coral, now home to many layed back iguanas who watched our approach with suspicious eyes.

I was amazed at the number of critters here. The island had a distinct smell which was only magnified by the heat. It was a pungent citrus/urine odor that came from the inhabitants in the trees.

Banana rats were not in the welcome aboard packet, but they were everywhere. You did not need to see them to know they had visited because they left banana shaped droppings wherever they roamed. To really see how many inhabited the island, all you had to do was shine your lights off the road at night. Their beady little eyes would stare back at the light, barely disturbed by the interruption.

We still had time to spare before we needed to pick the kids up so we checked out The Goat Locker. This was the Chief's Club in Gitmo and it was supposedly the place to be.

The last two weeks had been rough for all of us. My usual adjustment phase had kicked in with nightly tears and conversations with John about the fact that I would not make friends here. The island was so dead. I could not believe that we had to spend the next two and a half years here. No one seemed to be home. I had watched for kids in the neighborhood using Joe's purple, Discovery binoculars to no avail. It was so lonely.

I tried not to think about any of this as we made our way under the canopy. The smell of popcorn entered my nose and we could hear raucous laughter from behind the door.

Walking in, I was instantly transformed back to the states to a neighborhood bar. The patrons were sitting closely together avoiding their reflections in the mirror on the far wall. Tables were pushed together at the far end of the rectangular shaped room and were surrounded by several couples who seemed to be the source of the laughter.

I instantly recognized Dorothy Buckman, the woman from the first day. They had let us borrow a TV set until our household goods had arrived. I didn't think she liked me very much since I had woke her up twice on the same day trying to find a time to come and get the TV. Their three children were visiting their grandparents in Georgia and I think they had partied quite a bit the night before I had called.

John got us beers and within minutes she recognized us.

"Hey, ya'all! Come on over and join us!" she yelled over the noise of the bar.

She introduced us around the table to Mike and Cindy Armor who just happened to be our new next door neighbors.   We met Dave and Carla Blankenship, Lou and Nikki Losito and several other Chiefs. They were so much fun and John had already shared way too much information with this group to think that we would not be friends.

Dorothy was a talker and she was brutally honest. She shared her opinion of me on that first day in the terminal.

"Girl, you looked like an uptight, gold drippin' bitch."

She said this as she fondled one of four gold chains around her neck. We shared the story behind the story with Rockne and we laughed at how uptight I had been. They all loved to sing, and karaoke was on Saturdays so we knew we had found the right place.

Before long the Buckman's children came home and Joe and Erin found their friends too. We spent our time at Windmill Beach where Erin and Joe found heaven on earth. There were more critters on this island than either one of them had imagined. It did not take them long to become Caribbean kids!

Chapter 77

Mayberry Does Exist

The pace on the base picked up considerably as the school year approached. On a whim, I put my application in at the school. I would have loved to teach, but I thought it was a long shot without my stateside certification.

They needed substitutes badly and I thought this would be a good way to help the kids adjust and have some flexibility. A week before school I was called in and asked to begin the year as the Kindergarten teacher. They had hired a teacher, but she could not arrive in time to begin the year.

I jumped on the opportunity and was able to work almost full time as a sub. The kids loved school. Erin was in fifth grade and Joe was in first grade. I loved seeing them everyday and the extra cash was really nice.

I subbed for seven weeks in the first grade and this was the calalyst to get my paperwork submitted for certification through the Department of Defense Schools.

The staff at W.T. Sampson Elementary was so welcoming. Before long, we knew no strangers on the base. Mayberry does exist and we got to experience it. The 1500 personnel were made up of Navy, Marines, DOD contractors, teachers, and Jamaican Nationals. The base itself was almost 30 miles in diameter, however, we were only allowed to travel on 8-10 miles of that space. The speed limit did not go above 30 miles per hour.

John got started right away on his Masters degree at Troy State University, so his weekends were no longer his own. Troy State flew instructors to Cuba for two weeks at a time to teach the different classes in the Public Administration program. His goal was to finish before we left Cuba and he sacrificed a lot during this time.

I took up the slack by coaching the teams that he would have. I coached soccer and Little League and I truly had no idea what I was getting myself into. I also became very involved with the Catholic Church. This was the one thing I could always count on no matter where we lived. I became a Eucharistic Minister and a CCD teacher for the First Communion Class.

I was the Cub Scout Dad when John could not make the den meetings, and the Pinewood Derby. The beauty of small town life was that you could call on at least ten people to help you out if you were in a bind. They would come running. We spent many a night throwing horse shoes in the backyard at the Buckman's house.

Cold Beer was always flowing when we needed to unwind. Our mantra was, "The bird is in the tree." Erin and Joe made best friends with the Buckman kids, Little Bert and Brittney. Their oldest, Mandy, was our babysitter when the Youth Center was boring.

I have never felt so safe in my life. The kids had a standing manhunt game every Friday and Saturday night and we never thought twice about letting them stay out well past dark. We stayed busier than ever, but we loved our life on Gitmo.

Chapter 78

Friday Night Fights

I was blessed with subbing almost full time that first year at the elementary school on base. W.T. Johnson was the Assistant Principal and we hit if off from the beginning. He and his wife, Cynthia, were involved all over the base. Almost everyone on base was involved in an extra curricular activity. People would always volunteer to help with whatever needed to get done. This was why it was such a special place to be.

The school brought me a new group of teacher friends. They asked if John and I would like to join their Friday night fights on the golf course.

We had not golfed since we had arrived on Gitmo, so I was all for it. John had school, so I played with Al and Cassie, Mary and Henry, Debbie and Richard and Dave and Margie. They were teachers and administrators who were ready to let loose by Friday afternoon.

They were very different from our Chief friends and I hoped that John would like them as much as I did. Al really wanted to golf well. It took us so long to play Al decided that we should not start drinking beer until the sixth hole. This lasted until we teed off on number one the first night John was with us.

Everyone was having a good time, but I knew it was way to polite for John who was obviously scheming on how to liven up the party. On hole number two, Al was concentrating intensely on a four-foot putt. He was in the middle of his back swing when John said, "Has anyone noticed that Al has a saucy ass?" Friday night fights were up for grabs from this point forward and it was what we looked forward to all week.

Chapter 79

A Tour Like No Other

We spent just two years in Cuba, but it was the best two years of our lives. Pulling away from Ferry Landing for the last time was one of the hardest departures I have ever had.

We didn't just get stationed in Cuba, we lived Gitmo. They were some of the busiest years, but that is what happens when you live in a community.

You teach CCD and Pre-Kindergarten when they add another class. You go to the commissary for bread and see 20 people who want to talk. You sing the National Anthem at your husband's graduation ceremony and then run to the baseball field so he can coach. You become a Eucharistic Minister on Easter Sunday when Father needs help passing out communion. You celebrate holidays like Thanksgiving and Christmas with your best friends who cook turkeys in your house so it smells like you want it to.

You keep other people's children for a week while they go back to the states to house hunt and you never really notice the difference. Gitmo is signing up for a free sleigh ride home at Christmas, and looking forward to getting back to your island without cell phones or traffic. Gitmo Goodbyes were even special. Ferry Landing would fill with all who knew you during your time in Gitmo. If you were next to leave, you jumped in the bay to bid your friend's farewell as the Ferry pulled away.

It was something special that we will never have again, but thank God for everyday.

Chapter 80

Hey, It's Good To Be Back Home Again
July 2001

For the first time in our lives, we held one way tickets for our next duty station. My dream had come true for John's last tour. He had accepted orders to Hospital Corps School Great Lakes, Illinois as an instructor. We were just two hours from home.

We were not the only ones on the move. Mom and Dad had decided to be closer to Kelli and Mark. They had made the move to Pontiac during our time in Cuba.

This was still a bit weird for me since I associated Mom and Dad with every thought of home. Home was Dwight, but this move had nothing to do with me and everything to do with Mom and Dad. Kelli was the only one close by and even though Dwight and Pontiac were just 15 miles apart, it was a major hassle for her to get to Dwight.

Being home was so fun. The first summer we did all the little things that we had missed for so many years. Odell Days is not a big deal, but we were all there. Mom and Dad were so happy we were home. They had worried about us all the time and they finally had us close.

That weekend in Odell, I started to realize how much fun it was to just be with Mom and Dad. I could fight Dad all the time and still not be happy. I questioned what I was proving by being mad all the time. My Dr. Phil book had helped me see that I had the control to forgive him. He was just Dad. He was going to do what he wanted as long as he was alive. He wasn't doing any of it to hurt me. I would work towards finally letting go of all of my mess.

Chapter 81

That Terrible Day
Tuesday, September 11th, 2001

I got up earlier than usual today since Kelli was coming to our house for the first time. I had lots of cleaning to do and I had even thought about baking cookies, which is a big deal for me, the one who hates to cook. Over the weekend, John had put our second TV upstairs.

We were still working on moving in to our house in Fort Sheridan, Illinois. We were finally getting into a routine since school had just started on the fifth of September.

Erin had mentioned that Dad had not even kissed her goodbye this morning, so we called him on the car phone and she gave him grief. Joe said a quick hi too and the kids ate their cocoa puffs with the innocence that this day would be no different than any other for them. Little did we know that other calls were being made to family members for the last time.

The phone rang and it was Kelli. She was heading up to Downers Grove. We were so excited. She would stay tonight and then we were going to the Cubs game tomorrow. I gave her directions and realized how much I had to do.

Joe went upstairs to brush his teeth and watch cartoons and I took the luxury of some grown up TV time as I flipped on Good Morning America. I watched Charlie Gibson and Diane Sawyer watching a live shot of what looked at the time like a plane crash into the World Trade Center in New York City. They had very little information, but the picture showed that once again those poor people had to get out.

I am embarrassed to admit that with my busy morning, I did not give this single tragic event enough of my attention. Besides, it was in New York, which was so very far away from my mundane life.

As with most days, I was doing about 50 things at once so I did not sit down to watch. I yelled at Joe to come down and put his shoes on. He left the security of Cartoon Network only to be an actual eyewitness to the horror that so many Americans watched. I had a load of towels in my arms and I ran down to start the first of many loads of laundry for the day.

The scream from upstairs had me running with a fear that only a mother understands. My eight-year-old son was screaming,

"MOMMMMM!!! GET UP HERE!"

He and I stood and watched what we have all seen so many times, but with the new gripping fear that this was no accident. I could see the disbelief in his amazingly perfect face. I wanted to be able to understand what to tell him when he asked,

"Why would a pilot do that?"

His next question was even more haunting.

"Aren't those just like the planes we always fly on?"

I was unable to even speak. I did not want to hear what Charlie Gibson was saying that this was obviously a deliberate attack. Still in denial, one more time, my mundane life pushed on. Still unaffected to the level that I should have been, I prepared Joe's peanut butter and jelly sandwich. This time with hands that were not as steady as a few minutes before.

I put in his Scooby Doo snacks and answered his philosophical questions about, "What kind of person would do this?" with, "What fruit do you want to take in your lunch?"

This was what I knew. I knew exactly how much laundry detergent to put in my load of towels. I knew the way to curl Erin's hair to make it fall around her face. I knew how much peanut butter fit perfectly on one side of Joe's sandwich. I did not know what kind of person would do this. I did not know how much worse it would get and that the questions would only get harder to answer. I did not know that this day would change all of us forever.

Chapter 82

Get On Back To School

The winter of 2002, I got a job as an assistant at Sherwood School. This job helped me make a decision that I had been putting off for 16 years. I knew I wanted to teach, but I could not do it until I went back to school to get certified. The four teachers I worked for helped give me the confidence I needed to take the next step.

After doing the research, I realized that I would need almost 30 hours of undergraduate classes to get certified and I would still only have a Bachelors degree. I knew I could get a student loan since we had very little income with just my subbing.

National Louis University had a perfect Masters program for people wanting to do just what I needed to do. I would start in the summer of 2002. I told the kids they would just have to share their homework space with Mom.

The hardest part was doing without any extra income. After doing so well in Cuba and saving so much money, we were right back to living paycheck to paycheck. I should say paycheck to the week before the paycheck. This is a difficult way to live anywhere, but especially on the North Shore.

We were the minority in every sense of the word. We were Irish-Catholics in an area where they had school holidays for Rosh Hashanah, and Yom Kippur. We lived in military housing and paid $0 a year in property taxes, while many lived in half million dollar homes and paid $10,000 a year in property taxes. We went to Dwight for Spring Break, while many went to remote islands in the Caribbean. Joe and Erin were sent to McDonalds for lunch, while many children from our area were sent to exclusive camps for 12 weeks. We just did not fit too well. Erin and Joe had not felt any of the exclusion. Joe had been tested for the gifted program and was really showing just how smart he was. I had not made many friends which was rare for me. One of the first PTO meetings at Joe's school, I almost hit a woman who wanted to know if I lived in the development in Fort Sheridan or if I was military.

Her voice went down as she said "military" as if it were some dirty word! How dare she try to judge me for being married to a man who kept her and her family free every day!

I was not really lonely but I missed that sense of community that we had never been without. I had never started over in a community that was so cold. Military families were a rare bunch. Many people from Highland Park had known each other for years and they had no use for new friends that did not fit a certain profile. Erin made so many friends that her weekends were full with Bar Mitzvahs and trips to the mall.

Erin got a ride home with a girl's parents one night and she told us they had dropped off a girl who now lived where Scottie Pippen used to live. Like I said, we were in a whole new world.

Erin had wowed the Northwood crowd with her debut in "Annie" her seventh grade year. We invited half the town of Dwight to see the show! We needed 82 tickets for all who came to see her and she was amazing.

Chapter 83

Dad's Nurses
July 2002

The kids and I came down for a week to help Mom and Kelli. Dad had been struggling with kidney stones again. He had a stint placed to help him pass the stone, but it did not seem to be working. He was now in more pain than even before the stint had been inserted. He had gone to the Emergency Room on Sunday and he had been admitted.

Without knowing the damage it would do, the doctors had given Dad morphine. This was like poison to his system. Mark, Kelli, Mom and I spent the next four days at his bedside trying to keep him from ripping out his intravenous tubes, and falling out of bed. It took most of the week to get the morphine out of his system and after needless haggling between the doctors, he had the stint removed.

I got a glimpse into Dad's pain that week. I watched his body twitch and his face turn red as he struggled with pain I don't think I have ever felt. I listened to the heart monitors react when his heart felt the stress of what he was going through. I realized that week that we would lose him sooner rather than later and that all I had to do was love the man that was right here, right now.

Chapter 84

45 Years and Counting
November 2002

The limousine would arrive at 5:30, so we were all heading to Kelli and Mark's this afternoon. Mom and Dad thought the plan was that Kelli and Mark were to take them out for a quiet dinner, but they would be quite surprised when we all arrived by limo.

It was their 45th wedding anniversary and after all these years we had finally planned something for them. We were all excited to be together and John and I had just loaded the car and were ready to hit the road when the phone rang.

I could hear Kelli's hiccupped breathing before I even said hello.

"Dad says he is too sick to go," she busted out, letting go of fresh tears.

Not again. I felt so bad because she had worked hard at planning this whole thing.

"We just need to tell him to suck it up," I said. This time it was all about mom and we really wanted to surprise her. He had been struggling with kidney stones for a while, but I really thought he would be OK.

"Let me call him and talk to him."

"It's too late," she sighed,

"I already told Mom about the limo, but she doesn't know you guys are coming. She said Dad will come and not to worry."

It was always something. Last Christmas, John and I had the whole family for the first time in our married life. We were going to spend two days together but Dad had been too sick to stay. That time he had trouble breathing and had spent most of his day with his head in my freezer. He had ended up in the hospital with a kidney stone.

I had no idea how much he hurt today, but it was pretty important for him to go with us. Hopefully, Kelli's blowup got that message through. We had reservations at Jim's Steakhouse in Bloomington, Illinois, so I was sure he could make it that long.

They were both dressed to the hilt when the limo drove up to their apartment. Neither of them had ever been in a limo so they were pumped.

Hours later, I sat with tears streaming down my cheeks, watching Kelli and Dad sing 'My Way', with the man at the piano. Mom was in heaven. She had all of her kids and any of the hurt from earlier was forgotten. We had the best time and Dad did not complain once. I think he knew better than to try.

He and Mom were thrilled with their party and I had to laugh thinking about Dad trying to find the door handles inside the limo that were not there.

It was nothing short of amazing that we were celebrating their 45th wedding anniversary. The vows rang true every day for them. 'In good times and bad, in sickness and in health, till death do us part.'

Chapter 85

Are You Trying To Kill Me?

John was teaching at Great Lakes, and seemed to be enjoying the role of educator. We were a year away from his retirement and we had some major decisions to make. Where to settle down was the biggie.

As we sat down for dinner one night, I could not help but beam with pride over my afternoon's work. I could tell that even the kids were impressed.

"You made this mom?" Erin asked in disbelief.

"Yep I did!" I said with confidence. I spooned the steaming lasagna onto each plate with care and grabbed the garlic bread from the counter.

"This looks great sweetie!" John said as we prepared to pray. I had not attempted to make lasagna in ages, but this could have been in one of those cookbooks in my cupboard. We all dove in and I noticed John sticking his tongue out repeatedly across the table. He put his fingers to his lips and picked something off his tongue.

"What is it babe?" I said not really paying attention.

"Nothing," he said nonchalantly, "just a little something."

I was working on my salad and I was about half pissed when he started messing with his mouth again.

"What is wrong?" I barked, irritated that he didn't like it. I watched in horror as he pulled a large piece of paper out of his mouth.

"What the hell?" I yelled as I pushed my chair back to inspect the three-hour creation in the Pyrex. John had gone to the garbage can and was now spitting the remainder of pasta mixed in with paper.

As I lifted the middle layer of melted mozzarella cheese the evidence showed itself. A full layer of paper was wedged between the cheese and lasagna noodles. A full 9x12 dish of paper laced lasagna.

"What kind of cheese did you use honey?" he asked in a very patient voice for someone who could have just choked to death.

"The long strips of Mozzarella," I said defensively.

"Did you take the paper off the back of each slice?"

That patient voice was beginning to piss me off. "I did not know they had paper on them."

It was weeks before I attempted another dish in my kitchen. I hated cooking when I started this damn adventure and I am just damn lucky that I have not killed anyone, especially my husband.

Chapter 86

Finally a Spring Break
April 2003

Shirley came through for us once again by inviting us to share her condo in Clearwater Beach, Florida. This break was just what three crazed students and one overworked Dad needed. This trip also gave us a chance to meet Shirley's longtime friend, Brigitta who was in from Sweden. She was spending a few weeks with Shirley and did not mind sharing her with us.

We lounged in the sun and hit all the local hot spots at night. We ate at Frenchy's on the water and one night we tried a place called Guppy's. It was quite a drive but if the line outside the door was any indication, we had hit the jackpot.

As we sat and enjoyed our drinks, I watched Joe with alarm. He was facing the bar area and his face had turned a stark white shade.

"Joe what is wrong?" I asked starting to get up.

Trying to gather some air in his lungs he shared the reason for his sudden attack.

"HULK HOGAN IS AT THE BAR!" he said in disbelief.

We all tried to see over the wooden booth, but Joe watched as this large tan man with shocking blond hair was seated right across from us. He was with his family. We all tried not to stare since they just wanted to enjoy a normal dinner like the rest of us.

For the most part, people left them alone and it was not until we got up to leave that Shirley told Hulk that she hoped he was happy since he ruined her grandson's dinner.

He jokingly said, "Hey if he won't eat it, I will!"

Chapter 87

You Will Be Fine
May 14, 2003

What a crazy spring it had been. As I stole a few extra moments of quiet in Sammy's bed, I realized I better get moving. Dad's surgery was at 9:00 this morning and we wanted to see him before they took him up. I could hear the shower come on and I thanked God for the sister down the hall. She was so busy with her job and the boys, but she always made time for Mom and Dad too. They had gone down yesterday so that they did not have to get up so early this morning.

Knowing Dad, they were still up at the crack of dawn. He had been down this surgery road many times before so I imagine he knew the routine. I said one more silent prayer that this surgery would help his shoulder and hand. He hurt almost all the time and what he always called Arthur visiting (arthritis), was actually two vertebrae pressing on his spinal cord. He was a "fix me" kind of guy and he could not be talked out of this.

Before I could climb out of bed, Sammy came in and started my day with a warm hug.

"Are you going to stay here tonight?" he asked. "No bud! I've got to get back so I can be with Joe and Erin. But we will be down soon. I just have to finish school."

He smiled and said, "So you can be a teacher, right?"

"That's exactly right! Now let's go get ready for our day."

I headed to the shower to begin the longest day of my life.

"There you are!" Mom said as she folded her paper. She was sitting at the foot of Dad's bed where we had seen her so many times before. I squeezed her frail bony frame and then made my way to Dad who was sitting up, ready for his day.

"How's my Patti?" I breathed in his familiar smell as I hugged him tight.

"You smell like my Patti," he said this all the time.

We settled in for a visit since they were not taking him for about a half-hour.

"Mom, will you get me some ice chips?" His tone was more of a demand than a question and she shook her head and said he could not have any. One of the nurses had told him that maybe she could sneak him some, so he was not about to give up on this. Since there were no other chairs, I told Dad to scoot over. I sat with him and showed him our pictures from vacation and from Erin's play, Charlotte's Web.

"She looks just like she did when she was a baby." I watched as his blue eyes twinkled and misted.

"You have to promise me that she will not go to that big school where those girls did that to each other." He was referring to a hazing incident that took place at Glenbrook North the week before.

"That wasn't Erin's school Dad. I promise."

For some reason, no matter what happened in the suburbs, Dad thought it was at my front door.

"Mom, go find that nurse and get me some ice chips." He was not going to let up. Kelli, who had been reading the paper, leaned over and shook her finger at him.

"Dad! Drop it about the ice chips!" You can't have any!" Dad just looked at her and chuckled as he said, "Who invited the grump?"

Mom changed the subject without missing a beat as she told us about their night at Jumer's. They had checked in and the hotel staff told them to help themselves to the hors d'oeuvres and cocktails thinking they were with the group from an insurance company. Of course, Mom and Dad helped themselves and chatted with the people. It was not until they left, and saw the sign to the room, that they realized it was a private function.

"Is it any wonder we do these things?" I said to Kelli as we all laughed. Dad turned to Kelli and asked about her work.

"Oh, Dad it is so much right now!" she answered with a heavy sigh.

"I didn't bother to tell Brian you were having surgery, but I'll have to scoot after you are done!" She opened her black day planner to check what she needed to do. Dad reached over and rubbed her cheek.

"You work too hard, Sweetie!" he said with concern. She leaned into the hand that had held hers for 39 years.

"I'm tough Daddy, don't worry!" We were interrupted by a nurse, who brought in paperwork for Dad to sign. Kelli sat up and read it over with Dad.

"You make sure they do the right side or the correct side!" Dad whispered to the nurse,

"Sorry, she's my official body guard!" It wasn't five minutes after Dad signed the first sheet, that they were back with another one.

"I'm sorry, Mr. Slattery. We actually had the wrong terminology of your procedure on the other form so we need you to sign this one."

Kelli and I looked at each other warily. They seemed a bit disorganized, especially since it was 15 minutes before he was to be taken to surgery. As they came to take Dad, we moved into the hallway.

Kelli's cell phone rang and I could hear Ed on the other end. The nurses would not allow Kelli to take the phone into the room, but she yelled to Dad, "Eddie's on the phone Dad and he'll be here when you wake up."

We heard Dad's gravelly voice yell, "I Love you, Bum."

We stopped by the elevators and I leaned in for a quick kiss.

"I Love you Dad," I said. I watched as Kelli did the same. Mom leaned over, kissed him and patted his forehead.

"You will be fine, Sweetie." Dad pointed at Kelli and I and said to the nurse, "Have you ever seen two more beautiful daughters? And how about that third one? She has been married to me for 46 years."

The nurse laughed and said, "You have put up with him for 46 years?"

"Yes I have," Mom said in a thick voice. As she blew him one last kiss, she whispered softly to herself, "Yes I have."

Chapter 88

So Much Left To Do
August 2004

Had I known that this was to be my last kiss and my last "I love you," I would have never let go of my dad. He wanted to be able to play cards again. He wanted his shoulder to stop hurting. He did not think he was going to die on that operating table.

He had a full garden waiting for him to tend to. He had a best friend waiting with an empty glass that had been filled every afternoon. He had a big chair to sit in, and a paper to read. He had waitresses ready to pour him coffee at Baby Bulls. He had Pontiac football to watch.

He had sweet corn to eat and potatoes to butter. He had a bathroom to invade. He had Toni Bennett tickets. He had phone calls to make and messages to leave. More than any of this, he had the love of his life waiting to beat him at gin.

Maybe he actually was ready, but we were the ones caught off guard. Why can't I just know what he is doing now? Can he see me? Can he hear me? Does he know how much he is missed?

He has left a hole in my life unlike anything I have ever known. For the first few months, I would listen as people told me they were sorry to hear I lost my Dad. I would nod politely and thank them. What I really wanted to do was sit them down and tell them that it is not Dad that is lost, it is me!

I don't know what to do with the heavy feeling of missing him. I want to scream sometimes when I pick up the phone and it is never him. I want to see him laugh so hard that his whole body shakes. I want to smell him and hug him.

I want to cut his toenails and have him tell me that he once had a doctor tell him he had the finest feet of any patient he had ever seen. I even want to fight with him since this is what we did so often.

I want to tell him that even though we did not move to Dwight like he wanted us to, we did really good buying our new house. I want to scream that he can't be gone because he needs to see this house. He could pick it out from the street by the Ruskin family sign he had made for us.

I have needed him so many times since he died. Like that Saturday morning when I took my teacher certification tests. I needed him to tell me what Congress does and where the Ganges River is. I need him to drive with Erin and laugh so hard because another generation of bad drivers is just beginning.

The many things that made me crazy when I would spend time with him are now things I ache for. His constant coughing and hoiking made me just about throw up, but now when I hear an older man do this I can't help but smile.

I know he is with me everyday. I know I have more than angels watching over me. I knew on his birthday just a week after he died, when I got on the toll way to head home. I realized 50 feet from the tollbooth that I had no change. He put two quarters in the seam of my jacket. I felt them through the hole I had thought about sewing up a hundred times.

He was there on the day that Kelli got up to speak at John's retirement from the Navy. He was the train whistle reminding us that he was so very proud. He is every feather that blows through my window unexpectedly and every twinkling star that brightens the night sky.

He is there, each day, in his Patrick who shared more than anyone knew with his Papa. Patrick's loss was equal to Mom's since he shared nearly every day of his life with his Grandpa.

His death ended the biggest chapter of my life. Before his death, as I continued with my writing, I struggled with how to end my book. Dad gave me that ending. When a door closes, somewhere a window is opened.

He always told me to tell it like I felt it and he had read most of what I have written about the difficult years. As I said at his funeral, it was not a perfect life, but it was perfect love. I have so much of my mom and dad in me and I wouldn't want it any other way.

Tommy touched so many lives through his unselfish love and willingness to pick himself up over and over again. My mom has touched just as many lives as she has shown us over and over again what a commitment is and what true love can overcome. She did this in a world where marriages are tossed around like the piece of paper that certifies them. Where would I be without her unfailing love for me?

I have had an amazing life and I am only half way through it! I had this life because I was loved so unconditionally by my Mom and Dad. I have a chance to carry this on to Erin and Joe with John at my side. If I had it to do all over, I honestly think I would because.......... this was my damn adventure!

I will end with the words of my mother, Rita Slattery.

"There, I've said it! I'm glad I said it! Now I'm going to bed!"

Tom in Korea 1954

Rita Slattery 1958

Tom Slattery 1958

The Coughlin Family
Bill, Rita, Colleen, Joyce, Emmett, Eileen, Delores, Joanne, Betty

The Slattery Family
Tom, Francis, Bob, Bill, Joe, Monica, Bill, Lyde, Marie

Ed and Kelli, Christmas 1965

Me, Kelli and Eddie 1967

Mary Clausen
4 years old

Kelli
in Kindergarten

Ed in First Grade

Me in Kindergarten

The Slattery Family 1971

Me, Kelli and Mary
August 1972

Me and my best friend,
Brenda

Rita with her broken hip
April 1973

My First Communion Day
with Grandpa Slattery,
and Grandma and Grandpa Coughlin

Me in Third Grade,
Law Breaker

Ed with his first golf trophies
(the one Mom flushed is on his left)

Christmas 1974

Chippewa ball players
on Rambler

Ed's Eighth Grade Graduation
in front of
Grandma and Grandpa's
New House

Brenda and Me
in Sixth Grade

The Clausen Men and
the Slattery Men

John Ruskin
"The Hunk" 1978

Dad in front of Maurie's Tap

My first day of High
School
with Kelli 1980

Kelli and Mary
in Homecoming Parade 1981

The Girls ready for
Homecoming 1981

New Year's Eve 1981
Mary, Jim, Brenda, Me, John, Kim

Tammy

Moe

The Slattery Family 1982

Prom 1983
Tank, Me and Schultzie

My 17th Birthday
with my new puppy, Jake

Tank and Me
Ready for Homecoming

Mom, Dad and Me
Senior Night - Fall 1983

Brad and Me
Sweetheart February 1984

High School Graduation
May 1984
Mary, Brenda and Me

Lynn and Me
Western 1984

Susie and Lynn
Early Spring 1985

Joe

Kim and Brian

Jerry and Jonesy
Sophomore Year - Western

Billy and Me
Western 1985

Christmas 1985
Ed, Kelli and Me
Last Christmas in the old house

John and Me
January 1986

Bears Win! Julie, Me and Jonesy
Western 1986

E'd first year at Forest Hills
Rockford, Illinois

My boys, Sloaner, Joe and Opie
Fall 1986

What bodies!
Sloaner and Opie
Fall 1986

Jonesy and Me
Florida - Spring 1987

My 21st Birthday at Western
September 1987

Kelli's Wedding Day
November 1987

Mesha Marie
4 months old

Finally! Jonesy and Me
Western Graduation - December 1987

Kara and Me

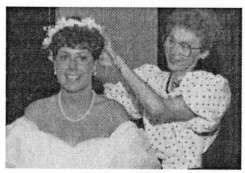

Mom and Me
My Wedding Day, May 21, 1988

Dad and Me
My Wedding Day, May 21, 1988

My Little Stick of Dynamite

Mr and Mrs. John Ruskin

Leaving for Key West

Our first home

My New Family
(Larry's daughter) Vicki, Larry, Shirley, Paula, Emily, Me and John

The Harley Newlyweds
June 25th 1988

Pregnant Patti

Jim and Mary
March 1989

Me and my Baby

Erin and Daddy

Erin meets her Aunts, Mesha, John,
Emily holding Erin, Me and Paula

Erin Eileen
Seven Weeks Old

Papa Tom and Grandma Rita
with Erin at Hemingway's
house in Key West

Papa Lar and Grandma Shirley with
Erin in front of our house on Sigbee

Aunt Kelli and Uncle Gerry
with Erin in Key West

Erin meets Jimmy Buffett

Drake and Vicki Miller
with Kevin and Samantha

Uncle Eddie and Erin

Kelli, Gerry and Patrick Miller
Christmas 1989

John and Dorie on their
Wedding Day
October 1990

Christmas 1990
with the Ruskins
Emily, John, Joe,Paula,
Erin, Bob, Ann, Mesha and
Me

Slattery Family
Christmas 1990

Jimmy T. and John on Pedro,
North Carolina, 1991

John, Mike and Jimmy T.
in Key West

Erin with Papa Larry, Shirl,
Eugene and Maynard

Grandma Shirl teaches
Erin to make pies

Papa Bob, Mesha and Erin

Our little singing star
Christmas 1991

The psychos on the beach
Fort Meyers, Florida 1992

Moe, Mary, Ronnie Woo Woo,
Brenda, Kelly and I keep busy during
a rain out at Wrigley

Erin meets Joe

John with his babies

Irish Grandma and
Grandpa with their Erin
October 1992

Go ND!
November 1992

Mary, Dan, John and Me
Belting out Danny Boy, St. Patrick's Day 1993

Tommy, the Politician

Our Little Sweeties

NC gang heads to Buffett in Raleigh

Ed and Sue's Wedding
November 1993

Mary and Joe at the Pacific Island
Club in Guam, January 1994

Talafofo Falls, Emily, Shelby,
Joe and Erin

Joe and Paula Krischel
May 1994

Paula's Wedding

Erin's first day of
Kindergarten

Erin and Joe
Guam, September 1994

Shirley's visit to Guam
Christmas 1994

Jonathan and John at a
Guamanian Fiesta

Kelli, Mark and Patrick at their
wedding, June 1995

Our growing family

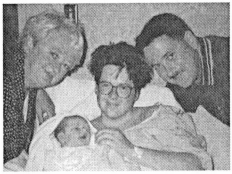

Paula with baby Mason, Grandma
Shirley and Uncle John, June 1995

Todd and John
on Guam

Sunset cruise with the Cavin's

Joe with his new buddy, Rockne

Nevada Kids

Zeke and Erin

Phil and Brenda on their
Wedding Day with Erin,
June 1996

Joe, Erin, Andy and Tanner at
Disneyland in CA, May 1997

Moe and Tim,
November 1996

Samuel Tomas with
his big brother,
Patrick

Erin holding Kyle with Joe and
Sean, Summer 1997

Chief wannabees Lora, Reggie,
Ron Brian and John

Kelly and Tony's
Wedding
August 1997

John's Chief pinning
September 1997

Al and John Ruskin at Al's
Retirement

The Hawaiian Master Chief's at the
Club, Nevada 1998

Baby Josh, Erin and Joe and Mason

Me and my God
Child, Jessica
September 1998

Ray and Ceci
February 1999

Ray's Retirement
July 1999

Erin, Joe, Stevie, Brianna
and Cristina
at Lake Tahoe, July 1999

The Northeast Gate
of Guantanamo Bay,
Cuba

Bert and Dorothy

Scuba Kids in Cuba

Holly, Brittney and Erin

Little Bert and Joe at the beach

Grandma Shirley holding Adin Joseph,
with Mason, Josh, Erin and Joe
December 1999

Papa Tom with Jessie, Patrick,
Kyle, Sean, Grandma Rita with
Sammy, Joe and Erin

The Ruskins in Cuba

My Master's Man

Friday Night Golf Gang
Henry, and Mary, Debbie and
Richard, Margie and David,
John and Me, and Cassie and Al

John in a cow suit jumping from the
pier at Ferry Landing Gitmo
July 2001

The Ruskin Family
Fort Sheridan, Illinois
Spring 2002

Dad with Ed on his birthday
May 21, 2002

Our favorite Annie
May 2002

Mom and Dad
Summer 2002

Our last family photo with Dad
Summer 2002

Spring Break with Grandma Shirley
and Brigitta in Clearwater Beach,
Florida 2003

John presenting Joe with a gift at
his retirement as we all look on
June 25, 2004

Patti Jo Ruskin lives with her family in northern Illinois.

Visit her website at www.pattijoruskin.npauthors.com.

Printed in the United States
35269LVS00006B/46-129